... Since having read your book, I have begun searching for my ancestors. I have since found 57 family names that I am researching and over 500 grandparents, aunts and uncles. I have found five Civil War veterans, two Revolutionary War veterans and an 1812 vet. Without your easy to follow and understand book none of this would have been possible. Two of my co-workers have read your book and now are researching their family trees as well.

—Adrian C. Sims

For cyber genealogy, try Genealogy Via the Internet...

—Southern Living

That's the best written instructions for getting a computer, getting on the net and doing whatever that I've ever read. The language is right and the facts are, too.

—Gus Seefluth

While Roberts' book is aimed at beginners, advanced genealogists will also find helpful tips. ...

—Family PC

Humorous, entertaining, and engaging. ...

—In The Spotlight

...quite readable and blends information, technology and humor into a compact package.

—*Linda Swisher,* The Star

... Genealogy via the Internet *is about two topics of exceptional interest—genealogy (one of America's fastest growing hobbies) and the internet itself.*

—Home Trends

The delight of Genealogy Via the Internet *is that the reader can approach the book with little or no computer experience. It is essentially a "How-to" book designed for practical use by ordinary people. Whether the reader is new to computers or familiar with the web, the book is an excellent genealogical tool.*

—UDC Magazine, *United Daughters of the Confederacy*

...gives a good overview of what is involved in getting started in genealogy in the computer age.

—Eastman's Online Genealogy Newsletter

My name is Slava Timashev. I live in Russia and am interested in finding the roots of my family which belongs to Russian nobility. ... Recently I got hold of your book Genealogy via the Internet *and read it in a few hours. I enjoyed it very much*

A must for beginning genealogy researchers and new users of the internet.Well worth the price.
                                    —*RQJO33@prodigy.net, Newport News, VA*

I have read several books about performing genealogy research on line, but this book is by far the best! It gives you hints, tips, software reviews, and, best of all, LOTS of links to genealogy sites on the WWW. This books is definitely worth its modest price for anyone who is, or is considering, performing genealogical research.
                                    —*vjones@aeneas.net, Martin, TN*

The Internet and the World Wide Web have made searching family histories fast, fun, and easy. In this humorous and informative book, readers will find genealogical programs, resources available through the Internet, and online databases where one can search for family information.
                                    —*www.hallgraphic.com/family_computing*

Genealogy Via the Internet *will make your search for family fun, easy, convenient and accurate. Toss out your well-used notebook, break your pencils and pick up this must-have Internet genealogical guide.*
                                    —Clan MacNeil in Canada Genealogy Pages

Genealogy via the Internet: Tracing Your Family Roots Quickly & Easily: Computerized Genealogy *by Ralph Roberts is a well-written, easy-to-understand book. Roberts also includes helpful genealogy software information (particularly on Family Tree Maker) and several links to start you off. The book is really geared toward beginning genealogists and beginning computer-users, so if you just got bit by the genealogy hobby bug, then this book's for you!*
                                    —The Broughton Family Tree

Computerized genealogy using the Internet! This book teaches you how to research your family history, covers genealogy computer programs, and points out dozens of online searchable genealogy databases. The perfect getting started guide. —Momsfamilies.com

A plain English guide to connecting your computer to the Internet and using it for genealogical research.
                                    —Rick and Lyn's Genealogy Page, *United Kingdom*

It is the most fundamental of how-to books, going out of the way to be personable and using stories and analogies for the purpose of allowing one to fearlessly approach self-instruction. There is a chapter on the basics of genealogy. Many people will be relieved to find so much help at such a reasonable price.
                                    —*Dr. Betsy C. Farlow, N.C. Genealogical Society*

GENEALOGY VIA THE INTERNET

INTERNET

TRACING YOUR FAMILY ROOTS QUICKLY AND EASILY

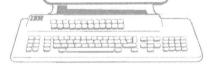

COMPUTERIZED GENEALOGY

IN PLAIN ENGLISH

SECOND EDITION

RALPH ROBERTS

Alexander Books

Alexander, N.C.

Publisher: Ralph Roberts

Editor: Pat Roberts

Cover Design: Ralph Roberts
Interior Design & Electronic Page Assembly: **WorldComm®**
Photographs and other graphics as indicated

2nd Edition

10   9   8   7   6   5   4   3   2   1

ISBN 1-57090-093-0 Trade Paper
ISBN 1-57090-129-5 Casebound

Library of Congress Number: 00-100284

Alexander Books—a division of Creativity, Inc.—is a full–service publisher located at 800 Macedonia Road, Alexander NC 28701. Phone (828) 252–9515, Fax (828) 255–8719. For orders only: 1-800-472-0438. Visa and MasterCard accepted.

Alexander Books iis distributed to the trade by **Midpoint Trade Books, Inc.**, 27 West 20th Street, New York NY 10011, (212) 727-0190, (212) 727-0195 fax.

and by **aBOOKS**, 65 Macedonia Road, Alexander NC 28701, sales@abooks.com

This book is also available on the internet at **http://abooks.com/genealogy**.

CONTENTS

PART III: Genealogy Software 151

PART IV: Out There on the Internet 205

COMPUTERIZED GENEALOGY

IN PLAIN ENGLISH

The author's great-great grandparents, James "Jimmy" Roberts (January, 1819—October, 1900) and Polly Goforth Roberts (October, 1818—June, 1903) of Madison County, North Carolina.

My 4th great grandfather, George Roberts, left Wilkes County, North Carolina, after fighting in the Revolutionary War to establish a new country, these United States, and—about 1800—he, his son George, Junior (Jimmy's father) and the rest of his family—headed for those high mist-enshrouded Great Smoky Mountains, settling in what is now the legendary Kingdom of Madison.* George, Junior married Sarah Payne (said to have been Cherokee), and soon had sons and daughters. One of these was James N. 'Uncle Bud' Roberts, who married Alice Matilda Correl. Their son George married Lottie Payne, who had a son named Carl. Carl married Ibbie Ball and my sister Marie and myself resulted. I still live here in these storied mountains. Knowing how you came to be; that's the true and wondrous magic of genealogy!

DEDICATION

This book is dedicated to every single ancestor and all collateral relatives in both mine and my wife's family all the way up from the very beginning of time.

That's a lot of people to dedicate a book to—pretty close to the entire human race—but, without them, it truly would not have been possible. We all exist only because of those who existed before us. Which is why any family history is so wonderfully fascinating.

* **The Kingdom of Madison** — Manly Wade Wellman — 1-56664-179-9 — WorldComm®. $16.95. Foreword by Ralph Roberts. 6x9, trade paper, 224 pages, b & w photographs. Call 1-800-472-0438 to order.

PREFACE

Genealogy via the internet and other online services is a marriage made in heaven. One of the fastest growing hobbies, worldwide, genealogy has always required a great deal of commitment and long years of research. This remains true today, but current genealogical resources, literally hundreds of thousands on the internet and the worldwide web, shortens your task dramatically.

When I wrote the first edition of this book in late 1997, the number of genealogy resources on the internet and the worldwide web was astounding, or so I truly thought—being many hundreds of thousands at the very least. Today (February, 2002) there are reported to be over *one billion pages* on the web! So there are several times more genealogical data now, than when the first edition was published, and this wondrous plethora of family research data will only continue to grow in leaps and bounds. Certainly my own researches into the history of my own and my wife's family histories has had tremendous success on the web. We now have over 130,000 relatives in our database dating back centuries that we never knew existed before.

What is it like today, tracing your roots on the worldwide web? Well, imagine having every major library in the world in your den. It's as if your bedroom was in the Library of Congress and a thousand county court-houses brimming with easy-to-find family records were just down the hall. And having access to thousands of family trees that might just very well tie into your own. Why reinvent the wheel if a lot of your research is already done? I'll show you how to find those records and much more!

Hours saved turn into days saved; then weeks saved become years saved! Your search for roots reaches a depth and an accuracy engendering pride and a sense of very real accomplishment. In researching and con-structing this proud family history of yours, you'll pass down to the generations following you that pride as a treasured family heirloom.

Preparing your family history is now fast, fun, and easily within the abilities of you, me, and everyone! No more the keeping of jumbled notebooks that made gene-alogy just too complex for most of us in the past. A personal computer and a telephone line are now your tools. The world is your library.

It's really easy, and I'll guide you through the starting process for both researching your family roots and the incredible *helpfulness* of using a personal computer to do so, all *in plain English*.

WHY THIS BOOK?

Now, a word about why I came to do this book, and my qualifications for writing it.

Before that justification, I will be frank and tell you another reason—not to brag, although authors are not overly modest creatures, but to say "thank you!"

The first edition of **Genealogy via the Internet** (Alexander Books, ISBN 1-57090-009-4, 1997) has been

Another set of my great-great grandparents, Henry Correll (July 1823—July, 1893) and Mary "Polly" McLean Correll (August 1823—June, 1903). I just recently found one of those wonderful human interest stories on the web about these two ancestors that makes genealogy so warm and rewarding. The young married couple moved to Madison County in the mountains of Western North Carolina because Mary abhorred slavery. The Corrells owned plantations. Henry followed his wife's lead, even fighting for the Union during the Civil War. (He got a pension for rupture and rheumatism—it was a long, cold, hard war.)

exceptionally well received and sold a *lot* of copies. The rewards have been substantial to myself and my publishing company, but what pleases me far more than the money is that wonderful warmth from knowing so many people have found this book so useful.

Now, on to even more personal reasons.

Two longtime fascinations exist for me—technology and history. In college, a good many years ago, I majored in engineering and minored in history. These choices of preference mirror themselves in my writing and reading. I've written over 90 books to date and read many thousands more, their topics being divided between computers and historical subjects, especially antiques and collectibles, and America's Civil War. The latter having no little interest to most of us whose ancestors fought in blue or gray, or were otherwise affected by this seminal event in the American experience.

Then came my own book publishing imprints—of which **Alexander Books** is one. As the company grew and expanded, you may have already guessed the two predominating subjects in our 500-plus titles now in print or soon to be so. Yep, computers and history/collectibles, including quite a few genealogical books.

So you might say I've been training to write this particular book for well over 30 years now. Even before college I combined a ham radio hobby with heavy reading and research in matters historic.

As computers have grown more powerful, so too has my love and use of them. As I've aged, so too has my fascination with the wonders and nostalgia of times past. My fifty-sixth birthday now past, interest in my own family and where they came from down through the misty centuries deepens as well.

A COMPLETE PACKAGE

The first edition of *Genealogy via the Internet* has been blessed with tons of great reviews—see the first two pages of this book for examples. Like most authors and publishers, we tend to use the good reviews and ignore the bad ones, but I'll mention them here to make a point. In fact, I was only able to find a couple. These reviews said that the book had too much in it about computers and the internet. I believe these reviewer folk missed the point.

Genealogy via the Internet is meant to be a *complete package*—taking you from dead stop (knowing nothing about computers) to joyfully seaching the internet and finding lots of good and useful information about your family's roots. Other books concentrate on just computers or just genealogy; this one ties it all up in a pretty ribbon and gives you the gift of understandable and useable techniques in plain English.

I take you from novice to the beginning of advanced internet genealogist in easy steps. If you are a beginner in computerized genealogy, this is wonderful. If you are already an advanced genealogist, the review won't hurt and you'll learn some handy-dandy stuff you may have otherwise overlooked.

Most importantly, I show you the joys of *full* genealogy (as opposed to just looking at your ancestors). Full genealogy lets you look at collateral lines (those parallel to yours) and find many more cousins than you ever believe possible. You'll find genealogy even more open and free and establish links to celebrities of all sorts using these research techniques. It's easy, it's fun, let's get started!

Therefore, I present this book to you—having stated qualifications that will result in a useful, informative family research adventure for you. We'll now sail the seas of cyberspace in search of long-lost but soon-to-be-found relatives.

Ralph Roberts

Ralph Roberts
65 Macedonia Road
Alexander, NC 28701 USA
email: *ralph@abooks.com*
web: **http://abooks.com/genealogy**

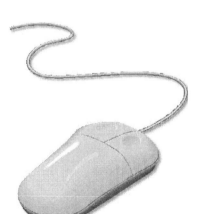

How far back can you trace *your* family? Pretty far if you can get though the 19th and 18th centuries and tie into one of the many well-researched European lines on the internet. My wife, Pat, and I are both descended from the Frankish Emperor Charlemagne (43 generations). Almost anyone decends from royalty if you go back far enough.

GENEALOGY VIA THE INTERNET

TRACING YOUR FAMILY ROOTS QUICKLY AND EASILY

PART I:

FULL GENEALOGY, COUSINS BY THE DOZENS

In this section we see the fruits of FULL genealogy, learn about cousins by the dozens (tens of millions actually), find out all presidents are related, and that most of us descend from the Prophet Muhammad, I kid you not.

Search RootsWeb.com | Search | **Search Ancestry.com** | Search | **Password Central** GO

First Name Last Name *By Keyword*   First Name Last Name *Advanced*

Passwords ~ Web Sites
Mailing Lists ~ Accounts

Getting Started
Getting Started at RootsWeb
RootsWeb's Guide To Tracing
Family Trees
RootsWeb Review Archives |
Subscribe
What's New

Search Engines and Databases
GenSeeker (Web Sites)
Meta Search (Multiple Databases and Files)
RootsWeb Surname List/RSL (Surname Listings)
SearchThingy (Multiple Databases and Files)
Social Security Death Index (Deaths)
Surname Helper (Message Boards, Web Sites)
U. S. Town/County Database (Locations)
WorldConnect Project (Family Trees)
USGenWeb Archives Search
Index of All Search Engines and Databases

Family Trees (WorldConnect)
WorldConnect Project Main Page
Search Family Trees
Submit Your Family Tree
Edit Your Family Tree

Mailing Lists
Index (Browse All Lists)
ROOTS-L Mailing List
Surname List Finder
Interactive Search
Threaded Archives
Requests for Mailing Lists (New or Adoptable)

Message Boards
Message Boards Home Page
Surnames | Localities | Topics
Requests for New Message Boards

Research Templates
Surnames (Most Common Names)
United States | Countries
Link Your Site to Research Templates

Web Sites
Web Sites at RootsWeb
Web Sites on RootsWeb's
Freepages
Notable Kin
US Presidential Ancestor Tables/Pedigrees
Requests for Web Space

Other Tools and Resources
ROOTS-L Library | State Resources
RootsLink URL Registry | Add A Link
Soundex Converter

Hosted Volunteer Projects
AOL Genealogy Forum
Books We Own
Cemetery Photos
Cyndi's List
FreeBMD (England and Wales)
FreeReg (UK)
Genealogy.org
Immigrant Ships Transcribers Guild
Obituary Daily Times
USGenWeb Project | Archives
WorldGenWeb Project | Archives

Help
FAQs & Help-Related Resources
Address Changes
Password Central
Contacting the HelpDesk

Buy or Sell
Affiliates Program
Genealogy Products

Contributing to RootsWeb
Share Your Research
Submitting Your Database to RootsWeb
Personalized Mailing Lists (A Sponsor Benefit)

Free Genealogy Newsletters:

RootsWeb Review	RootsWeb Product Watch Review	Ancestry Daily News
Each Wednesday you will learn the latest news about RootsWeb, new databases, mailing lists, home pages, and Web sites to maximize your genealogy research.	This newsletter will introduce you to new products from The Shops@Ancestry.com and offer periodic savings exclusive to Product Watch subscribers.	Every weekday you will find a new column on family history practices and current events with articles from a team of the best and brightest family history columnists.
Subscribe or Unsubscribe (via e-mail) View Archives Submit Story (plain text, no html or attachments)	Subscribe The Shops@Ancestry.com	Subscribe View Archives

A great starting point for online research is **rootsweb.com**, the largest and oldest free genealogy site on the web!

FULL GENEALOGY
AND ONLINE ACCURACY

A CLASH OF CULTURES

The presence of humans, in a system containing high-speed electronic computers and high-speed, accurate communications, is quite inhibiting. —Stuart Luman Seaton
Time, 17 Feb 1958

Researchers are to be cautioned against the notion of relying strictly on internet research to compile evidence of their pedigrees. Until all source documents (birth, marriage, death, etc.) are on the internet, you'll be using the online indexes as a "guide."

—in emails sent by the Old Buncombe County Genealogical Society

I've added 30,000 relatives in the last three months. —me

L ike cymbals clashing, arguments flow back and forth about the accuracy of doing online genealogi- cal research. It's a "hot potato" topic that many prefer not to touch, but I've got my oven mitts on.

The following examines both sides, attempts to re- solve the ongoing argument, lays out techniques for achieving better results online, and shows the positive side of internet genealogy (and it's a lot more positive than some would have you believe).

So, on to controversy and could I have some chives and sour cream with this hot potato?

ONLINE RESOURCES

My favorite genealogy site on the web is RootsWeb's WorldConnect Project (**worldconnect.genealogy. rootsweb.com**). With over 192 million names (as of this writing) and growing rapidly, you can find most any family connection quickly and easily, and download *gedcoms* with hundreds or even thousands of new kinfolk several times an evening. A GEDCOM (GEnealogical Data COMmunication file) is a standard developed by the Family History Department of The Church of Jesus Christ of Latter-day Saints (the Mormons) for exchanging data between genealogical programs. You'll use it often.

The internet now teems with many, many thousands of sites related to genealogical research. You, too, can download hundreds of your relatives a night. Sounds good, huh?

Well, yes it is and that's what this book, *Genealogy via the Internet*, is all about. Yet, like any powerful tool, you need some guidance in how to use it.

As in the quote at the first of this chapter, I really did add 30,000 relatives in the last three months.

"Not accurate! Wrong! Full of mistakes! Unproven!" So say the old-line genealogists, growling in disgust from their positions perched in the front of microfiche readers in a thousand libraries; and from a legion of dusty, dimly lit courthouses. "Not primary documentation. Unconfirmed!"

Who's right? Who's wrong? Both of us—yes, both sides are right and both wrong, but here exists the future of genealogy. It's more wonderful and promising than you might at first imagine. Yet, there's a clash of cultures occurring, causing a mini war over online accuracy.

To understand, let's first look at how genealogy has been done in the past?

ANCESTOR GENEALOGY

For centuries, serious genealogists exercised the only choice possible, their feet. They visited the towns where ancestors had lived; spending hours in libraries, halls of records such as courthouses, and reading tombstones in cemeteries. They pored over near illegible and often vastly illiterate ledgers of public record full of whimsical spellings, examined local histories, thoughtfully analyzed census records, and translated reams of wills signed with a spidery 'X'. Slowly and painstakingly they accumulated the primary documentation proving specific life events of BMDB (birth, marriage, death, burial) by which classic genealogy is accomplished and recorded for each individual ancestor.

These mighty genealogists of yore prepared careful charts of their results; recording pedigrees and constructing family trees. Years, decades, often even a lifetime was spent in expanding their data for only a few generations of their ancestors. The sum total of their findings now fill shelves of books, populate millions of microfiche and, well, where do you think most of the 192 million name plus database at WorldConnect and other online databases came from mostly?

Serious genealogists today continue this Herculean task; digging out and verifying BMDBs for more and more of our ancestors. We owe a great debt of gratitude to their untiring efforts. So, don't get me wrong here, I *respect* serious genealogists.

The immense difficulty in this type of genealogy favors specialization. Years are spent on the lines of one's own ancestry, looking *only* at those individuals from which the genealogist himself or herself is descended. Indeed, when you and I take up the hobby of genealogy, our first tasks involve tracing back our grandfathers and grandmothers, their fathers and mothers, and so on. We also look only at ancestors. This type of study is called, logically enough, *ancestor* genealogy.

"Well?" you ask. "Isn't that what genealogy is all about? Ancestors?"

No, it's not. Genealogy is about all *relationships*— more about that in a moment.

A certain limiting mindset exists in some professional genealogists and in quite a few newcomers because of ancestor genealogy and the often rather narrow viewpoint it sometimes engenders.

The professionals, rightly proud of years of experience in sifting through records for rare gems of information about the families from whence they came, have a vested interest in protecting the *status quo*. They maintain you need to examine the actual source records for life events in your ancestors, that you must prove each ancestor before proceeding to an earlier generation. They say genealogy is hard, tedious, painstaking work. In that context, they are right.

Newcomers to genealogy (called *newbies* on the internet*) at first see great progress, adding a great number of ancestors to their databases. Because they start at nothing, they find lots of good stuff immediately—adding five, six, seven generations almost overnight. They say ancestor genealogy is easy. In that context, *they*, too, are right.

So, for differing reasons, ancestor genealogy has strong proponents who defend it as being the *only* kind of family research. Old-line professionals scoff at the internet as not providing actual documentation—copies of wills, birth and death records, and marriage records. "How can you *prove* anything?" they demand.

---

* A note of explanation, I do not capitalize the word 'internet' (albeit that's the style usage these days) unless forced to (sometimes a publisher demands it), because the internet is a collection of thousands upon thousands of interconnected nets, not one huge entity as a few technically illiterate journalists view it.

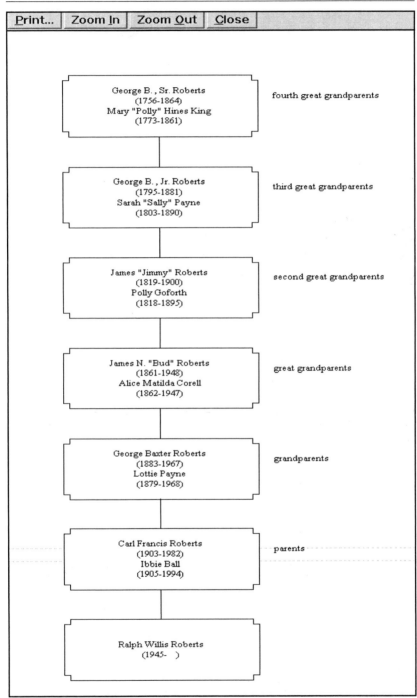

George B. , Sr. Roberts
(1756-1864)
Mary "Polly" Hines King
(1773-1861)

fourth great grandparents

George B. , Jr. Roberts
(1795-1881)
Sarah "Sally" Payne
(1803-1890)

third great grandparents

James "Jimmy" Roberts
(1819-1900)
Polly Goforth
(1818-1895)

second great grandparents

James N. "Bud" Roberts
(1861-1948)
Alice Matilda Corell
(1862-1947)

great grandparents

George Baxter Roberts
(1883-1967)
Lottie Payne
(1879-1968)

grandparents

Carl Francis Roberts
(1903-1982)
Ibbie Ball
(1905-1994)

parents

Ralph Willis Roberts
(1945-   )

Ancestor genealogy looks at direct lines back to your ancestors, like this one from my father's side of the family.

Newcomers, after that initial flush of success, become enmeshed in the minutia of proving their lineages. After that heady rush of rapid victories, months may go by before another ancestor is found and added. "The internet is only good for *clues*," they say, adopting the mindset of admired professionals.

And nothing is wrong with this mindset in so far as it promotes accuracy. We *all* should strive to make our family data as correct as possible. But some of these people have no sense of humor; they believe everything published in books, online, or anywhere should be one hundred percent correct *according to what they have found*. They growl and groan at incorrect data posted online, send emails (some polite, some nasty) to anyone who dares go against their view of who is the father

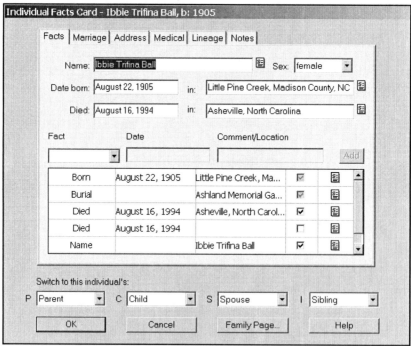

The more data you can accumulate on each person, the better. The basic information should include birth, marriage, death, burial. Good genealogy software (like the Individual Facts Card shown here in Family Tree Maker) simplifies your task of keeping proper records.

of whom. All this only reinforces the mindset that online genealogy lacks validity and is not to be respected when the opposite is true with proper caution.

Yes, what's the use of having computers and access to the vastness of the internet if you can't use all that *power*? Many of us do use it, and that's when the cymbals start banging away.

CLASH OF CULTURES

I've seen the clash of cultures that are now ongoing in genealogical circles often before, and it's always technology-driven. Classic examples include the industrial age of the early 19th century, when steam power, programmable looms, and such brought automation to manual manufacturing processes. There were those who claimed weaving by hand remained the best way of making cloth. Well, yes it is, but darned slow (pun, as ever, intended). The superior quality of handmade garments remains true today, but we all tend to mostly buy the mass produced socks at Wallymart. They're cheaper.

A more recent example—one which I've spent the last twenty-some years observing and participating in—concerns exactly what I do at this very moment, writing! I saw the advantage of the personal computer for writing back in 1978 and it jumpstarted my career. In those days, "serious" professional writers mostly espoused the typewriter or—if you really wanted to do it right—scribble your work by hand and, if you must, then type it up for the publishers (who, not being purists) insist on something they can actually decipher instead of a handwritten manuscript.

The exact same arguments for maintaining the *status quo* and dire warnings about a rapid decrease in quality of writing were promulgated by these serious writers as were voiced by those against automatically-knitted socks and by those professional genealogists today aghast at online "mass produced" family research.

With writing, it took only a few years before most writers saw the power of using word processing software. Just try to find a ribbon for an Underwood manual typewriter today—it's a thing of the past. Yet, admittedly, the fact that personal computers made the process of writing so easy, and generate professional-looking manuscripts, did lower the overall quality of work sent to publishers. As a publisher, I can tell you, 99% of the stuff submitted is crap... but it's *good-looking* crap.

So, I can and do subscribe to the conclusions made by serious writers 20 years ago, serious genealogists today, and those sock weavers of yore—automation lowers the overall quality. What I *don't* accept is their argument that it's not worthwhile. Millions more people today write, wear socks, and share the thrill of online family research.

That's what I mean about mindset. Just like machines spin out more socks (yeah, another pun) in a shorter time and word processing software makes authoring books *much easier*, online genealogical research greatly magnifies our efficiency in corralling our relatives and shortens the time frame by *years*. More about responsibly using this power while still reaping its benefits shortly.

FULL GENEALOGY

Okay, we looked at ancestor genealogy, which is much like a horse wearing blinders; you see only the path ahead (actually, *behind*, since we move back into the past). You can travel it faster online, but the ancestor-only mindset keeps one from experiencing the complete richness and diversity of data that online research offers. It's like petting your cat with a shoe on your hand—neither one of you receive much enjoyment out of the process.

The term *full genealogy* refers to *all* relationships, not just those of your ancestors. It adds zest and body, scope and vision, and much more.

George Washington, for example, is my second cousin, eight times removed. This doesn't mean I'm descended from the first president of the United States and "Father of His County" (no one is, he had no children)—however, Washington's mother, Mary Ball, was my first cousin, nine times removed.

What does that mean, the oft heard, seldom understood term "removed?" The next chapter ("Cousins by the Dozen") explains kin relationships in detail, a subject extremely important for the enjoyment of full genealogy instead being bound by the limitations of ancestor genealogy. Below is the condensed definition.

Cousins have the same ancestor. If you and I share common grandparents, you are my first cousin. If we are related through our great grandparents, you are my second cousin, and so on.

However, if your mother is my second cousin, that makes you my second cousin *once removed* and your sons and daughters would be my second cousins *twice* removed. "Removed" simply refers to the difference in number of generations (good genealogical software figures relationships automatically, saving you much headache).

So George Washington and my direct ancestor, Daniel Ball, had the same great-grandfather (Colonel William Ball), making them second cousins. I am in the eighth generation of descendants from Daniel, making me the second cousin of *George eight* times removed—a reasonably close relationship.

I'm a writer so other authors stand among my heroes. One such is the writer Samuel Langhorne Clemens (1835-1910), better known by his penname,

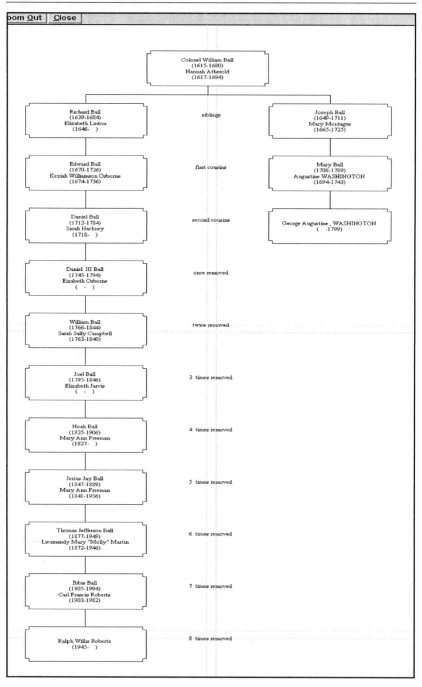

Because George and Martha Washington had no children (he was only "the Father of His Country"), my relationship to him is through a common ancestor instead of directly.

"Mark Twain." I derived great pleasure in proving that he is my fourteenth cousin, six times removed. Our common ancestor is Robert III, King of Scotland (1350-1401).

How far can you go with full genealogy? Well, as my 17th cousin, twice removed—President George W. Bush—might say, "all the way to the White House." In a very satisfying exercise of full genealogy, I proved my relationship to *all* 43 U.S. Presidents! (Counting Grover Cleveland twice, of course, since he is the only president to serve separated terms.) I also determind George Bush as being related to all the other presidents. Details on all that in Chapter 3 of this book.

Neither President Bush nor myself are too excited about being related to ex-President Clinton, but all families have their black sheep, eh? Clinton is my 23rd cousin once removed and President Bush's 19th cousin two times removed.

How I did all this (and how you can do it for yourself) is detailed throughout this books but, following, are the basics.

MY COUSIN, "VEE"

We are, one and all, the Family of Humanity. You go back far enough and everyone's related, no matter the race or geographic homeland of your ancestors. Thanks to intermarriage, we humans are marvelous mongrels and lines of kinships a lot closer than you think.

Full genealogy, again, is all possible relationships. Not just your direct ancestors but also their descendants; all of your many, many cousins.

How many cousins do you have? Assume this: If we conservatively say that each generation of your ancestors had only two children and that each of those had two children, then going back only 20 generations means you have the possibility of over *one million* cousins today. Actually—since the old folks in medieval and colonial times tended to have large families—you have *many millions* of cousins.

The trick, of course, is finding out *who* these cousins are and managing a database with tens or hundreds of thousands of relatives. Online genealogy and good family research software on your personal computer now gives us the power to do all this.

And the key to proving a relationship to a distant cousin is the *vee* technique. (That's vee, like in the letter 'V.') Take, as an example, the son of your uncle, your first cousin. To prove a relation to him, you go from yourself to your mother to her parents (your maternal grandparents), back up to their son (your uncle), to your first cousin. It's a simple 'V' shape, down and up.

All cousin relationships, no matter how complex or how many generations are involved, are a simple vee. The only other type is a straight line back to a direct ancestor (one side of the vee).

To prove a relationship to any distant cousin, celebrity

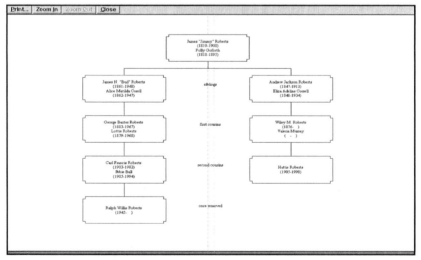

An example of a vee relationship (upside down vee) with the common ancestor being the tip of the vee.

or not, requires tracing down lines of descendants, looking for a place that intersects with one of your own direct
lines. In short, making that vee we just discussed. Occasionally, you many need to go back through quite a few
generations.

Hardest of the presidents for me was Martin Van
Buren (1782-1862), our eighth president. Martin has all
Dutch ancestors back for many generations and I have
very few. For a time, it looked impossible; but, in full
genealogy, *nothing* is impossible! Just keep looking.

President Van Buren, as it turns out, is my 26th
cousin, once removed (and the 26th cousin, three times
removed of President George W. Bush). The common
ancestor to both President Bush and myself to Martin
Van Buren is William the Conqueror, Duke of Normandy
and King of England (old William, he invaded and took
England and he hasn't given it back yet, bubba—he
changed the course of history, but that's another book,
the one I'll write about my 28th great grandfather). The
common ancestor is the bottom point of any relationship vee.

In establishing a distant relationship like the one
with Van Buren, you'll find yourself adding hundreds
of people looking for that magic intersection, the
common ancestor completing the vee and establishing
kinship. In researching Van Buren's ancestors, I went
through hundreds of his ancestors—all Dutch—before
finding a marriage into the Norman French nobility in
the 13th century. After that it was a breeze—all the
European nobility intermarried and once you hit them,
you can fly through relationships. The techniques
used in finding and adding these relationships are
covered at length in the pages of this books.

"How long did *that* take?" you ask.

Oh, the best part of one evening. When you can add
lines of scores or hundreds of people by merely download-

ing and merging a GEDCOM into your database, events move quickly.

Which brings us back to accuracy. Our friends the professional and other "serious" genealogists no doubt already have raised hackles when I mention dropping hundreds of people into your database without checking them. I know some genealogy clubs have requirements like you must show at least two pieces of primary documentation (wills, birth or death certificates, other recognized items of public record) before claiming an ancestor. It can take years to find those and, meanwhile, you are stopped on that line.

In full genealogy, you do such fact checking *later*—and make no mistake, you'll still need to eventually prove your relationships. So you find a likely looking GEDCOM on the internet, download it in seconds, and add 10 generations worth of people (hundreds perhaps) in a few seconds more.

I hear gasping out there from the old line genealogists, but bear with me here, this is the way to get away from that mindset and use the power of computers and the internet, making real progress in your family research.

ONLINE ACCURACY

Just how good is all that family stuff you get off the internet? Well, it ranges from precisely the same accuracy that any serious genealogist would approve of—because it *is* reports from professionals that someone has published on the net—to the patently absurd, even whimsical. The trick lies in determining which is which.

A good example of the last can be found sometimes in the data from FamilySearch™ (**familysearch.com**). This site, and it's overall an excellent resource, is provided by the Church of Jesus Christ of Latter-day Saints (popularly known as the Mormons). Genealogical research is a tenet of this religion and the Mormons lead the world in accumulating and disseminating family data, adding over a hundred million records a year. This is good.

Unfortunately, some Mormons treat the requirement of supplying information on their ancestors the way you and I looked at our homework in the fourth grade—we turned in whatever we thought would get us off the hook. So do not take FamilySearch™ (and all sources for that matter—internet, book, whatever) as permanent proof, but do use them.

If the old-line genealogists fairly characterize the accuracy of data from books and other sources, which are not primary documentation, they'll readily admit about the same percentage of mistakes, occur as do in internet data. You have births happening when the mother is

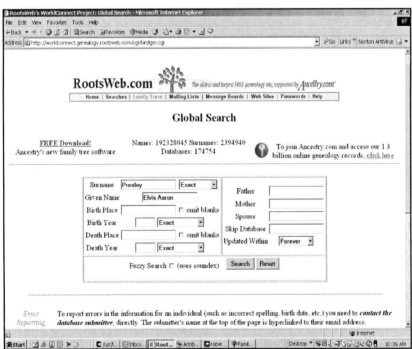

The search screen at **worldconnect.genealogy/rootsweb.com/cgi-bin/ igm.cgi** allows you instant access to over 192 million genealogy records. **Ancestry.com** (a leading for pay service) can up that to 1.3 billion!

three years old or years after the father has died. Entire generations get skipped, wrong parents are assigned to children, and other mistakes both obvious and not so obvious. In short, no family research you may find *anywhere* is going to be 100% accurate.

In old style ancestor genealogy, mistakes in source material might hold the researcher up for months or years. Remember the requirement I mentioned earlier of two primary sources being required to claim an ancestor? That does find mistakes but certainly stops the flow of research.

Downloading a GEDCOM with several hundred real or potential relatives from the internet and importing it into your family database certainly speeds things up. You're getting the same number of mistakes that serious genealogists find, but a whole lot faster. Computers don't make mistakes, but they certainly *magnify* the errors of humans.

USING ONLINE DATA

Discard that mindset I spoke of earlier that hampers genealogical research. Yes, you want to avoid erroneous data if possible, but don't let the possibility of their existence slow you down. If you want to dump a thousand new entries into your database in seconds, *do it*! This freedom allows you to take complete and efficient advantage of the amazing power of the internet and personal computing.

Do the errors stay in there forever? Well, of course they do if you don't make corrections, and you *should*. Accuracy always counts. The real secret here is that correcting your data is an ongoing process rather than a stop and start one. Whenever you find a mistake in birth, marriage, death, or burial (BMDBs), or any other fact in your database, correct it. You'll find these as you are in the process of adding other data, or people will call them to your attention if you publish your findings on the net—sometimes politely, sometimes not.

By the way, you should publish your results—always give back in thanks to those providing you with so much information). Withholding family research data is simply selfish; help others achieve the same satisfaction and fun you do. One good way of doing this is to place a GEDCOM of your family tree on the WorldConnect project (**worldconnect.genealogy. rootsweb.com**). I show you how in the chapter about using RootsWeb.

But as wonderful as places like WorldConnect are—with over 192 million entries, some are bound to be *your* relatives—you still need to exercise care to get the best accuracy possible.

"Remember that information found at WorldConnect," reads a warning on their website, "like any other genealogical material you find published on the Internet or in traditional sources, provides clues and contacts, not proof."

Here are some basic rules for using online data:

1. *Does any of the data match up with what your research has already uncovered?*
2. *Are sources given?*
3. *Do BMDB dates appear logical (i.e. children not born when the mother is three years old, and so forth).*
4. *Is the data free of typos (carelessness in language often reflects carelessness in entering data—spelling counts, especially in family and place names!).*
5. *Does the person publishing the information seem to know what he or she is doing (after a while, you learn which people publishing GEDCOMs take that extra effort to provide good data).*

WHAT ARE YOUR GOALS?

Finally, consider what your goals are in doing family research. If all you want is the immediate few generations of your ancestors as accurately as possible, old style genealogy works well, albeit mighty slowly. On the other hand, if you yearn for the wide open vistas of having a few hundred thousand cousins and knowing your relationship to tons of famous and even infamous people, then *full* genealogy and the power of the internet awaits you.

In full genealogy and celebrity genealogy, having total proof of each and every person is not as important as in ancestor research. The *path* (that relationship *vee* we discussed) counts for more. So what if you have some incorrect dates, you'll eventually find and correct them, or not. Keep the vision going and don't slow down your research. Develop an internet mindset!

Did I mention Her Majesty Queen Elizabeth II of England is my 10th cousin once removed? Or that singer Bing Crosby was my half 7th cousin twice removed? Or that the highly respected and much beloved icon of the South, General Robert E. Lee is my third cousin, six times removed?

Perhaps you, too, are related to all the noted personages above, and many more besides. The odds are certainly with you. The power of *full* genealogy lets you find out and record all those satisfying kinships.

You've got the world's greatest genealogical research library setting on your desktop—your personal computer and the internet. So, on to fun!

COUSINS BY THE DOZENS

If your grandparents had children (often enough the case if you exist) then the children of your parents' siblings (your uncles and aunts) are your first cousins, their children your first cousins once removed, and so forth.

The basic concepts of kinship are simple. You'll find a little knowledge of how family relations work both useful and fascinating.

TYPES OF KIN

The kind of kinship most interesting and meaningful in genealogical research is called *consanguinity*. That's a four-dollar word (excluding tax, batteries not included) simply meaning a direct *blood relationship* as opposed to one just through marriage or adoption.

This chapter deals only with kinship by blood; it does not cover step or in-law or marital connections. There are three sorts of blood relationships:

- **Lineal** — The word *lineal* means a straight line. You are descended directly from your great grandparents through your grandparents to your parents to you. Your grandchildren (should or when you have them) descend in a straight line from your children to you. Most people—when they first start researching their roots, concern themselves mostly with this type of relationship, i.e. *ancestor* genealogy.

- **Collateral** — What about your brothers and sisters? You are related to them collaterally. That doesn't mean you can use your relatives as collateral in getting a bank loan—another definition of *collateral* is parallel (side by side). You share common ancestors with your brother and sister but you are not in a direct line of descent from or to them. Other types of parallel relatives include cousins, uncles, grand aunts, or anyone else you share a common ancestor with but are not in a direct line from or to. All this falls under *full genealogy*, our favorite kind!

- **Half** — "Half" relationships are really simple— in these you share only one common ancestor, that common ancestor having more than one spouse. Your mother remarries and has another child, that's your half sister. Your great great grandfather remarried and all the descendants of that marriage are your half cousins.

YOUR RELATIVES... AND LOTS OF THEM!

How many relatives do you have? Here's some simple math just to establish scope:

- Grandparents: Your mother's father and mother plus your dad's father and mother = 4
- Great Grandparents: 4 sets of man and wife x 2 = 8
- Great Greats: 8 x 2 = 16

- Eight Generations back: 256 eighth great grand-parents
- 20 Generations back: 1,048,576 20th great grand-parents.

Yep, that's right; over *one million* direct ancestors only 20 generations back—that's somewhere around the 1400s for those of us now living.

These are all lineal ancestors of yours.

Now, let's come back up the generations. Consider your one million 20th great grandparents averaged two kids each. That's also 1,048,576 because we have to divide the parents by two, men and women (and if you don't understand *that*, you need a birds and bees type book, not this one).

And each of those kids got married and had two kids (low for back then, people tended to run to big families)—and so forth, and so forth. And, by the time we get back to *now*, you have literally tens of millions of collateral relatives—cousins and half cousins.

"Wow," you say, "with tens of millions of cousins that means that you and I are probably related."

Not just 'probably' cuz, we *are* related. Everyone is!

Alexander, Rhoda C.	November 06, 1785	Half 14th cousin 5 times remo
Alexander, Robert	1610	Half 8th cousin 11 times removed
Alexander, Robert	Bet 1620 - 1625	Half 7th cousin 12 times removed
Alexander, Robert G.		Husband of the 8th cousin once rem
Alexander, Robert S.	September 02, 1795	Half 14th cousin 5 times removed
Alexander, Sarah M.	1827	Half 15th cousin 4 times removed
Alexander, Strong	Abt. 1632	Half 9th cousin 10 times removed
Alexander, Thomas	1770	Half 13th cousin 6 times removed
Alexander, Thomas, Jr	1676	Half 10th cousin 9 times removed
Alexander, Thomas, Sr.	1630	Half 9th cousin 10 times removed
Alexander, William	1604	Half 7th cousin 12 times removed
Alexander, William	Abt. 1634	Half 9th cousin 10 times removed
Alexander, William	1668	Half 10th cousin 9 times removed
Alexander, William	1676	Half 9th cousin 10 times removed
Alexander, William	March 22, 1737/38	Half 12th cousin 7 times removed
Alexander, William Davidson	January 28, 1798	Half 14th cousin 5 times removed
Alexander, William Davidson	December 10, 1800	Half 14th cousin 5 times removed
Alexander, William, 1st Earl of Stirling	Abt. 1567	Husband of the half 6th cousin 13 tin
Alexander, William, Sr	1624	Half 8th cousin 11 times removed
AlexanderII, King of Scotland	1198	Half 25th great-granduncle
AlexanderIII, King of Scotland		Half 2nd cousin 23 times removed
Alexandra Fedorovna 'Alix'	June 06, 1872	Half 9th cousin 11 times removed
Alexios, Emperor of /BYZANTINE EMPIRE/	February 1105/06	7th cousin 26 times removed
Alexios, II, Emperor /BYZANTINE EMPIRE/	September 10, 1169	Husband of the 2nd cousin 27 times
Alfgar	1002	4th cousin 31 times removed
Alfonso	Abt. 1220	23rd great-granduncle
Alfonso (Affonso) I Henriques	1109	Half 1st cousin 26 times removed
Alfonso II	March 1156/57	Husband of the half 25th great-grand
Alfonso IX "the Slobberer"	August 15, 1171	1st cousin 26 times removed

Part of my kinship report from the Family Tree Maker genealogy software. The program calculates degrees of kin quickly and easily.

Ain't genealogy wonderful? Thankfully, computers now let us manage huge databases with tens or hundreds of thousands of relatives with the greatest of ease. This is good because you'll find you have not just one relationship to distant cousins but dozens or hundreds because of all the intermarrying of cousins down through the years. For example, my mother and dad were cousins, so I have a common set of great great grandparents on both sides of the family. This happens quite often and only a computer can track it all for you.

Your most plentiful type of relatives, naturally, are cousins. By the dozens? Nah, try by the tens of *millions*.

Here's a broad definition:

> **COUSIN:** *In colonial usage, it most often meant nephew or niece. In the broadest sense, it could also mean any family relationship, lineal or collateral (except mother, father, sister, or brother), or the modern-day meaning of a child of one's aunt or uncle. Usage today includes qualifiers like first, second, third, once removed, twice removed, etc.*

HE'S MY COUSIN, ONCE REMOVED

Okay, what does *removed* mean? You already know about your grandparents. Move back one generation—to your *great* grandparents. The brothers and sisters of your grandparents are your grand uncles and grand aunts. Their children are your first cousins *once* removed. Your great great grandparents produce children who have first cousins twice removed, and your great great great grandparents supply first cousins three times removed.

Removed is a simple count of the generations between you and that relative—just pure addition and subtraction to get that number of generations different.

Here's how it works. Your great grandparents are three generations back—first generation back, parents; second generation back, grandparents, third generation back, great grandparents. Which means your grand uncles and grand aunts (siblings of your grandparents) are two generations back (same as your grandparents). So the sons and daughters of your grand uncles and grand aunts are only one generation back, or *once removed*.

As you come forward, subtract one for each generation; as you go back, add one for each generation.

With each generation of descendants of those first cousins, the number of the cousin relationship increases but the removed number decreases (since there are fewer generations between you and that relative. In other words, your first cousin eight times removed fathers your second cousin seven times removed who bears your third cousin six times removed.

Obviously, if we are subtracting as we come forward in generations, we reach *zero*. If someone is your first cousin, second cousin, fifth cousin, or 23rd cousin with no 'removed' attached, it means they are in the *same generation* as you.

Moving forward from your generations, the number for the removed relationship continues to add, but having passed zero now becomes a positive number. And the degree of cousinship remains the same. The children of your second cousin become your second cousins once removed, their children your second cousins twice removed, and so on.

Getting a little confused? Now is the time to study the "Your Kinship Chart" illustration which appears on the next two pages. This chart visually explains cousin relationships. At first, this whole concept appears confusing and complex. I studied various attempts at showing cousin relationships, and this is my go at it.

Generations	YOUR K				
-8				6th	
-7				5th great grar	
-6				4th great grandparents	
-5				3rd great grandparents (32)	
-4			great-great grandparents (16)		
-3			great grandparents (8)		
-2		your grandparents (4)		grand uncles/aunts	1
-1	your parents (2)		uncles/aunts	1st cousin 1x removed	2
0	**YOU**	**your brothers/ sisters**	**1st cousins**	**2nd cousins**	3
+1	your children	nephew/ nieces	1st cousins 1x removed	2nd cousins 1x removed	3
+2	your grandkids	grand nephew/ nieces	1st cousins 2x removed	2nd cousins 2x removed	3
+3	your great grandkids	2nd grand nephew/ nieces	1st cousins 3x removed	2nd cousins 3x removed	3

x = times as in 2 times removed   ©2002 Ralph Roberts

HIP CHART

dparents (256)					
(128)					5th great grand uncles/aunts
				4th great grand uncles/aunts	1st cousins 6x removed
			3rd great grand uncles/aunts	1st cousins 5x removed	2nd cousins 5x removed
		2nd great grand uncles/aunts	1st cousins 4x removed	2nd cousins 4x removed	3rd cousins 4x removed
	1d ts	1st cousins 3x removed	2nd cousins 3x removed	3rd cousins 3x removed	4th cousins 3x removed
	2x	2nd cousins 2x removed	3rd cousins 2x removed	4th cousins 2x removed	5th cousins 2x removed
	1x	3rd cousins 1x removed	4th cousins 1x removed	5th cousins 1x removed	6th cousins 1x removed
	ns	**4th cousins**	**5th cousins**	**6th cousins**	**7th cousins**
	1x	4th cousins 1x removed	5th cousins 1x removed	6th cousins 1x removed	7th cousins 1x removed
	2x	4th cousins 2x removed	5th cousins 2x removed	6th cousins 2x removed	7th cousins 2x removed
	3x	4th cousins 3x removed	5th cousins 3x removed	6th cousins 3x removed	7th cousins 3x removed

Using this relationship chart is simple. The white boxes (YOU and your siblings, and cousins in white) are all the same generation as yourself). Negative numbers in the 'Generations' column goes back towards your ancestors, postive numbers come forward toward your kids, grandkids.

Looking at the "Your Kinship Chart" the pattern of cousin kinship becomes clearer. Look at generation 0, your generation—call the white horizontal line of blocks your *generation line*. In your generation are first cousins, second cousins, third cousins, etc. Anyone not in your generation is in a *removed* generation, above or below your line. One generation previous is once removed but so is one generation forward. This is not nearly as confusing as it might sound at first.

Going across your generation line, we see these basic rules:

- You and your first cousins share grandparents in common.
- You and your second cousins have the same great grandparents.
- You and your third cousins have the same great great grandparents.
- You and your fourth cousins have the same great great great grandparents ... and so forth.

The number of cousin—first, second, third, etc.—denotes the number of generations you have to go back to the one that shares common parents. Your first cousins and you are one generation removed from your parents and their siblings (your uncles and aunts) who share the same parents, which happen to be your grandparents. Your second cousins are two generations removed from the generation that shares common parents, your great grandparents.

It's an elegant pattern, the pattern of human blood relationships!

Here's a quick rule of thumb for determining how many times removed a cousin is: for ancestors subtract, for descendants from your generation level, add. Look on "Your Kinship Chart" and find your 5th cousins. Your 5th cousin's father (one generation back) would be your 4th cousin, once removed. Note on the line in the chart (the line the 4th cousin once removed is on) has a –1 in the left hand column.

Your 5th cousin's *daughter* would be your 5th cousin once removed (+1 instead of –1). The big difference in cousins above and below your generation line is that *above* your generation line, the number of cousin subtracts with each generation—fourth to third to second to first to granduncle and grandaunt to great grandparent. *Below* (later generations), the number of cousin remains the same, only the removed number increases—fifth cousin once removed, fifth cousin two times removed, and so on.

Yes, removed relationships are not immediately obvious. In learning degrees of kinship, I've studied a lot of charts and read a lot of articles about cousins. From that, I developed the chart above, which makes these connections as visually obvious as possible. You don't have to memorize the chart, just be familiar with how it works.

The *really nice thing* about computerized genealogy is *not* having to figure relationships out; any good program does it for you by examining your entries. If I want to know George Washington's kinship to me, I just ask my family roots database (I use Family Tree Maker the most) and find he's my second cousin, eight times removed.

OUR GRANDPARENTS ARE GREAT!

In genealogy—to get away from having to write all those "greats" in front of ancestors in our direct line—we shorten it by saying our great great great grandmother is our third great grandmother. Her mother would be our fourth great grandmother and her children (our third grand uncles and third grand aunts) procreate our first cousins four times removed.

George Washington's relationship to me is through my *ninth* great grandfather Colonel William Ball, who is our common ancestor. Colonel Ball was the father of Richard, my eighth great grandfather, and Joseph, my eighth great uncle and George's grandfather. Joseph's daughter Mary Ball, my first cousin nine times removed, married Lawrence Washington and had George. Old George, of course, went on to chop down a cherry tree and become the first President of the United States.

Such relationships and the study of full genealogy as opposed to the more limited ancestor genealogy are great fun. Let's get on with it.

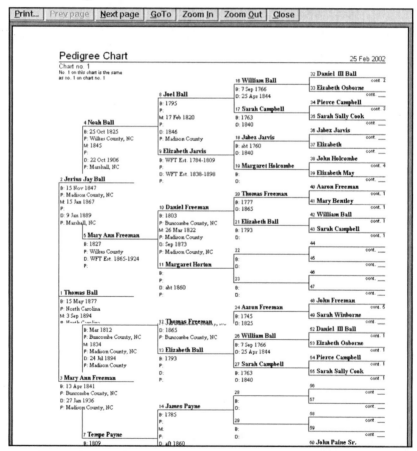

Good genealogy software generates numerous reports that help you see family relationships. Above, a pedigree chart from Family Origins.

PRESIDENT BUSH AND HIS COUSINS: ALL THE OTHER PRESIDENTS!

George W. Bush and the 41 Other Men Who Have Been President All Have One Thing in Common, They ALL Are Relatives

> *"We've uncovered some embarrassing ancestors in the not-too-distant past. Some horse thieves, and some people killed on Saturday nights. One of my relatives, unfortunately, was even in the newspaper business."*
> —James Earl "Jimmy" Carter
> President: 1977-1981

"Black sheep"—relatives we'd just as soon not be related to—exist in all families. President George W. Bush might or might not be happy with his cousin, former president Bill Clinton, but Clinton's part of Bush's family and vice versa. Then, too, there's that Tennessee country cousin to both of them, Al Gore.

Bush and Clinton are 19th cousins, twice removed. Gore, interestingly enough, has a closer relationship to Bush (23rd cousin, 3 times removed) than he does to his former boss Clinton (27th cousin, 2 times removed).

Yep, the trying election of 2000 was conducted by kinfolk; the little spat that resulted was all in the family, although I doubt any of the grandkids or other descendants of these three men will be named 'Chad' anytime soon.

Bush, Clinton, Gore, myself, and almost certainly *you*, as well, can trace our kinship through common ancestors. In the case of George Bush and William Jefferson Blythe IV (whose last name was changed to 'Clinton'), their closest common ancestor happens to be John, Duke of Gaunt—the son of King Edward III of England—and Katherine de Roelt (spelled variously).

As a matter of trivia, Bill Clinton is not the only president we've elected who has a different name than he was born with. The other is Leslie Lynch King, Jr., whose name was changed to Gerald Rudolf Ford when his mother remarried. This changes a lot in genealogy research; since we have to trace the King line instead of the Fords, who are not related to him by blood.

THE WONDER OF KINSHIP

To understand how everyone can be (and definitely is) so interrelated, consider the fact that you have four grandparents, eight great grandparents, sixteen great great grandparents, and so forth. In fact, go back a mere 20 generations and we all have over a million grandparents each! Come back to the present time figuring just an average number of children for each generation and you wind up with *tens of millions* of relatives.

Your parents, grandparents, their parents, and so on are your direct ancestors and you are their descendant. And descendants in lines up from a common ancestor parallel to your own are your cousins. In figuring family relationship, these folk—all cousins—are called collateral kin. Your uncle's son is your first cousin, he's in a collateral line. Your great grandfather's sister's daughter is your first cousin two times removed. (See Chapter 2)

Tracing kinship brings up all sorts of fascinating facts. Former president Clinton has often been likened to that king of rock and roll, Elvis Aaron Presley. However

President Bush is actually closer related to the King (half 17th cousins once removed) than Mr. Clinton (half 21st cousin, thee times removed).

Half cousins share only one common ancestor. In other words, the common ancestor remarried and you descend from a stepson or stepdaughter.

What about *removed*? We see this term a lot in extended cousin relationships, but it's pretty simple. Visualize kinship lines as looking like the letter 'V'. You're at the top on one side, Elvis is at the top on the other side, and your common ancestor is at the bottom point of the 'V'. Ah, but people live different length lives, have children at varying times in life, so each leg of the 'V' is not necessarily the same length. Visualize those cases as the 'V' being a checkmark (with one side longer than the other). The difference in length between the legs is measured in generations. Your 15th cousin, twice removed, even though she's your age, took two more generations to reach this point than your side of the family did.

Fortunately—as we saw in the last chapter—with a good genealogy program on your personal computer, calculating these often very complicated degrees of kinship becomes child's play—the genealogy software does it for you and your son or daughter can show you how. See... child's play.

A good genealogy program—I use Family Tree Maker the most, but there are many other good ones—allows you to manage a huge database of relatives. I have over 130,000 relatives now and it just keeps growing. Lots of fun chasing down family connections!

Now, looking in my database, I can tell you that Her Royal Highness Queen Elizabeth II of England is the half 18th cousin, once removed of President George Bush (he's perhaps two zillionth in line for the throne). Is that his only possible relationship to Her Majesty? Not at all—

recall if you will all those millions of ancestors everyone shares. Hundreds, thousands, even more degrees of kinship exist for any two people.

The relationships I give you here are the nearest ones I have *based on my database.* My database, of course, is oriented toward my own relatives, so certainly closer relationships can and probably do exist. By the way, Queen Elizabeth is my 10th cousin, once removed and President Bush is my half 17th cousin, twice removed. While my kinship to the Queen is closer than the president's, I doubt either of us will ever rule Britannia. Nice work if you can get it, though. Eh?

THOSE COUSINS, THE PRESIDENTS

At the beginning of this chapter I said that George W. Bush, and the 41 other men who have also been president, all have one thing in common—they are relatives. Which is true. And—lest you think I'm miscounting since Bush is the 43rd president—Grover Cleveland served two terms separated by the presidency of Benjamin Harrison, so he was both the 22nd and the 24th president. Again, good work if you can get it.

Grover Cleveland was both the 22nd and 24th president of the United States, because he served separated terms. He is George Bush's 14th cousin, 3 times removed.

It's common knowledge that some of the presidents were related. President Bush and his father, George Herbert Walker Bush, became our second father/son team upon the election of

The other father and son presidential team, John Adams (our second president and John Quincy Adams (our sixth president. Adams the father is President George Bush's 23rd cousin, 4 times removed and J.Q. Adams is Bush's 24th cousin 3 times removed.

the present President Bush. Our second president, John Adams, and his son, John Quincy Adams, also served. William Henry Harrison and his grandson, Benjamin Harrison made up another closely related duo of residents at 1600 Pennsylvania Avenue. But, of course, every single president who has ever been elected is related to every other president, and to the majority of us Americans as well!

I came up with the brainstorm one day recently of proving I was kin to all 42 U.S. presidents. Thanks to all the information on the internet these days, and the fact that I already had a huge database of relatives, it took me very little time to realize this goal. I hoped to use this achievement in promoting my book, *Genealogy via the Internet* (2nd edition). However, even I quickly concluded that nobody much gave a durn about *my* relatives except us homefolk. So, I did some more research (which I enjoy doing anyway) to prove that President Bush is related to all U.S. presidents.

All our presidents being cousins is a bit more noteworthy than my own genealogy (as much as it may fascinate me) and part of the magic of *full* genealogy. Full genealogy is where you research your collateral relations instead of just direct lines (ancestor genealogy). Full genealogy is a lot more fun and much more rewarding.

Martin van Buren, the eighth president, was the hardest to research because of his exclusive Dutch roots. He is President Bush's half 26th cousin, once removed.

Not that it was any sort of snap in finding these relationships. In fact, two were very hard. Take our eighth president, Martin van Buren. His people were Dutch, from those who settled the colony of New Amsterdam, now part of New York state. The van Burens married only their own kind. Tying President van Buren to both President Bush and myself, took the most digging.

After a great deal of research slogging back through Dutch families and learning lots about the Netherlands, I finally hit some nobility back around the 13th century. Once that occurred, the rest was easy.

THE "SECRET" OF FULL GENEALOGY

Now, here's the secret of full genealogical research—tie into the nobility. The noble and royal families of medieval Europe intermarried like bunnies. All of them; just lump all the different countries together and it's cousin Duke de This and cousin Baron le Brave, etc. Those folks got around all over the place and had kids everywhere. And, best of all, they have been heavily researched by genealogists for centuries. Your work is already done for you once you get that far—just enter the

President George W. Bush's Kinship with All The Other Presidents

1	George Washington	10th cousin, 8 times removed
2	John Adams	23rd cousin, 4 times removed
3	Thomas Jefferson	15th cousin, 6 times removed
4	James Madison	Half 11th cousin, 7 times removed
5	James Monroe	19th cousin
6	John Quincy Adams	24th cousin, 3 times removed
7	Andrew Jackson	11th cousin, 6 times removed
8	Martin Van Buren	Half 26th cousin, once removed
9	William Henry Harrison	20th cousin, 5 times removed
10	John Tyler	Half 13th cousin, 5 times removed
11	James K. Polk	Half 19th cousin, 2 times removed
12	Zachary Taylor	Half 13th cousin, 4 times removed
13	Millard Fillmore	18th cousin, 4 times removed
14	Franklin Pierce	17th cousin, 2 times removed
15	James Buchanan	21st cousin, 4 times removed
16	Abraham Lincoln	22nd cousin, 3 times removed
17	Andrew Johnson	3rd cousin, 5 times removed
18	Ulysses S. Grant	Half 10th cousin, 6 times removed
19	Rutherford B. Hayes	Half 17th cousin, 5 times removed
20	James Garfield	9th cousin, 3 times removed
21	Chester A. Arthur	Half 17th cousin, 4 times removed
22	Grover Cleveland	14th cousin, 3 times removed
23	Benjamin Harrison	22nd cousin, 3 times removed
24	Grover Cleveland	14th cousin, 3 times removed
25	William McKinley	Half 21st cousin, 5 times removed
26	Theodore Roosevelt	15th cousin, 4 times removed
27	William Taft	6th cousin, 5 times removed
28	Woodrow Wilson	17th cousin, 2 times removed
29	Warren G. Harding	19th cousin, 3 times removed
30	Calvin Coolidge	Half 20th cousin, once removed
31	Herbert Hoover	Half 10th cousin, once removed
32	Franklin D. Roosevelt	Half 11th cousin, 5 times removed
33	Harry S. Truman	15th cousin, 9 times removed
34	Dwight D. Eisenhower	19th cousin, 5 times removed
35	John F. Kennedy	*see note
36	Lyndon B. Johnson	16th cousin, 2 times removed
37	Richard Nixon	16th cousin, once removed
38	Gerald Ford	Half 15th cousin, 2 times removed
39	Jimmy Carter	19th cousin, 3 times removed
40	Ronald Reagan	19th cousin, 3 times removed
41	George H.W. Bush	Father
42	Bill Clinton	19th cousin, 2 times removed

* John Fitzgerald Kennedy is the only U.S. President whose ancestors cannot be traced prior to the mid 18th century. The reason, they're all Irish and until late in the 19th century, only the nobility enjoyed reliable birth and death records; the parish priest—whose responsibility it was—ignored everyone else. So there is a gap in Kennedy's recorded ancestors related to Bush (and everyone else) of about 200 years, from the mid 1500s to the mid 1700s. However, President Bush's 28th great grandfather is Roger De Bellesme De Alencon De Montgomery. Roger's granddaughter, Alice de Montgomery, married Maurice "the Invader" FitzGerald (b. 1100) and their descendants ruled Ireland for the next 600 years. All the Fitzgeralds descend from Maurice and Alice. So JFK, at worst, would be something like Bush's 27th cousin. Since there are more recent ties, he's probably more like the 20th; I just can't prove the exact degree of relationship. But, there's no doubt JFK and Bush are cousins.

material on the internet, always checking it against other postings and other sources to decide which is correct.

To give President Bush a relationship to President van Buren, we have to travel all the way back to about the year 1050 for their common ancestors— Hugh "the Great" Crepi and Adelaide, Countess of Vermandois. So Bush and van Buren have a rather distant kinship, 26th cousins, once removed.

One president's exact ancestors remain rather elusive, so far as documention and proof goes. John Fitzgerald Kennedy is the only U.S. President whose ancestors cannot be traced prior to the mid 18th century. The reason, they're all Irish and until late in the 19th century, only the nobility enjoyed reliable birth and death records;

John Fitzgerald Kennedy, the 35th U.S. president

the parish priests—whose responsibility it was—ignored everyone else. So there is a gap in Kennedy's recorded ancestors related to me (and everyone else) of about 200 years, from the mid 1500s to the mid 1700s.

However, President Bush's 28th great grandfather is Roger De Bellesme De Alencon De Montgomery. Roger's granddaughter, Alice de Montgomery, married Maurice "the Invader" FitzGerald (b. 1100) and their descendants ruled Ireland for the next 600 years. All the Fitzgeralds descend from Maurice and Alice. So JFK, at worse, would be something like Bush's 27th cousin. Since there are more recent ties, he's probably more like the 20th. Neither I nor anyone else can prove the exact degree of relationship. But, there's no doubt JFK and Bush are cousins.

In fact the net of kinship covers far more than President Bush's relationship to all the other U.S. presidents. The Arabs who stormed out of Arabia in the 700s at the behest of the Prophet Muhammad controlled Spain for several hundred years and intermarried, thus adding their bloodlines to that of the Spanish nobility, who married about everyone else in Europe. Bush is the 43rd great grandson of the Prophet Muhammad, and we look at that astounding relationship in the next chapter.

In fact, as we'll see, over 70% of Americans are direct descendants of Muhammad. Since we have common ancestors in the Arab world, it means that we are cousins to most Arabs living today.

What if you are African-American, are you excluded from this great gene pool? Not at all! It only takes intermarriage of one Arab back centuries ago (and this happened many, many times), or one person of European descent (and, like it or not, during the centuries of slavery, white owners and slaves often had children). So *everyone* is related—that's what's wonderful about researching genealogy.

A couple of examples concerning African-American genealogy, the *real* "Roots" if you will.

It's now pretty much an established (albeit controversial) fact that our third president, Thomas Jefferson, had children and a long time relationship with Sally Hemings, the daughter of a slave. Since Jefferson is related to all other presidents, then the descendants of Sally Hemings are as well.

Thomas Jefferson, author of the Declaration of Independence and our third president, is President Bush's 15th cousin, 6 times removed.

And most recently—as I was writing this—a Reuters wire article (February 8, 2002) reports that boxing legend Muhammad Ali has Irish roots! No kidding.

"Researchers at the Clare Heritage Centre in southwest Ireland," the article read, "said they have evidence that a great grandfather of the three-times world champion hailed from the county town of Ennis, close to the west coast.

"Antoinette O'Brien, a genealogist at the center, told Reuters that Ali's great grandfather, Abe Grady, emigrated to the United States from County Clare in the 1860s, settled in Kentucky and married an African-American woman. ..."

Their son, the article continues, also married an African-American, and one of that couple's daughters, Odessa Grady, married Cassius Clay in the 1930s. They settled in Louisville, Kentucky where their son, also called Cassius, was born in 1942.

The young Cassius Clay, of course, changed his name to Muhammad Ali when he converted to the Nation of Islam after winning the world heavyweight title against Sonny Liston in 1964. It is interesting that Muhammad Ali—now an adherent of Isalm—is descended from his namesake, the Prophet Muhammad, through his European roots and, thanks to Irish, English, and Spanish ancestors, is entitled to wear the green turban specified in that religion for descendants of the Prophet. But, then, so are most Americans, Islamic or not. At least 70% of us are direct descendants, again thanks to European ancestors.

Many, many more examples exist. The same is true for us Native Americans (I'm proud to be part Cherokee) and just about any other ethnic group you can think of.

Chinese? No problem. Lots of Europeans from Marco Polo on visited China. Portuguese, Dutch, British, French—nature took its course.

Name any ethnic group. Somewhere back there (okay, sometimes *really* far back) we all share common ancestors.

We are one big family, this humanity of ours!

The nice thing about all of the above is you can easily prove tons of relationships for your own family. The techniques are easy and documented in this book. There are hundreds of millions of sources out on the internet. I recommend starting first with your own family (get your ancestors back four or five generations). Once you get back into the early 19th or 18th centuries, it's easy to go to places like **rootsweb.com** (my favorite—it's free!) which has hundreds of millions of family records, and start running your own lines back into medieval times and beyond.

You'll find you have plenty of celebrities in the family. In addition to all the other presidents, President Bush is also akin to:

- Winston Churchill — half 17th cousin, once removed
- General Robert E. Lee — half 7th cousin, 7 times removed
- King Henry VIII — half 2nd cousin, 15 times removed
- General George S. Patton III — half 17th cousin, once removed
- William Shakespeare — 12th cousin, 16 times removed
- Crooner Bing Crosby — 19th cousin
- Emperor Charlemagne — 34th great grandfather
- Ernest Hemmingway, author — 10th cousin, once removed
- Emperor Napoleon Buonparte I — 15th cousin, 3 times removed

Winston Churchill, half 17th cousin, once removed

Emperor Napoleon, 15th cousin, 3 times removed

Elizabeth I, Half 3rd cousin, 14 times removed

- First Lady "Dolley" Madison — half 20th cousin, 6 times removed
- Colonel "Davey" Crockett — half 19th cousin, 7 times removed
- Queen Elizbeth I of England — Half 3rd cousin, 14 times removed
- Sir Walter Raleigh — half 5th cousin, 5 times removed
- General "Stonewall" Jackson — half 14th cousin, 4 times removed
- Grand Duchess Anastasia Romanov — half 18th cousin, 8 times removed
- First Lady Eleanor Roosevelt — 19th cousin, 3 times removed

And many more.
We're all cousins, cousin!

MOST AMERICANS OF EUROPEAN ANCESTRY DESCEND DIRECTLY FROM MUHAMMAD

A shereef (or descendent of the Prophet) wears a green turban, or is privileged to do so, but no other person; and it is not common for any but a shereef to wear a bright green dress.

—Thomas Patrick Hughes
A Dictionary of Islam

Here's a real shocker to lots of people, especially us Southern Baptists and probably any number of Moslems. As direct descendants of the Prophet Muhammad, founder of Islam—like millions of other Americans—President George W. Bush and I both are entitled to wear a green turban. President Bush is, in direct line, the great grandson 43 generations removed of the Prophet, as am I.

No doubt it comes as a surprise that so many of us Americans find ourselves related to the founder of Islam in these days of conflict with and hate for this country from many in the Muslim world. And it may provide even more of a shock to the Arab or other Muslim in the street, but we are all truly cousins and the Prophet our common ancestor.

How can this be? Three good reasons exist making it easy for an American of European ancestry to prove descent from Muhammad.

The forces of Islam agressively spread their religious empire after the death of Muhammad. By the 700s, they had conquererd Spain—their largest foothold in Europe, held until the 1200s—and throughout the Middle East. The victorious descendants of the Prophet intermarried with European women (and vice versa) and now almost all of us of European ancestry descend directly from Muhammad.

MUHAMMAD'S GENEALOGY WELL DOCUMENTED

First, as founder of both a religion and an empire, much better records were kept about the Prophet than, for example, Christ. Christ—living on Earth more than 600 years earlier—belonged to a race then subjugated by the Romans and recordkeeping for enslaved people was sparse. So, while one cannot do a genealogy chart for Jesus (even of his earthly parents, Mary and Joseph), a few minutes browsing on the Internet results in scores of charts showing relatives of Muhammad with verified lines of descent. A good starting point—I highly recommend it and use it a lot—is the World Connect project (**worldconnect. genealogy.rootsweb.com**), which has over 192 million genealogy records. Access is free! And please share your results as so many of us do.

Muhammad, by the way, was certainly not as celibate as some religious figures; he had at least 12 wives at one time or another. This adds greatly to the number of progeny permitted the green turban.

Why a green turban? For the Muslims green is the color of the Prophet Muhammad. He himself declared it as his favorite color and wore a green coat and a green turban. Even today, among those believing in Islam, only his successors are allowed to wear a green turban.

We in the Western world have a hard time matching the number of marriages of Muslims like Muhammad, but the Prophet's 28th great grandson, Henry VIII of England, came close with 8 wives.

CHILDREN OF THE PROPHET

Of Muhammad's 12 wives (or 9, depending on source), the most important was his first, Khadija Bint Khuwalyid, who lived from 555 to 619. Not only are most Americans

The Battle of Tours in France in 732 determined the fate of Western civilization. Charles Martel (Charles "the Hammer") led a Frankish army that defeated the Moslem armies and ended their dream of conquering Europe for Islam.

related to the Prophet descended from her, as is the present royal family of Jordan, but she is also the mother of Muhammad's best-known daughter, Fatima, "Fatima the Resplendent."

Fatima, while revered by both of the major factions of Islam, the Sunni and the Shi'ite, still is a symbol of its greatest division, a controversy over who the legitimate successors of the Prophet really were. Today, Iran is the most powerful Shi'ite country while the Sunni faction controls most others. Part of the factional fighting in Afghanistan pits Sunni against Shi'ite. Fatima was the 42nd great grandaunt of President Bush.

We Americans—at least those of us descended from Muhammad through European roots—come down from

Fatima's sister, Umm Kulthum—who married Yazid, the 6th Caliph (ruler and leader) of Islam.

THE DESCENDANTS SPREAD

The second reason for our kinship to the Prophet is the rapid expansion of Islam. Muhammad died in 632 A.D., but by 711 Arab armies had spread like triumphant wildfire out of Arabia and rolled over Egypt, Persia, Turkey, Palestine, across the Indus River into India, through all of North Africa, and into Spain. They appeared unstoppable!

Europe came very close to becoming completely Muslim. After the conquest of Spain—except for a few small Christian enclaves such as the kingdoms of Castile, Leon, Navarre, and others—the Islamic armies crossed the Pyrenees and invaded France.

In 732—at Tours in France—there occurred what many historians consider the most important battle ever fought. The Muslims finally met their match in a French army commanded by Charles Martel (Charles "the Hammer"—grandfather of the Emperor Charlemagne and another personage many Americans descend from). This battle determined that Christianity rather than Islam would dominate Europe.

The forces of Islam retreated back into Spain, but it took another 700 years to fully dislodge them from this European toehold. And this time of occupation was actually good. The Muslims had a far more advanced culture than the rest of feudal Europe. Spain became more civilized, making great strides in learning and in everyday life. For example, the Moors (as the Muslims came to be called in Spain) introduced an efficient irrigation system still in use by Spanish farmers today.

Moors gave the Moorish arch to Spanish architecture. Moorish cities were magnificent—these included Córdoba, Toledo, and Valencia. Some of the most beautiful buildings in the world were built at Grenada. The armorers of Toledo became famous for their flawless and wonderfully flexible steel swords inlaid with gold. The craftsmen of Córdoba were well known throughout Europe for their unsurpassed leatherwork.

SPAIN BECOMES A MELTING POT

During these seven centuries of Moorish rule, there was much intermarrying between the Moors and the rest of the population. The royal families of the small Christian kingdoms would form alliances by marriage with various Moorish rulers, who quite often were related to Muhammad, hence their positions of importance.

Within only about 300 years after the death of Muhammad, the Moors were not only firmly settled in Spain but had married into various of the Christian royal families. In the main line we Americans relate to, Aurea Ibn Lopo Ibn Musa, the daughter of the Muslim governor of Saragossa, a direct descendant of the Prophet, was married in 845 to Fortun Garces, King Of Pamplona, firmly linking Muhammad's bloodline to that of almost all royal families of Europe, which later married into the Spanish royal lines.

A good example of how the Moors and the other Spaniards were intertwined so closely in not just marriage but all aspects of life in general is the Spanish national hero, *El Cid*. Many of us will recall "El Cid," the 1961 classic movie about this legendary fighter, starring Charlton Heston.

El Cid lived in the 1000s and worked both sides of the castle drawbridge, selling his strong sword arm in the service of various Moorish and Christian kings. He defeated the armies of several Christian noblemen while fighting for the Moorish king of Zaragoza. Finally, again working for the Christians, he conquered Valencia in 1094 and locked in his legend of courage and skill by not just being on but helping to create the winning side.

The tide was now turning against the Moors. Christian kings stopped making alliances with the Moors (or at least, not so many) and united to drive the Muslims from Spain. By 1276, only the Moorish kingdom of Grenada in southern Spain remained and, by the 1400s, it was gone and the Christian kingdoms of Spain were uniting into one powerful country. This unification was achieved

El Cid

An old drawing reputed to be of Rodrigo "El Cid" Diaz de Vivar, hero of Spain and the 28th great grandfather of President George Bush. Interestingly enough, and evocative of the Spanish/Moslem intermarriages, El Cid's wife—Ximina (Jimena) of Asturias—was the 15th great granddaughter of the Prophet Muhammad.

totally in 1469 when the two most powerful kingdoms, Aragon and Castile, were joined by the marriage of King Ferdinand V of Aragon to Queen Isabella of Castile (who later used her jewels to finance the oceanic explorations of one Christopher Columbus).

Yet, while the Moorish political presence in Spain and the Islamic religion both faded away, Moorish blood remained, flowing in the veins of the Spanish people, then and today. Nor had this unification of Spain gone unnoticed in England and France and among the nobility of other European countries, duchies, princedoms, and various smaller fiefs.

KISSING COUSINS, THE ROYALS AND NOBILITY

Which brings us to the third of the reasons why so many Americans descend from the Prophet Muhammad, intermarriage among the royal and noble families of Europe. Just as the Christian and Moorish kings had cemented relationships for several hundred years by marrying off daughters to the other side, the ruling families of other European states now sought the same ties with the increasingly powerful Spanish.

These marriages on both the royal level and in the lower ranks of nobility have made for complicated webs of kinships. Take, for instance, Henry III of England who married Eleanor of Provence (a French fiefdom). Eleanor's father and grandfather were both Counts of Provence, but her great-grandfather was Alfonso II, King of Aragon and the 16th great grandson of Muhammad.

In genealogy, by the way, the father of a great grandfather (your great great grandfather, for example) is called the 2nd great grandfather, his mother is the 3rd great grandmother, and so forth. It's a shortcut avoiding having to use terms like great great great ... etc. etc. ... grandfather. So instead of putting 16 *greats* in front of grandson in Alfonso II's relationship to Muhammad above, we just say he's the 16th great grandson. Isn't that great?

Alfonso's Aragon, of course, was one of those small Christian kingdoms in Spain that survived by forming alliances—often by marriage—with the Moors. So Queen Eleanor brought into the English royal family bloodlines from the French, the Spanish, and the Arabs/Muslims.

The English nobility already had plenty of French blood, still being mostly Norman French themselves, from when William the Conqueror had taken England from the old Saxon kings.

But, keep your eye on the line of the Prophet, it gets more convoluted. Henry III's son, who became King Edward I ("Longshanks") of England who, thanks to his mother, is the 20th great grandson of the Prophet, marries Eleanor (same name as his mother for you fans of Oedipus), daughter of Ferdinand III, King of Castile. This Queen Eleanor is the 22nd great-granddaughter of Muhammad, meaning she is related to her new royal husband through this shared common ancestor, which does not matter since they were already third cousins through the many recent intermarriages of the French, Normans, English, Dutch, Germans—well, you name it, all those Europeans got around more than just a little bit.

The above may seem rather complicated, but you don't have to understand it other than

Edward I of England is about half way up the direct line of descent from Muhammad to President Bush.

to realize this is only one of the many lines and tangles of relationships bringing the Prophet's bloodlines to us in America today.

Why are the English nobility and all their bloodlines important? Edward I, for example, happens to be my 22nd great grandfather and probably bears a similar relationship to a multitude of Americans (tens of millions of us according to some sources). That means he's 22 generations back. If we assume Edward had two children (and he had considerably more) and each of those two children had two, and so forth, that totes up to over four million people alive today who are descended from Edward I, spread throughout the U.S., U.K., Canada, Australia, etc. Every single one of these is a direct descendant of Muhammad!

The leading internet website, **ancestry.com**, reports that: "Seventy percent of Americans can trace their family history back to the United Kingdom or Ireland."

Additionally, a multitude of other lines of descent from the Prophet exist as well—many not even passing through the English but coming up from the French, Germans, Italians, and others whose nobility intermingled with the Moors. This even includes places like Albania, Bulgaria, Poland, Greece, Serbia, and Russia. So even those of Eastern European ancestry are very likely related to Muhammad.

Of course, commoners intermarried as well, but the nobility kept far better records, thus it's easier to prove births, marriages, deaths, and burials (BMDB, one of the underlying concepts of scientific genealogy).

In short, based on all above, we can say that the *majority* of Americans descend directly from the founder of Islam. Sort of makes one wonder why some Muslims are so mad at us when they should, instead, be venerating us as descendants of their Prophet.

PRESIDENT BUSH'S LINE OF DESCENT

43rd great grandparents
The Prophet Muhammad (570-632)
Khadija Bint Khuwalyid (555-619)

42nd great grandparents
Kuttum Umm Kashim
Yazid I, Caliph of Umayyad (-683)

41st great grandparents
Abd Al Malik Umayyad
Unknown Umayyad

40th great grandparents
Abdul Yazid Al Walid Umayyad
Egilom Umm Assim Balthas

39th great grandparents
Aisha Umayyad
Fortun, Governor of Saragosa

38th great grandparents
Musa Ibn Governor of Saragosa

37th great grandparents
Musa Ibn Governor of Saragosa (-863)
Assona, de Pamplona Iniguez

36th great grandparents
Lopo Ibn Governor of Saragosa
Ayab Al Bulatiya

35th great grandparents
Aurea Ibn Lopo Ibn Musa
Garcia Fortun, King (-905)

34th great grandparents
Oneca, de Pamplona Fortunez (847-)
Aznar Sanchez de Larraun (-893)

33rd great grandparents
Toda Aznarez (885-970)
Sancho I King of Pamplona (865-925)

32nd great grandparents
Garcia II Jimena Sanchez (919-970)
Andregoto, Countess Galindez (-972)

31st great grandparents
King Sancho II Garces Abarca (935-994)
Urraca, de Castile Fernandez (-1007)

30th great grandparents
Garcia III Sanchez, King (964-999)
Jimena, de Leon Fernandez (-1035)

29th great grandparents
Sancho III King of Castile (990-1034)
Sancha de Aybar (995-)

28th great grandparents
Ramiro I Sanchez, King (-1094)
Felice de Montdidier (-1086)

27th great grandparents
Ramiro II Sanchez, King (1075-1147)
Maud of Aquitaine (1100-)

26th great grandparents
Petronella of Aragon (1135-1172)
Count Raymond Berenger V Barcelona (-1162)

25th great grandparents
King of Aragon Alphonso II (-1196)
Sanchia of Castile (1154-1208)

24th great grandparents
Count of Provence Alphonso II (1180-1208)
Gersenda II of Sabran (1165-1224)

23rd great grandparents
Raymond IV Count of Berenger (-1245)
Beatrix of Savoy (1198-1266)

22nd great grandparents
Eleanor of Provence (1217-1291)
King Henry III Plantagenet (1206-1272)

21st great grandparents
Edward I Plantagenet (1239-1307)
Alice de Lusignan (1238-1270)

20th great grandparents
John de Botetourte (1262-1324)
Maud FitzThomas (-1328)

nineteenth great grandparents
Thomas de Botetourte (1285-1322)
Joan de Somery (-1326)

eighteenth great grandparents
John, Lord de Botetourte (1318-1385)
Joyce La Zouche (1325-1372)

seventeenth great grandparents
Joyce de Botetourte (1368-)
Sir Adam de Peshall (1352-1419)

sixteenth great grandparents
Margaret Pershall (1393-1420)
Sir Richard Mytton (1389-1419)

fifteenth great grandparents
Sir William Mytton Lord Weston (1416-)
Margaret Corbett (1416-)

fourteenth great grandparents
Joan Mytton (1455-)
John Washbourne (1422-1517)

thirteenth great grandparents
John Washbourne (1480-1545)
Emme (1479-1547)

twelfth great grandparents
John Washburn (1512-1588)
Jone WHITEHEAD (1557-1567)

eleventh great grandparents
John III Washbourne (1566-1624)
Martha Stevens (1572-)

tenth great grandparents
John Washburn (1597-1670)
Margery (Or Margaret) Moore (1608-)

ninth great grandparents
John II Washburn (1620-1686)
Elizabeth Mitchell (1628-1684)

eighth great grandparents
Mary Washbourne (- after 1693)
Samuel Kingsley (- after 1693)

seventh great grandparents
Samuel Kingsley (1693-1730)
Mary (1700-1727)

sixth great grandparents
Silence Kingsley (1727-1764)
Samuel Herrick (1732-1797)

fifth great grandparents
Sarah Herrick (1764-1823)
Reverend Nathaniel Butler (1761-1829)

fourth great grandparents
Samuel Herrick Butler (1785-1851)
Judith Livingston (1785-1858)

third great grandparents
Courtland Philip Butler (1813-1891)
Elizabeth Slade Pierce (1822-1901)

second great grandparents
Mary Elizabeth Butler (1850-1897)
Robert Emmet Sheldon (1845-1917)

great grandparents
Flora Sheldon (1872-1920)
Samuel Prescott Bush (1863-1948)

Grandparents
Prescott Sheldon Bush (1895-1972)
Dorothy Walker (1901-1992)

Parents
President George Herbert Walker Bush (1924-)
Barbara Pierce (1925-)

President George Walker Bush (1946-)

OTHERS DESCENDED FROM MUHAMMAD

Some other notables descended from the Prophet Muhammad include:

- President George H.W. Bush — 42nd great grandson
- President George Washington — 36th great grandson
- General Robert E. Lee — 39th great grandson
- Queen Elizabeth II of England — 43rd great granddaughter
- President Jimmy Carter — 44th great grandson
- William Frederick "Buffalo Bill" Cody — 43rd great grandson
- Princess Diana of England — 43rd great granddaughter
- President Thomas Jefferson — 40th great grandson
- General George S. Patton III — 42nd great grandson
- Author Laura Elizabeth Ingalls — 43rd great granddaughter
- President Theodore Roosevelt — 39th great grandson
- President Richard Nixon — 42nd great grandson
- Pope Calixtus II — 15th great grandson

General Robert E. Lee, 39th great grandson

Buffalo Bill, 42nd great grandson

Teddy Roosevelt, 39th great grandson

Sir Walter Raleigh, 32nd great grandson

Lord Nelson, 40th great grandson

Woodrow Wilson, 41st great grandson

- Pope Felix V — 25th great grandson
- General Ulysses S. Grant — 42nd great grandson
- President Andrew Jackson — 41st great grandson
- Winston Spencer Churchill — 42nd great grandson
- Sir Walter Raleigh — 32nd great grandson
- President Lyndon Baines Johnson — 44th great grandson
- Playwright Tennessee Williams — 42nd great grandson
- General Stonewall Jackson — 39th great grandson
- Author H.P. Lovecraft — 40th great grandson
- President Grover Cleveland — 41st great grandson
- Lord Horatio Nelson of Trafalgar — 40th great grandson
- President Woodrow Wilson — 41st great grandson

IT'S A SMALL GREEN WORLD AFTER ALL

How to put this strongly enough? If *any* of your ancestors came from Europe, you have royal blood of some sort and, because of that, you are very, very likely descended directly from the founder of Islam and you can start shopping for a green turban.

MY COUSIN, THE QUEEN
ARE WE—YOU AND I—IN LINE FOR THE THRONE?

We lost the American colonies because we lacked the statesmanship to know the right time and the manner of yielding what is impossible to keep.

—HM Queen Elizabeth II of England
In Philadelphia on a six-day
Bicentennial visit, July 1976

Royalty—especially *English* royalty—holds much fascination for us Americans. I was pleased, for example, when my own family research determined that Elizabeth Alexandra Mary Windsor— Her Majesty Queen Elizabeth II—is my 10th cousin, once removed. After that revelation, I tended to joke that I was now in line to the throne, like two millionth maybe.

The British royal family may or may not be excited in hearing my own relationship to them. Like the famous quote often attributed to Queen Victoria (my half 7th cousin, 13 times removed), their position might very well be "We are not amused." Still, "kinfolk is kinfolk," as we say up here in the Carolina mountains.

With that wonderful tool, the internet and the world wide web, it occurred to me that finding out *exactly* how close I am to wearing the crown of England would be only a few minutes searching. I *did* find out exactly and I'll share that with you in just a few pages.

First, let me hasten to explain the pointing out and namedropping of my celebrity kin here and there in this book is by no means being stuck up. A wonderful truth exists: we are *all* related. You have just as many royal and other famous kinfolk as I do; you just haven't researched them yet. That's what this book's about, showing you how to do that. My examples, I hope, help you see the fun inherent in knowing your kin—noble and otherwise.

PRESIDENTS AND ROYALS

Prince Charles (Charles Philip Arthur Windsor), heir apparent to the throne, is about my age and we belong to the same generation, hence he is my 11th cousin. His wife, the late Diana Frances Spencer, Princess Diana, was my half 19th cousin, once removed—i.e. she was born in 1961, a generation later than Prince Charles and myself.

President George W. Bush shares royal connections as well. He and HM Queen Elizabeth are half 18th cousins, twice removed (two generations difference). The intermarriage of royal families gets covered later in this chapter but it leads to interesting relationships. For example, President Bush and the Queen share the same kinship—because of this intermarriage centuries previous—with the present Spanish king, Juan Carlos II—both being half 18th cousins, once removed to His Majesty of Spain.

Our own gracious queen in this country—First Lady Laura Lane Welch Bush—enjoys a slightly closer kinship to the British monarch than her husband, half 18th cousin once removed. But where it gets interesting, she and Her Majesty's husband, Prince Philip Mountblatten, share an even closer relationship, half 11th cousins, 7 times removed. This stems from Mrs. Bush's connections through the Hellenic (Greek) royal family, Prince Philip's direct ancestors.

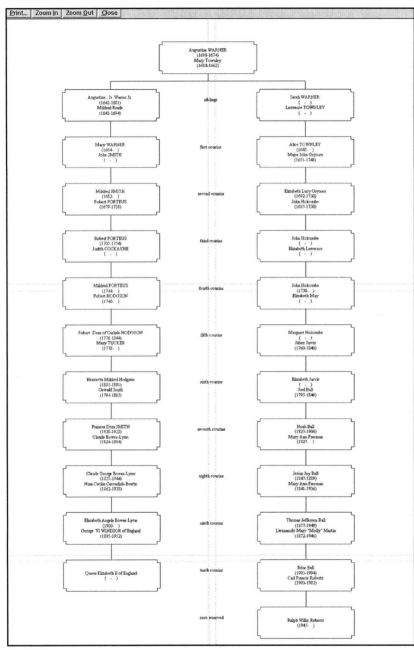

Her Majesty Queen Elizabeth II and I share common ancestors, Augustine Warner and Mary Townley. The true fun in FULL genealogy is finding your own common ancestors with notables. No matter your family heritage, I guarantee you descend from thousands of years of kings and queens. (This relationship report generated by *Family Origins* software.)

Again, the calculation of all these degrees of kin come from my personal database of 130,000 relatives—closer relationships may very well exist. Also, I give only the closest kinship—many *hundreds* of cousin relationships almost always exist between any two people. This great human family tree of ours is incredibly intertwined.

And speaking of that:

INCREDIBLE IMPORTANCE OF ROYAL MARRIAGES

Due to royal intermarriages over the centuries—using the techniques of full genealogy, we find the great majority of Americans today related to English royalty, and indeed all the royal houses of Europe—whether *regnant* (a three dollar word meaning 'ruling') or pretenders to the throne like the Bourbon family in France. The latter family may no longer rule in the splendor of Versailles—like their ancestor Louis "I am the state" XIV (my 9th cousin, 15 times removed) did, but they lent their name as a generic description of a fine Kentucky sippin' whiskey—certainly immortality of sorts.

King Louis XIV of France, the half 8th cousin, 12 times removed of Queen Elizabeth II and also the half 8th cousin, 11 times removed of President Bush. Mr. Bush and Her Majesty share many common ancestors.

So, why does it matter if you descend from kings and queens?

Royal and noble families carry great importance in genealogical research—they are the glue that bind us all together. For literally thousands of years, royal and noble families have intermarried for political advantage. The King of Spain would give a daughter in marriage to the future King of

Many royal families today maintain the own websites. Above is that of the Dutch royal family (in English, at **http://www.koninklijkhuis. nl/UK/welcome.html**). Below, the British royal family's official site at **http://www.royal.gov.uk/**.

England, England a princess daughter to France, and so on down the levels of royalty and nobility. Thousands of these intermarriages mean that all the royal families and the lesser nobility of Europe share a common ancestry and that, indeed, they are all cousins. This includes every royal family you can mention—England, Scotland, France, Denmark, Norway, Sweden, Greece, Italy, Bulgaria, the Czars of Russia, the Holy Roman Empire (that was "neither Holy nor Roman nor an Empire), Austria-Hungary... All of them and more!

Two thousand years and more of such intermarriages—in Europe, Asia, Africa, and more—mean the royals of Europe have *hundreds of millions* of living relatives.

That's the importance of proving your descent from royalty in your own personal family research. Because of our long fascination with royals and nobility, their genealogy remains the best documented; after all, who married who and who sired who is *history*.

Find a connection through your own ancestors back to a noble family of medieval times and you've tapped into that great pool of common ancestors. You can now use full genealogy techniques and connect via collateral lines to thousands upon thousands of your relatives, close and distant (remember collateral relationships are described in Chapter 2, "Cousins by the Dozens").

Royal connections can also be fun. My attention was recently drawn to the Dutch royal family. I injured my mousing arm (very important to us computer types) a couple of years ago and the repetitive act of using the mouse many hours a day (it's how I earn my living) became painful. I was induced finally to seek physical therapy, which is doing an amazing job in restoring the old wing back to full flight duty.

My therapist from Thoms Rehabilitation Hospital in Asheville, North Carolina, Edwin, is from the Netherlands. Very professional, highly trained, and we have these great conversations about polders and windmills and the Dutch royal family while he treats my arm with ultrasound and other soothing techniques. So, out of our interesting conversations, I was moved to look at the Dutch royal family.

The current royal ruler in this charming land of tulips and farmland wrestled from the sea's cold embrace is HM Queen Beatrix Wilhelmina Armgard—Queen of the Netherlands, Princess of Orange Nassau, Princess of Lippe-Biesterfeld. She is, I'm proud to relate, my half 11th cousin, 9 times removed. Her Dutch Majesty is also a half 11th cousin (8 times removed) to Queen Elizabeth II of Britain. President Bush's relationship to Queen Beatrix is a bit more distant, half 19th cousin, 7 times removed.

Once you have your own connection to royal and noble families, establishing such relationships for yourself becomes exceptionally easy, and I show you how later in this book.

KING RALPH?

The 1991 movie "King Ralph" starred John Goodman as a Vegas lounge singer who ascended the throne of England when an unlikely accident wiped out the royal family of Britain and most of the heirs. It's a great movie and I own a tape of it.

As promised earlier—since my relationship to the British royals is relatively close (pun, as always, intended)—could I or you get tapped to wear the crown in real life? Could I become King Ralph.

Well... the short answer is "nah!"

The longer answer involves the Act of Settlement of 1701. I found the following about it on **alt.talk.royalty** (a Usenet discussion group and a super source for lots of information about the British and other royal families). A frequently asked questions (FAQ) is presented by them at **http://www.heraldica. org/faqs/britfaq.html**).

The Act of Settlement, this website informs me, was a law enacted during the reign of King William III (William and Mary) of England. It was designed to ensure a Protestant succession to the throne.

This law "set the succession as William III (the then sovereign) for his life, then Princess Anne Oldenburg of Denmark (later Queen Anne of England), then Princess

Anne's descendants (the last had already died), then William III's descendants (he had none), then Princess Sophia, electress and duchess dowager of Hanover, then the heirs of Sophia's body being Protestants."

Sophia Stuart was the granddaughter of James I of England, thus her role in the line of succession. The Law of Settlement explains to us how the German-speaking Hanovers, beginning with George I, became kings of England. George III Hanover was king when England managed to lose her 13 American colonies (see HM Queen Elizabeth's quote at the top of this chapter).

George III Hanover, King of England, managed to lose the American colonies. He is my half fifth cousin, 15 times removed. He and President George Washington were half 7th cousins, 5 times removed.

The law does not go into who succeeds to the throne if Sophia's heirs died out. This means that there is a finite number of persons who are eligible, under this Act, to become king or queen of England. In other words, they must be a descendent of Sophia Stuart Hanover (1630-1714) and Protestant as well (which is spelled out in yet another Act).

Well, I am Protestant but not a direct descendent of Sophia—albeit we are half eighth cousins, 12 times removed. President Bush is also out of the running, being a half 16th cousin, 9 nines removed. As the eighth great granddaughter, HM Queen Elizabeth, of course, had no problem qualifying (now in her 50th year as Queen) nor does Prince Charles, the ninth great grandson of Electress Sophia.

Royal links

Sweden Norway Denmark The United Kingdom Belgium

The Netherlands Luxembourg Spain Monaco Liechtenstein

Other German-speaking countries

France Portugal Italy Greece Yugoslavia Bulgaria Romania Albania Georgia Russia Poland

The rest of the World

Royal Genealogy Different Royal subjects Message Boards

Sweden

Royal Family of Sweden
Kings of Sweden (by Robert Warholm)
The Royal Family of Sweden (by Henri van Oene)
Ritva's site about the Swedish Royal Family
Swedish Kings (in Swedish)
Gustaf Wasa (in Swedish)
Sveriges Kungafamilj (in Swedish)
Princess Madeleine Online
Rojalistiska Föreningen

Norway

Royal Family of Norway
Kings of Norway (by Robert Warholm)
The Royal Family of Norway (by Henri van Oene)
Documents relating to the Royal House of Norway (by Dag Hoelseth)
The Royal Wedding of 1968

Denmark

Royal Family of Denmark
Kings of Denmark (by Robert Warholm)
The Royal Family of Denmark (by Henri van Oene)
Danske Konger (in Danish)

The United Kingdom

Royal Family of the United Kingdom
HRH The Prince of Wales
HRH Prince Michael of Kent
The Royal Family of the United Kingdom (by Henri van Oene)
Alt.talk.royalty FAQ about British Royalties
Windsor Street
Descendants of Electress Sophia

Belgium

Royal Family of Belgium
Kings of the Belgians (by Robert Warholm)
The Royal Family of Belgium (by Henri van Oene)
Kings of Belgium

The Netherlands

Royal Family of the Netherlands
The Dutch Monarchs (by Robert Warholm)
The Royal Family of the Netherlands (by Henri van Oene)
About the Dutch Royal Family

Luxembourg

The Grand Dukes of Luxemburg
The Grand Dukes of Luxembourg (by Robert Warholm)

Excellent royal links: **http://www.warholm.nu/Royallinks.html**

The monarchy
The Royal Family
The Royal Palace
Properties
News
Home Page

Norske sider

Developed by Itera Future
Powered by Digimaker

The Royal House of Norway

www.kongehuset.no

Press Release: 21.01.2002 HRH Princess Mårtha Louise goes out to work

The official website of the Norwegian royal family may be found in English at **http://www.kongehuset.no/default.asp?lang=eng**.

So, because of the Act of Settlement, again, a finite list of people qualified to sit on the English throne exists. The question occurs, who is *last* in line? Again, **alt.talk.royalty** supplies the answer.

"The persons who are genealogically last in line to succeed to the British throne under the Act of Settlement are found among the von Keudell descendants of Prince Ernst of Württemberg (1807-1868). (Prince Ernst is a descendant of King George I's daughter, Sophie Dorothea (1687-1757), wife of Friedrich Wilhelm, King in Prussia, himself the only son of Sophia Charlotte (1668-1705), last child of the Electress Sohpia). The last three people in the line of succession are therefore Frau Vogel (née Ilse von der Trenck, b. 1930) and her two children Martin (b. 1963) and Klaus (b. 1964)."

How much did I miss it by? Oh, about eight generations or so. Our common ancestor is Robert II, King of Scotland. Still, exploring royal connections makes history come alive and can be lots of fun. I hope you enjoy it as much as I do.

GENEALOGY VIA THE
INTERNET

TRACING YOUR FAMILY ROOTS QUICKLY
AND EASILY

PART II:

BASIC COMPUTER STUFF,
BASIC GENEALOGY STUFF

In this section we learn computers are not only our friends but pretty darn simple to use as well. We'll also take a look at the basics of genealogy, things which make your family research a lot more understandable and enjoyable.

Computers only *look* complicated. In truth, they are idiots. Being idiots, they must have *exact* instructions. Learn the few basics of how to communicate in their language, and computers become your lifelong friend. They will do absolutely *anything* for you and you can run any program, even if you've never seen it before. This chapter reveals that secret language and you'll find it incredibly simple, just like computers themselves. Don't bother to learn it and computers will drive you totally insane in about three days. Maybe two.

THE EASY WONDER OF COMPUTERS

We found the following on the internet. "According to an *American Demographics Magazine* survey, more than 40% of American adults express an interest in genealogy, and some 100 million of us are tracing our family trees." Worldwide, that number grows rapidly.

Why would you want to use personal computers and the internet in researching and constructing family records? Because it's one heck of a lot *easier*.

First, let's get the misconceptions out of the way. We deal here, in this book, with no less than three subjects generally perceived under such headings as *complicated, esoteric, hard, obscure, confused*, and downright *difficult*. I speak, naturally, of genealogy, computers, and that vast cyberspace expanse containing millions upon millions of things about millions of things—the internet itself.

You'll find, as we move along—I certainly hope to your very pleasant surprise—that these three subjects are simple, highly useful, and quite enjoyable. Admittedly, the initial opinion most of us hold is somewhat contrary. To the layperson—and that's all of us when we start—genealogy, computers, and the internet all appear beyond both our ken and our reasonable abilities. Not so!

Take the personal computer—as the late famed comedian Henny Youngman said about his wife—*please*. Many people consider the personal computer more antagonist than friend. Books achieve great commercial success with titles like *Genealogy for Dummies* ... or *The Complete Idiots Guide to* ... These titles play upon the average beginning computer user's frustration with manipulating computers. There are, we all find, only three basic ways of using the computer—the right way, the wrong way, and the computer's way. Only one of which works. (You guessed it! The computer's way.)

Add to this bewildering entanglement of exact syntax and other computer jargon the massive complexities of the *internet*. The internet is in reality many thousands upon thousands of computers worldwide, all exchanging data at high speed with each other and to your personal desktop machine if you are connected (called being *online*). Millions of computers at any one time—clucking and gabbing and gossiping amongst themselves like a sea of chickens in some planet-sized henhouse (and just about as intelligible, or so it seems at first). Probably talking about you, right? Or me! Urk.

Then comes the subject of genealogy, itself. To all the computerized puzzlement and mystification just described, we add the equal complexities of tracing your family's history. We'll be delving into pedigree charts, birth records, death records, census results, and much more.

Yes, indeed, three very complicated topics. Right?

Nope. Not at all!

COMPUTERS NOW SIMPLE. HONEST!

Remember when we were kids (oh, so long ago) and

the bicycle first entered our awareness? My, but we wanted to ride a bicycle. Riding was something big kids did! That was for us, yes sirree!

The problem with bicycles, as we all soon discovered, was the fact that they only have two wheels. Learning the fine art of keeping a bicycle upright and moving forward seemed just as daunting a task to us then as using a computer might today. How the heck, we asked ourselves, do the big kids do it?

Few of us failed to master riding, however. Even today, at the ripe old age of fifty-six I can plop my aged carcass on a bicycle and more or less keep up with the rest of the big kids. Old skills, once learned, are not forgotten. Of course, the bicycle I now ride most is the stationary one in front of the TV—some of us big kids, you see, have gotten quite a bit bigger with age.

The subject of fitness and middle-age spread aside, riding... er... using the computer is much similar to our bicycling experiences of yore. The effort of just keeping the darn bike moving forward while desperately wobbling the front wheel from side to side in a barely successful (and sometimes not so successful) try at achieving

Little kids want to ride like big kids. uprightness is equivalent to our first use of a personal computer. We wobble just as much, pushing the mouse around and wobbling the arrow on the screen, it refusing to go where it's supposed ta go!

In learning bike riding, with practice, came proficiency and expertise. We then whizzed about neighborhood streets with great aplomb, enjoying the scenery and the envious stares of little kids admiring the *big kid* riding his or her bike.

Once that stage of effortless riding ability was achieved, the only hindrance to progress was the occasionally ill-tempered, snarling dog. Being chased, while on a bike, by a fearsome monster pooch the size of a horse intent on making a glutinous meal of your tender ankle wakes any kid up. Your heart pounds, your legs pump for all they're worth. If luck is on your side, you escape the mangling molars of the bloodthirsty, ravaging canine.

What I found to be quite effective, growing up in the 1950s and riding country roads patrolled by large farm dogs hugely disinclined toward any friendliness, was a water pistol. We'd fill the pistol with simple household ammonia. One squirt of that noxious mixture at a dog and the brute left you alone the next

Chased by a fearsome monster pooch the size of a horse! (Or so it seemed.)

time you cycled through his territory. He *remembered*! And he gave you the right of way.

All of which (the learning how to bicycle analogy) has direct bearing on understanding, using, and even coming to love the personal computer.

Take the matter of merely staying upright.

Having only two wheels, and those in tandem, bicycles fall over at the least provocation. As kids, we quickly learn that only our own balance keeps the bike upright, and that this balance is more easily achieved and maintained while pedaling the bicycle in some semblance of forward motion.

A simple enough sounding principle, *uprightness*. Yet, I remember to this day the first time a well-meaning relative (a first cousin, no less—supposedly older and wiser) coaxed me up onto a bike. Poor little kid was I, feet barely reaching the pedals. A frightened little tyke, but did my cuz show mercy? Nah! With a quick shove, I was flying down the gentle slope of our front yard (a great precipice, it seemed).

Did I immediately triumph and sail serenely off into the sunset on my red Western Auto Flyer? No, but by dint of strenuously sawing the handlebars back and forth, I survived for 15 or 20 feet. It was a first, and I've never looked back. I learned not to move the handlebars so much and it became easy.

That experience might be similar to yours upon first encountering Windows 95, 98, ME, and now XP (Mr. Gates, he loves those weird names) or whatever operating system came installed on your new personal computer. Forget family history research, or even connecting to the internet, you just want to stay upright!

Well, two and only two things make that computer "uprightness" possible, and they are the same you needed in learning to ride a bike—lots of practice and *training wheels*.

More about training wheels in a moment, but first, let's consider a definition of terms.

JARGON AND THE LIKE

Many writers—myself included in the past—sugarcoat computers. They gloss over technicalities instead of explaining them. They ignore practicalities. They *trivialize* stuff you really have to know. They encourage you to forego jargon and learn the operation of specific programs by rote.

By rote is not the way to learn anything—memorizing a bunch of stuff does not help you to comprehend how the information is used. Instead, understand the basics and your ability to use the computer is far more flexible. In place of reacting by rote and dumping a year's work irretrievably, you'll know computers well enough to solve the immediate problem. You'll also use your machine and programs more powerfully and efficiently.

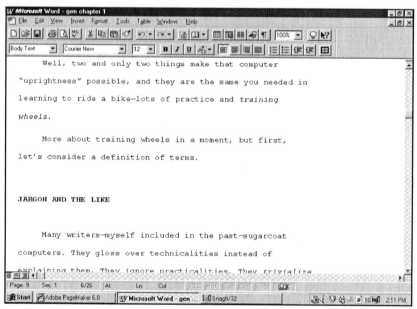

Software in action—the way my computer screen looked as I wrote this book using Microsoft's Word word processing program.

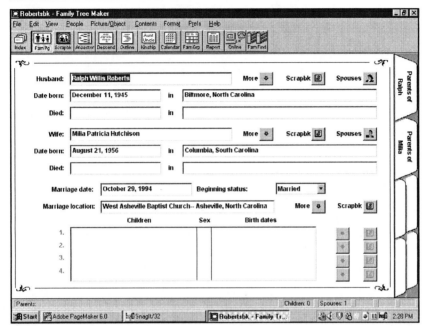

Genealogy software in action—the top record (mine) of my personal
family tree using Family Tree Maker.

It's not that hard. Kids do it every day. It's as easy as...
well... right... riding a bicycle!

Reaching your end goal of just using the computer in
aiding family history research requires some limited
familiarity with various concepts and terms relating to
both computers and genealogy. Like the old joke "eschew
obfuscation" (which means "avoid complication" or "keep
it simple"), understanding the words makes speaking the
language easier.

To ride our "bike," requires knowing and understanding such concepts as "handlebars," "seat,"
and "pedals."

Fortunately—while not immediately appearing so—
computerized genealogy and computers in general are
about that same degree of uncomplicated. Don't worry,
I'll lead you by the hand, if necessary, and we'll explain
everything as we go.

Computerized genealogy is not a new concept. Various computer bulletin board services (referred to as *BBS* or *BBSes*) have been around for well over 25 years now. Many of those bulletin board services offered files and message posting services to family history researchers almost from the first.

Online services such as CompuServe and Delphi appeared in the early eighties. Genealogical resources were available on them almost from their inception.

The internet—while a new discovery to most people—has been alive, constantly evolving, and flourishing since the late sixties! There was lots of good genealogical stuff there, even 20 years ago, albeit much harder to find and use.

The personal computer, itself, is now over 25 years old. From that wondrous dawn of the personal information age, people were using the PC as a research tool and an aid to collecting and maintaining family records.

From at least the early 80s, commercial software companies have offered genealogy-related packages.

Software, by the way, is computer jargon for any program or collection of instructions that causes a computer to perform a specific group of tasks. For example, I am using Microsoft Word in writing this book. Word is a *word processing* program; a collection of computerized tasks relating to entering, formatting, and printing text.

Genealogy software, of course, provides various computer routines aiding in the recording and maintenance of family history records.

Computer programs, then, is/are software and software is/are programs.

Why don't we just call programs *programs*? Hmmm. Why are we human? The use of technical jargon in any field just seems part and parcel of being what we are—people. As a computer user, traveler of the cyberspace realms of the internet,

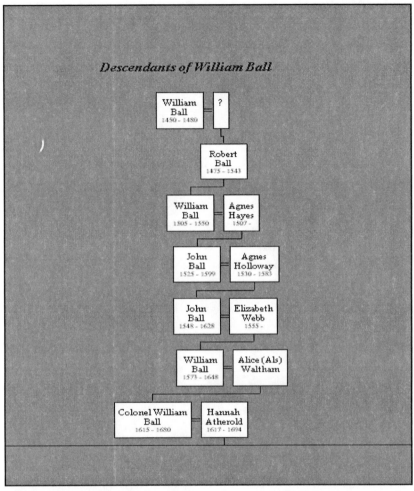

Descendants of William Ball

One huge advantage of using a computer for your family history research is the ease with which you can track the relationships of many hundreds of your relatives. Here's some of my Ball line dating back to 1450 (my mother was a Ball). The figure above is a descendant tree chart. To the right is a descendant outline. Any family history gets quite complex after a few generations. A computer is the answer!

Descendants of William Ball

```
1   William Ball 1450 - 1480
    ..+?
........2   Robert Ball 1475 - 1543
............3   William Ball 1505 - 1550
................+Agnes Hayes 1507 -
....................4   John Ball 1525 - 1599
........................+Agnes Holloway 1530 - 1583
............................5...John Ball 1548 - 1628
................................+Elizabeth Webb 1555 -
....................................6....William Ball 1573 - 1648
........................................+Alice (Als) Waltham
............................................7...Colonel William Ball 1615 - 1680
................................................+Hannah Atherold 1617 - 1694
....................................................8....Hannah Ball 1638 -
........................................................+Daniel Fox
....................................................8....Richard Ball 1639 - 1684
........................................................+Elizabeth Linton 1646 -
............................................................9...John Ball
............................................................9...Edward Ball 1670 - 1726
................................................................+Keziah Williamson Ozborne 1674 - 1736
....................................................................10.Edward Ball
........................................................................+Sarah Owens
....................................................................10.Benjamin Ball
........................................................................+Ann Owens
....................................................................10.Catherine Ball 1695 -
....................................................................10.Arthur Ball 1695 -
....................................................................10.Johannah Ball 1699 -
........................................................................+John Blake
....................................................................10.Edward Ball 1700 -
........................................................................+Sarah Owens
```

and family researcher, exposure to three sets of jargon happens constantly.

Fighting it merely wastes your time and annoys your computer. Accept and learn such terms as *RAM* for random access memory (where a computer keeps programs actually running) and hard disk (where inactive programs and data are stored) in the personal computer world.

Master internet terminology like *worldwide web* (the web is that system of tens of millions of "pages" with text and pictures accessible via the internet), *FTP* (file transfer protocol used in retrieving information from a remote computer to yours), and *e-mail* (electronic mail allowing you to send to and receive messages from anyone on the internet and many of the online services such as CompuServe or AOL which are tied to the internet).

Happily grasp genealogical terms such as *ancestor chart* (a chart showing an individual, his or her parents, grandparents, and so forth as far back as accurate information is available), *descendant chart* (which takes one of your ancestors and brings his or her line forward), the *birth record* (when and where a person was born), and the *death record* (the record of someone's passing from this life).

A Help screen in Family Tree Maker

When you encounter a new word, term, or acronym (a collection of letters meaning who knows what) and it seems significant, either puzzle it out in the context it appears, or look it up. Learning jargon is not like studying Croatian or Sanskrit, it only *seems like it*. Seriously, mastering a few dozen terms in all three fields—personal computers, the internet, and genealogy—speeds you along your way.

You can now pedal without thinking about it and enjoy the scenery!

Each time we fall upon a new piece of jargon in this book—or at least by the first *appropriate* time—I'll define and explain it to you. We'll also look at plentiful, useful, and enjoyable examples of how various concepts apply in practice.

So, do not fight jargon; embrace it. Life will be ever so much easier. The darned stuff just ain't gonna go away.

TRAINING WHEELS

What's really nice about using a personal computer in today's world of advanced technology is its ease-of-use. We mentioned earlier that people have been using computers in genealogical research for at least the last 25 years. True, but it was *hard*.

The first personal computers—from 1976 to around 1984 when the Apple Macintosh appeared—had display screens that were *character based*. This means only letters and numbers instead of the many colorful icons and other graphics on today's computers. The displays on current computers are referred to as graphic user interfaces (GUI or "*gooeys*"), and are much more powerful in depicting program results.

Character-based computers were complicated, difficult to understand and use, and generally repellant to the average person. Only after GUIs like the Mac's and the all pervasive Microsoft Windows, did personal computers explode into the popularity and almost universal usage they enjoy today.

Now, back to training wheels. When you were that little kid in training for big kid status, the initial concept of riding that bicycle was a dismaying one. How the heck could you make that puppy stay *upright*? That's when your parents might have introduced *training wheels*, those two little wheels on either side of the bike's rear wheel. These treasures kept you from falling over and skinning your cute little kid knees.

In a few weeks, or even less, your confidence and ability to ride without going over onto one or other of the training wheels meant you had graduated. You were a big kid now and the training wheels hung out to rust in the garage.

Yet, you needed those extra wheels at first, and this is just as true in computers. Luckily, you've got them, and they'll always be there for you, not rusting out in the garage.

One strong feature (training wheel) of both the Mac OS (operating system—the GUI) and Windows is built-in *Help*. Almost all programs designed for use with a GUI have a Help feature. This is a selection usually located on the top *menu bar*. The menu bar is that line across the top of the window in which a particular program is running. It normally has such words as FILE, EDIT, VIEW ... HELP. The Help selection is almost invariably the rightmost one. Move the selection arrow over the word Help with your mouse and *click* (depress the left-hand mouse button)—to bring up the Help window.

The above procedure works the same for practically every current model computer and software package available today, whether running Microsoft Windows or the Apple Macintosh system.

Windows are framed portions of the screen in which a program runs. There may be several windows on the screen at any one time, although you might have to move other windows around, or temporarily collapse them to see what's underneath.

Again, both the Mac- and Microsoft-based operating systems have windows, as do a number of other more powerful systems, such as X-Windows in the Unix/Linux world.

Another part of your training wheels is that any program designed to operate in a GUI-type system basically runs the same as any other program.

It's a beautiful and simple truth once grasped. If you learn how to work *any* program under Windows— be it word processing software such as Word or Word Perfect, a personal accounting package like Quicken or Microsoft Money, family history software such as Family Tree, a drawing program like Corel Draw, or any of thousands upon thousands of other programs, you know the basics of using every windows-based program. Tens of thousands of them!

Such important submenus as FILE, EDIT, and HELP are all in the same place up at the top of the window in all these many, many programs. You can open files, save files, cut, paste, and do all the other basic operations of running any program just the same in *all* programs.

COMPUTER LITERACY

The above concept bears repetition and emphasis: all windows programs work the same way; they just do different things. Learn and accept this incredibly simple concept and you're now a computer whiz, just like the rest of the big kids.

Computer literacy happens to be another of my pet

subjects. Most computer books, teachers, courses, *ad infinitum* isolate each program and teach you the steps needed for that piece of software alone. You learn Word Perfect, you suffer through the course on Excel or Lotus 1-2-3, you master Corel Draw in six weeks or PageMaker, or any of the other five or six programs you have immediate need of, or can afford its course.

Excuse me, but that's an exceptionally counterproductive way of learning the personal computer. It's equivalent of reading Mark Twain's *Tom Sawyer* by one set of rules and John Grisham's latest lawyer thriller by another. They are, after all, still written in the same language.

No! That would be and is ridiculous. If you can read—assuming the book is in a language you know, like English—millions of books pour their information and excitement through your beautiful (and/or handsome) eyes into your highly intelligent brain.

Software of all types may be "read," just like books, magazines, newspapers, and so forth. Instead of memorizing a few steps for one program, it's as easy to learn how tens of thousands of programs basically work. Then you are truly computer literate and immediately take advantage of new programs. The computer world changes *fast*, and you'll be constantly deluged with software updates and new programs. The ability to use these programs from the first time you see them on the screen vastly enhances productivity and lowers your general level of frustration.

Admittedly and even emphatically, "reading" programs requires a basic familiarity with computer jargon, just as we've already emphasized earlier in this chapter. Unlike English, there are far fewer words to learn, grammar and syntax are at least logical (English, you should not ask about—such a weird language, I want to tell you!)

Here, I'll make it even easier for you, because I like you! (Why? You bought my book, or at least checked it out of the library. Thanks, friend!)

Following is *Ralph's Mastering 100,000 Programs in Four Minutes* (Let's see the *Dummy* series beat that record!) This should boost your confidence and give you a sometimes much-needed head start.

RALPH'S MASTERING 100,000 PROGRAMS IN FOUR MINUTES!

Windows-based programs—whether in Microsoft Windows or the Macintosh operating system—have a very standardized set of basics. Appearance may vary slightly, wording might and probably will differ minutely, but the general concepts below always are there in some form or the other. Learn them and you'll never get lost again... at least not on the computer.

A menu bar is along the top of the window in which the program appears with words such as FILE, EDIT, VIEW, WINDOW, HELP. Words differ, but almost invariably FILE, EDIT, WINDOW, and HELP will be there,

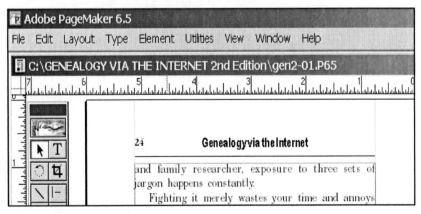

All Windows-based programs have the same type of menu selections across the top of the window. This example is from Adobe PageMaker, which was used in typesetting this book. If you learn one Windows program, you'll have the ability to run *thousands* of others!

with other selections depending on the type of program. Moving the mouse arrow over one of these words and clicking the mouse's lefthand button causes a submenu to drop down, which has more selections.

FILE: the FILE menu has selections such as but not limited to NEW, OPEN, SAVE, SAVE AS, PRINT, CLOSE, and EXIT. These are your basic navigation aids.

NEW: Opens a new, empty file for new data. In a word processing program, this would be a blank page. In a genealogy program, this would be a blank family tree with no entries yet.

OPEN: Opens a saved file that already contains data. You'll need to know where you left the file to find it again. Computers have *directories* or *folders* (interchangeable terms) that correspond to drawers in a file cabinet. Go to the right drawer and you see the file name. Click on it (move the arrow over the selection with the mouse and press the lefthand mouse button to open).

SAVE: Records a file you are currently working on to disk. Take a moment to note which directory or folder it goes into, making finding it again much easier.

SAVE AS: Gives you a chance to record a file under a different name. This is an important feature, allowing you to make backup copies of your work, or to experiment knowing you always could drop back to the original file. In other words, SAVE AS makes a *copy* of a file.

PRINT: Lets you print all or part of a file on whatever printer is attached to your computer.

CLOSE: Closes the current file but leaves the program running. You then might use NEW to start a new file, or OPEN to load in another file.

EXIT: Closes all open files and shuts down the program.

EDIT: The FILE submenu, just described above, lets you manipulate files. The EDIT submenu is for manipulating objects within files, such as words, pictures, or numbers. Typical EDIT submenu selections for any windows-type program are UNDO, CUT, COPY, and PASTE. There may well be others, but these four are most common.

UNDO: A most fortuitous command! UNDO is a real friend, a super *oops* eliminator. (OOPS is an acronym meaning Oh! Ouch! Puck! Shucks! As in, "Gee, I made a mistake, didn't I?") So, UNDO, simply undoes your last action. It's a wonderfully handy tool, even if most of us might occasionally use somewhat stronger language than the above.

CUT: If you select something in the program window—words, pictures, numerical data, then click on CUT, that object is *cut* from the screen but stays in the computer's memory until the next item is cut or copied.

COPY: COPY is similiar to CUT, except it leaves the object on the screen and only *copies* it into memory. The use of CUT or COPY lets you move and duplicate objects with ease. Why type in a lengthy family description eight times? Right, type it once, then copy and past it seven more times. Takes but seconds.

PASTE: Using the PASTE selection on the EDIT submenu, the last object cut or copied is placed wherever you have indicated in the file (i.e. on the screen). We are assuming here that you've learned how to use the mouse to point and click menu selections, and to indicate where the *cursor* goes in the file.

Riding with the big kids is the way to go!

WorldConnect Project
CONNECTING THE WORLD ONE GEDCOM AT A TIME

RootsWeb – The Oldest & Largest FREE Genealogy Site

Home | Boards | Lists | Searches | Sites | Passwords | Contribute | Help

Global Search

Names: 48835183 Surnames: 1031554 Databases: 19308

Results 1-25 of 45

Name	Birth/Christening Date	Birth/Christening Place	Death/Burial Date	Death/Burial Place	Database
Roberts,	ABT 1876	of,Scotland,Missouri			mkitchen
Father: Andrew Jackson Roberts Mother: Agnes Ann Pruett					
Roberts,	ABT 1878	of,Scotland,Missouri			mkitchen
Father: Andrew Jackson Roberts Mother: Agnes Ann Pruett					
Roberts,	ABT 1880	of,Scotland,Missouri			mkitchen
Father: Andrew Jackson Roberts Mother: Agnes Ann Pruett					
Roberts, Addie Agnes	AUG 1891	of,Scotland,Missouri	1971		mkitchen
Father: Andrew Jackson Roberts Mother: Agnes Ann Pruett Spouse: Elmer Wright					
ROBERTS, Alexander I	1716	Scotland			jtbenson
Father: Thomas ROBERTS Mother: Hannah					
Roberts, Alpha L.	JUN 1896	,Scotland,Missouri	1966		mkitchen
Father: Andrew Jackson Roberts Mother: Agnes Ann Pruett					
ROBERTS, Andrew	ABT 1824	Scotland			orbenton
Roberts, Andrew Jr.	BEF 1682	Scotland Co., VA	1772	Craven Prec., Bath Co., NC	edithj
Father: Andrew Roberts Sr. Mother: Ann - Mrs. Andrew Roberts Sr. Spouse: Hannah Shackleford					
Roberts, Ann	ABT 1680	Scotland Co., VA			edithj
Father: Andrew Roberts Sr. Mother: Ann - Mrs. Andrew Roberts Sr.					
ROBERTS, Betsy Smith	14 Sep 1897	Arbroath, Angus, Scotland	23 Dec 1969	Aberdeen, Scotland	jlovie
Spouse: Francis LOVIE					
Roberts, Clarence L.	FEB 1883	of,Scotland,Missouri	1930		mkitchen
Father: Andrew Jackson Roberts Mother: Agnes Ann Pruett					
ROBERTS, Edward		Scotland			lindamonks
Spouse: Margaret CONWAY					
ROBERTS, Edward	1736	Hawarden Flintshire Scotland	1802		lindamonks
Father: Thomas ROBERTS Mother: Mary HICKCOCK					
Roberts, Elizabeth	ABT 1679	Scotland Co., VA	4 MAR 1754	Carteret Co., NC	edithj
Father: Andrew Roberts Sr. Mother: Ann - Mrs. Andrew Roberts Sr. Spouses: Mr. Noble, William Webster					
Roberts, Elizabeth	ABT 1854	Bervie, Kincardine, Scotland	03 JUL 1908		iburness
Spouse: James Burness Stephen					
Roberts, Elizabeth	ABT 1872	Glasgow, Lanark, Scotland			jlk

One of my favorite places on the worldwide web for genealogical research is **http://worldconnect.genealogy.rootsweb.com**, a free service with now over *192 million names* quickly searchable! It's the RootsWeb's World Connect project, "Connecting the World, One Gedcom at a Time." Check it out and support it by contributing your own research. Great place! Above, searching for Scottish Roberts links.

The cursor being an indicator of varying shapes (underline, block, "I-beam") which shows the point where new material will be inserted, whether you type it in or PASTE it in.

WINDOW: This submenu has selections relating to how the program window is displayed on the screen. Remember, you might have three or four programs running at once, each in their own window. Up in the upper right-hand corner of a window are two or three little symbols (depending on your version of Windows) that (left to right) collapses the window entirely (but leaves the program active), makes the window take up less of the screen (revealing other windows that might be underneath), or causes the active window to take up all of the screen for easier viewing. The WINDOW submenu offers additional ways of manipulating windows. These also vary depending on the program but, for example, you might see a selection like SPLIT, which splits the screen and gives you, in essence, two independent views into the file. This is handy in such word processing tasks as writing this chapter where I can have an earlier page on the screen just to make sure I'm properly explaining all necessary points.

HELP: Back to those training wheels again, big kid. The help menu has selections like CONTENTS and INDEX, all of which help you to find, well, *help*. That is explanations of how the program works. It covers the selections on the main menu bar that are unique to the program, and all the various selections on all of the menus, plus many hints and tips and examples of whatever tasks the program is designed to aid you in accomplishing.

Learn the basics described above in *Ralph's Mastering 100,000 Programs in Four Minutes*, even if it takes you longer than four minutes (so my watch is fast, sorry). Once you have these simple steps down, the computer holds no fear for you. Hundreds of thousands of programs all running the same way. Neat, huh? No wonder Bill Gates became the richest man in the world for pushing Windows and getting (the unkind say "forcing") so many software manufacturers to standardize on this system.

A WATER PISTOL FULL OF AMMONIA

Okay, there remains but one loose end in our learning-to-ride-a-bicycle analogy as applied to mastering the personal computer. We've seen how to stay upright, become confident enough in using the computer to enjoy the scenery, and the importance of "training wheels" in getting us started.

Out there in the beautiful countryside of using the computer, you do get chased occasionally by those huge farm dogs "hugely disinclined toward friendliness" (to quote myself). This takes the form of computer glitches, blips in the power (which tend to drive computers insane), or (*gasp*) your own *oops!*-type mistakes (to quote you, kind but sometimes frustrated friend).

So, then, here's your ammonia-filled water pistol.

Not only does understanding some computer jargon and the basics of window-based programs make you more productive, it keeps you that way. Things happen with computers, weird things. That's just part of computing. Knowing how to recover from a mistake, be it yours or the machine's, is the true secret of being a power computer user instead of a frustrated neophyte.

You "squirt the dog" by knowing how to revert to a previously saved file in case of a mistake by yourself. "Save early, save often," says Al Lowe, creator of Leisure Suit Larry. It works in computer games. It works in writing books (man, *how* it works!), and it works always while you are constructing your family history. More on this in later chapters.

You "squirt the dog" if the computer acts up by knowing the options on the menu bar—how to step back, or how to stop the program if it's locked up without having to reboot the computer. An example of the latter—in Microsoft Windows—is to hit the key combination CTRL-ALT-DEL. This brings up a window that usually lets you end the stuck program while retaining everything else you have running. We'll elaborate later.

Knowledge is power, and a quick squirt of it usually makes that "dog" of a computer heel and obey its master or mistress. (That's you! That's you!)

Just don't challenge it to a chess game.

WINDOWS, WHAT THE BIG KIDS RIDE

What computer should I get?

This is the question I'm most often asked.

What follows is my educated opinion, based on living and breathing and writing about computers for the last 22 years and more. Take it or leave it, agree or disagree, but this is the *easy* solution.

You, of course, want the most bang for your buck, and a system that grows as you do by having the capacity to be easily expanded and upgraded, and which will always run the latest and greatest software. This latter, being the most important! If the machine and operating system are obsolete and/or no longer supported, you're stuck at a level which increasingly falls further and further behind the current technology.

This book covers using all sorts of computers for family history research via the internet. It includes machines using the Macintosh, MS-DOS, Windows, and Unix operating systems, and even "legacy" systems long gone from the stores like the Apple II and Atari.

However, we must also be realistic. The operating system holding the current championship as the fastest-selling, most widely supported, and easiest to use with the internet is Microsoft's Windows 95, 98, ME (Millenium Edition), XP (the latest) or whatever. Any other choice is a poor one.

Alas, I own no Microsoft stock and receive nothing for this endorsement. I don't even particularly like Microsoft, but facts are facts. Microsoft rules the desktop computer and all the new, great, powerful genealogy programs run on Windows 95, 98, ME, XP or whatever—indeed, *require* Windows 95, 98, ME, XP or the current version of that system to run at all.

The nice thing about this market dominance is that you get Windows 95, 98, ME, XP or whatever free with new computers these days, and that those new computers are *cheap*. An exceptionally fast and adequate machine for surfing the internet and constructing your family history sells today in the thousand dollar range or less!

The advantages of why you should have a Windows 95, 98, ME, XP or whatever computer would fill this book. Yes, you can construct your family history with an older machine or a Macintosh, but it's harder, especially the internet connectivity part. Don't fight the flow, just go with it—life will be a lot easier.

Personally, I much prefer Unix or Linux systems,

but they are a good deal more complicated, what I call "expert friendly," although that is changing.

But, for now, the logical choice is Windows. By the way, here's a tip for any computer running *any* windows-based system. The more memory, the better. The quickest and easiest way to speed up your computer is by adding more memory. For a now ancient Microsoft Windows 3.1 computer, have at least 8 megabytes of RAM (random access memory). For a Windows 95, 98, ME, XP or whatever computer, don't even turn it on unless you have a minimum of 64 megabytes, with 128 or 256 megabytes or move (I use 512 Mb. in this computer) being more preferable. Memory's cheap now and the simple upgrade of adding more RAM yields dramatic dividends.

RIDING ALONG

Okay, now we've learned the easy wonders of computers. In the next chapter, we'll look at genealogy itself. You'll find it just as simple and just as much fun.

Ready to pedal, big kid? Got your water pistol handy? Great, here we go!

THE BASICS OF GENEALOGY

*G*enealogy, to define the term, is the study of family relationships and the pattern they follow back through the years. Careful research may enable a person to trace his or her descent up through many generations from quite distant ancestors. From this research, the family history researcher then has the necessary information to construct an accurate and interesting family tree.

The word itself, *genealogy*, is from the Greek words meaning "family" and "study."

In this book, we will show you ways of doing that basic genealogical research, constructing your family tree, and even proceeding onward by publishing a limited edition, inexpensive book of your family's history. All of this is made far easier than it ever has been before by using the personal computer and the wide open resources of the internet and worldwide web to trace your roots.

What's more, we will all have fun!

WHY DO IT?

It's no secret—researching and constructing a family

history is both work and a quite long, sometimes tedious process. You do not complete it overnight, even with computers and the internet. Why do it?

Having come this far, you no doubt possess well thought out reasons of your own. I will, however, state the obvious.

People like people, that's a basic reason. All of literature from time immemorial concerns interesting characters and what happens to them. Even more fascinating than what happens to fictional heroes and heroines are those stories concerning your ancestors—the flesh and blood that eventually resulted in you, your mother and father, your sisters and brothers, and those cousins by the dozens.

Genealogy hooks you into a wonderful and fascinating hobby. Was great-great uncle Fabius really hanged as a horse thief, or was he a Texas Ranger, brave beyond all measure? Or just a poor but honest farmer who kept his family fed and clothed in hard times? Knowing for sure is nice. Most any family has its share of rogues and rascals but, in general, you'll find your forebearers a sturdy lot. After all, you turned out well, right?

So your reasons for researching your family back many generations are probably sentimental and include a curiosity about the past and historic fact as relating to your family. Did they fight in the War Between the States? Were they here in colonial times, or arrive via Ellis Island, emmigrating from some distant land to one of greater promise?

Another reason you might harbor (and nothing wrong with it) is a desire to show descent from nobility or royalty. This may turn out to be easier than you think. The farther you go back, the wider your ancestor pool becomes. Besides, those kings, princes, barons, dukes, counts, and earls of olden days did tend to get around a bit, so to speak. Not having the internet to roam, they

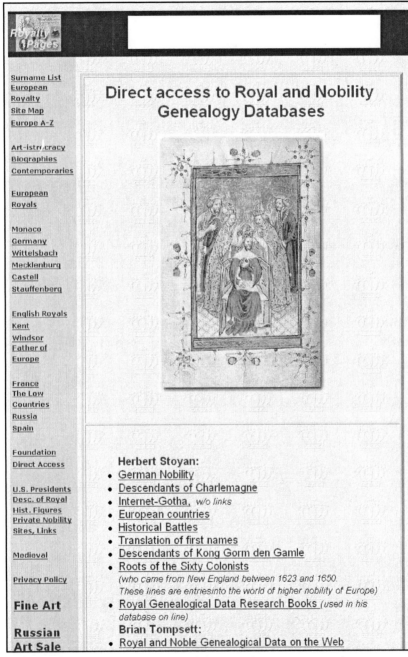

Surname List
European
Royalty
Site Map
Europe A-Z

Art-istr/cracy
Biographies
Contemporaries

European
Royals

Monaco
Germany
Wittelsbach
Mecklenburg
Castell
Stauffenberg

English Royals
Kent
Windsor
Father of
Europe

France
The Low
Countries
Russia
Spain

Foundation
Direct Access

U.S. Presidents
Desc. of Royal
Hist. Figures
Private Nobility
Sites, Links

Medieval

Privacy Policy

Fine Art

**Russian
Art Sale**

Direct access to Royal and Nobility Genealogy Databases

Herbert Stoyan:
- German Nobility
- Descendants of Charlemagne
- Internet-Gotha, w/o links
- European countries
- Historical Battles
- Translation of first names
- Descendants of Kong Gorm den Gamle
- Roots of the Sixty Colonists
  (who came from New England between 1623 and 1650. These lines are entriesinto the world of higher nobility of Europe)
- Royal Genealogical Data Research Books *(used in his database on line)*

Brian Tompsett:
- Royal and Noble Genealogical Data on the Web

Many excellent sites about royal genealogy exist on the internet. You'll find this very extensive one maintained by Brigitte Gastel Lloyd on the *rootsweb.com* site at **http://worldroots.com/ brigitte/royal/directaccess.html**.

roamed the local villages resulting in a number of descendents—some legitimate, some not; some acknowledged, some not. A few of these people might possibly be your or my ancestors. We'll see.

Or, you might want to trace your lineage from ancestors who arrived in America on the *Mayflower* in 1620. Or from well-known historic figures in any other era of this or any other country's history.

It's an interesting story, your family's history and mine. An absorbing hobby that will last you for years.

All of us living today came from those who lived before us. Parents, grandparents, great grandparents, and so on back through the generations to the remotest dawn of history when the world was young. Think I exaggerate? What about the guy in England who recently was found to have DNA in common with human remains from the same area that were prehistoric (i.e. thousands of years old). Talk about a family living in the same neighborhood for a long time!

Even more, some scientists claim we all descend from a common gene pool from some 250,000 to 300,000 years ago. Those of a more religious bent proclaim our common ancestors to be Adam and Eve in the Garden of Eden.

However, let us not get into such a controversial discussion. Suffice it to say that the family tree of us all—humankind in general—grows strong and very, very tall. Any of us, with greater or lesser digging required, have the possibility of tracing our roots back many generations. Later, we look at ways of making this easier. It's not quite as daunting as it may sound at first.

While the tracing of family histories has been with us from Biblical times to the present, in the last 20 years or so, its popularity has suddenly taken on an explosive growth in popularity.

The late author, Alex Haley, deserves a good portion of the credit for this. In his 1976 book—upon which a

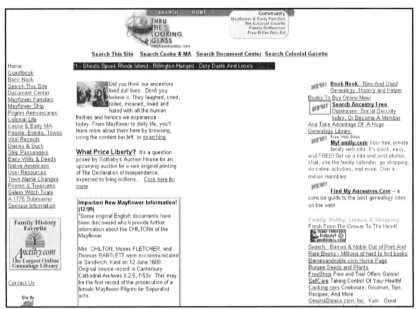

To determine if your ancestors came over on the *Mayflower*, check out this super web site at **http://mayflowerfamilies.com**. It has lots of other colonial data also. By the way, more than one ship brought these families over—they were the *Mayflower* (1620), *Fortune* (1621), and the *Anne* (1623).

blockbuster television miniseries was based—he called these ancestral lines into our past, "Roots." That term is now popularly applied to our family tree ... We search for our *roots*.

Yes, but what is the first step?

DECIDE WHAT YOU WANT TO ACCOMPLISH

First, decide on your end goal. What do you want to have accomplished when all the research is finally over? Genealogical research, as we have already intimated, can rapidly become very complex.

For example, you had two parents, four grandparents, eight great grandparents, 16 great great grandparents, and 32 great great-great grandparents. That's only six generations counting your own, for a

minimum of 63 people if every one of these six generations were an only child. Add in sisters and brothers for
all of the generations and the possibilities rise into the
hundreds.

Continue tracing backwards only four more generations and the very smallest number of your ancestors
(and highly unlikely) is now 1,023. Even if all these
forebearers of yours only averaged one sister or brother,
a mere ten generations back you have well over 2,000
ancestors. Since families in previous centuries tended to
be larger than today's 2.4 people or whatever, you'll find
even 2,000 a low figure for all of the people who got
together over the centuries to produce *you*.

As you see, the numbers rapidly multiply. Yep—you
gotta admit—it's downright fascinating.

Still, I'll not kid you, to research every single relative
you've ever had could take more time than you really
want to spend in the pursuit of ancestors. That's okay,
you have the choice of drawing a line of exclusion anywhere you like. The nice thing, as you'll find, about
computerized genealogy is that you'll always have the
option of returning and adding more information later.
Or passing your files along to another family member
who wants to pick up where you left off.

Three types of basic plans or approaches exist for the
construction of a family history. We start with the sim-
plest and move to the most complex.

THE FAMILY TREE

The *Family Tree* shows your male-line ancestors
such as father, grandfather, great-grandfather, and so on
along with their wives, brothers, and sisters.

"Whoa, *sexist*," the more politically correct might
yell. Yet, in our Western society which is non matriarch-
oriented—that is, the daddy gets all the credit whether he

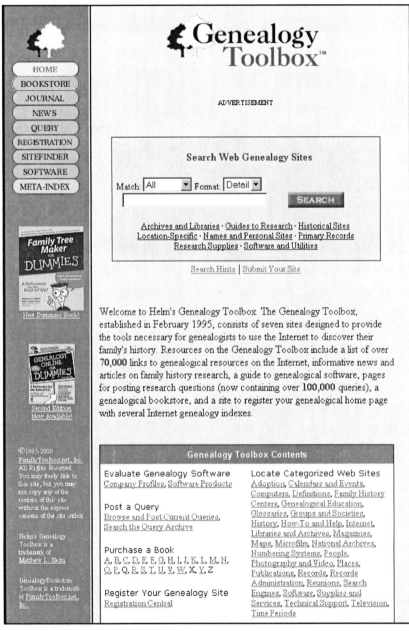

Matthew L. Helm's Genealogy Toolbox web site is one of the best all around genealogical resources on the worldwide web. Among ever so many other things are links to thousands of pages featuring family surnames. Look for your family's genealogical homepage, it could save you months of research. The Toolbox is at **http://genealogytoolbox.com**.

deserves it or not—doing a family tree based on female-line ancestors is really, really hard. The main problem being the fact that for centuries wives have taken their husbands surname. Hundreds of years of birth and death records reflect this fact.

Which is not to say that female ancestors aren't important—we know better than that, right? Of course! So, I suggest, you add in whatever female-line information you can glean as it is encountered.

There is no such thing as having your family history too complete, but time may limit just how extensive you let it grow.

With a bit more time and effort to spare, you might consider the next, more comprehensive type of family records.

THE EXTENDED FAMILY TREE

The *Extended Family Tree* is just that, you plan from the first to have more information, including such an end in your basic research techniques. An extended family tree shows all *collateral* branches of a family. Collateral branches are where you bring forward the lines of all descendants on your family tree including their spouses and children, not just your direct male-line ancestors. You can even start with an earliest known ancestor in either male- or female-line.

The result in your generation is that the old cliché of "cousins by the dozens" becomes literally true. And how!

The easiest way to envision the difference between a Family Tree and an Extended Family Tree is by thinking of a plain old pine tree, that conical shaped evergreen we see so many of at Christmas or, if you live out in the North Carolina mountains like me, you get to see them all year round—them little green suckers grow like weeds hereabouts!

Anyway, a Family Tree is that conical- or triangular-shaped tree right-side up. You (your generation) is at the top and each level down of ancestors causes the tree to become wider and wider, having more branches. Remember, we all have four grandparents, eight great grandparents, and so forth.

The Extended Family Tree is like that pine tree upside down! The point of the triangle or cone is some distant, early ancestor, and his or her descendents become greater in number as we go up in generations until at your generation, there may be hundreds or thousands of branches. All of these people, having a common ancestor, are your cousins, both near and distant.

Obviously, an Extended Family Tree requires an incredible amount of additional research and work. So, at first, you probably will start with the easier to accomplish Family Tree. As already indicated, a Family Tree can be turned into an Extended one by you or someone else.

ANCESTRY CHART

An *Ancestry Chart* can and should be even more complex than the Extended Family Tree. It includes as many of your direct ancestors as possible in *both* male and female lines! A truly complete Ancestry Chart might very well wind up with tens of thousands of entries. Sounds like a book to me! (See Chapter 12).

TWO GENERAL RULES AND HELPMATES

No matter which of the three types of family histories you elect to start with, two general rules will always prove helpful.

If you come across information about an ancestor who might not fall into your plan, it is still wise to record that information. This may very well help you to identify a later or earlier ancestor (so and so was the

SERVICE DATA	11F20 INTELL SPEC	NONE	b. TOTAL ACTIVE SERVICE	2	7	3
			c. FOREIGN AND/OR SEA SERVICE	2	1	10

24. DECORATIONS, MEDALS, BADGES, COMMENDATIONS, CITATIONS AND CAMPAIGN RIBBONS AWARDED OR AUTHORIZED

NATIONAL DEFENSE SERVICE MEDAL   VIETNAM CROSS OF GALLANTRY W/PALM
VIETNAM SERVICE MEDAL   BRONZE STAR MEDAL
VIETNAM CAMPAIGN MEDAL

25. EDUCATION AND TRAINING COMPLETED

NONE

REGISTERED JANUARY 16, 1970
AT 1:41 P.M. AND RECORDED   WODL03-L
IN BOOK 71 AT PAGE 257.

William E. Diggs REGISTER OF DEEDS
BY _Brenda S. Allen_ Deputy

26a. NON-PAY PERIODS TIME LOST	3. DAYS ACCRUED LEAVE PAID	27. INSURANCE IN FORCE	b. AMOUNT OF ALLOTMENT	c. MONTH ALLOTMENT DISCONTINUED
NONE	39	☐ YES ☐ NO	NA	NA
	28. VA CLAIM NUMBER	29. SERVICEMEN'S GROUP LIFE INSURANCE COVERAGE		
	c NA	☑ $10,000 ☐ $5,000 ☐ NONE		

(Above) The DD (U.S. Department of Defense) Form 214 is a good way of obtaining data on veterans of the modern era. Above is a portion of the author's DD Form 214 showing the stamp of the Buncombe County (N.C.) Register of Deeds where I had it recorded after returning from Vietnam in 1970. DD Form 214s, other military records, and land records along with birth, marriage, and death records as well as other legal documents are all public records at county courthouses and all available to the genealogical researcher. (Right) The author from his military days when he was a lot younger and slimmer.

son or daughter of so and so, etc.). Plus, if you ever decide to expand your tree more, it's that much less work you'll have to find again.

No matter which of the trees or chart you are trying to research, concentrate on one small part at a time. This makes it far easier to follow what you are doing. Should you get stuck in any area, work on other parts for a while. You'll be surprised how often problems of finding a particular ancestor can solve themselves that way, and you keep moving forward as well. You will still be accomplishing your task even if it is not necessarily in the direction of your original research plan.

Which brings us to the fact that we need to talk about working backwards.

WORKING BACKWARDS

It may sound like I'm belaboring the obvious but, in doing family history research, work backwards. You most likely know who your parents were, a distinct starting point in finding your ancestors.

We are not being funny here. Your near ancestors—parents, grandparents, great grandparents—are easiest to determine and to trace lines from down through the generations. Many people still living will be able to give you tips in the directions to proceed.

"Yep, sonny, I remember hearing your grandpa say his parents moved up here from Roberts, Georgia."

Now you possess a starting place for carrying your family tree on back. This working backwards technique is far simpler than, for instance, taking a family legend that your folks descended from George Washington or Robert E. Lee and trying to work forward. Famous people of antiquity usually have thousands of branches by the time you reach generations close to you own. This makes attempting to tie them into your family tree a very laborious and time-consuming process.

Work *backwards*. It's much easier. Besides, who knows, you might really be descended from Robert E. Lee. If so, you'll find out faster going backwards.

VERIFYING INFORMATION

Tips, of course, are only tips—you have to actually research and verify the information. In the example above, you would query the birth, death, and marriage records in the county seat of whatever county Roberts, Georgia lies in (Jones County, southeast of Atlanta, near Macon). The Georgia census records would also assist you in placing your grandfather's parents (your great grandparents) as having been residents of that county.

Such records are called *civil registration records*. In addition to those already named, such items as real estate property deeds, probated wills, and various other legal papers including court-granted changes of name are in the public record and available to you.

In the past, genealogical research required a lot of travelling and visiting where these records were kept in person. The conscientious family historian also became an expert on the widely varied architectural design of county courthouses since he or she certainly had to visit a lot of them.

Using the internet and various other online methods, this book shows you how to avoid a good deal of travel, while not totally eliminating it.

Back to working backwards: having traced a set of your great grandparents to a particular locality, the next step is indeed verification. This means finding some sort of documentation in civil registration records confirming they were there.

For birth, death, marriage, wills, and other legal papers of public record, the starting point is the county courthouse for the county in which the locality is, well, located.

The office that keeps county records goes by varying names in different states. In North Carolina counties, the Register of Deeds is responsible for recording not only deeds but marriage licenses, death certificates, birth certificates, changes of name, and lots of other helpful material to the family researcher.

For example, when I came back from Vietnam in 1970 and was honorably discharged from active duty, one of the last things the Army told me to do was to register my DD Form 214 at my local courthouse. The DD Form 214, while relatively recent, shows details of a veteran's military service including awards and medals, all of which make nice additions to family histories. Veterans who served prior to the DD Form 214s advent have various other types of military records available at this local level.

The courthouse may only be your first stop—the actual records could be maintained elsewhere. Most county clerks are well familiar with genealogical research by now and usually very helpful if approached in a courteous manner.

Okay, we said in North Carolina the Register of Deeds if the first office to check. However the name can and does vary widely from state to state. In South Carolina, many counties call this office the *Register of Mesne Conveyance*—the term *mesne conveyance* being a rather obscure archaic legal term meaning "Register of Deeds." (Okay, sorry, us North Carolinians sometimes give our southern neighbors a hard time cause they like that mustard-based barbecue sauce instead of the good tomato/vinegar nectar we use up here, but we still loves them, and the world's best pit-cooked pork barbecue simmers and savors in these two states!)

Seriously, if you are not sure of the correct term for that state, just ask who keeps birth, death, and marriage records.

DO THESE THINGS FIRST

Back once more to working backwards: As we said, start with your parents in accumulating the raw data that goes into your family history. In fact, you'll get a real jump start in the beginning by talking with or writing to all the kinsfolk you can find.

This is really important! Do it now, while they are still alive. Find out what sort of family documentation they hold, and get Xerox copies of it whenever possible for your own records. Items to inquire about include birth certificates, clippings about family members from newspapers, family bibles, diaries or journals, old letters, and anything else that mentions persons in the family.

Also, while these kinspeople are available, record as many genealogical facts about them as possible along with any other family members who they have knowledge about. These facts include date and location of birth, baptism, and marriage. If the person is deceased, include date and place of death, and the place of burial. Later in this chapter we'll list all this stuff in far greater detail for you (see "What to Look for Exactly" which follows this section).

Do the above for as many of your near relatives as you can. However, *do not take* their word as gospel. Sure, sure, old Great Aunt Bessie Mae looks truthful enough, but either her memory could be faulty (the old dear is getting along in years) or else someone could have misinformed her back in 1947. You don't know.

Again, verify everything through civil registration records or via other trustworthy sources of data. One we haven't mentioned yet are cemeteries. Genealogical researchers have spent a lot of time in cemeteries. The names and dates on tombstones often are invaluable information. Luckily, there are resources now on line which include cemetery records.

Generally, your kinsfolk comprise a tremendous wealth of information in the initial stages of constructing your family history. They are also a fantastic source of photographs and other materials to dress up your history. This is true regardless of whether you just "publish" it in the form of a single copy notebook, or actually do a limited edition book. The latter might well become a family heirloom and spur later generations into an appreciation of all those who went before them, including *you*.

Genealogy Help and Guides

The following are some of the many guides about how to do genealogy research that are available on the internet.

- JellyJar.com has has a good introduction for beginners starting genealogy research
- Jeffery Johnson gives Genealogy Instruction for Beginners, Teenagers, and Kids
- Maura Petzolt's Helpful Hints for Successful Searching has a variety of good tips both for those starting and well into researching their ancestors.
- The Genealogy Records Service has a free collection of printable genealogy and research charts as well as some help documents available for download.
- A number of general and specific genealogy help and information files are available from the ROOTS-L Library, which is associated with the ROOTS-L mailing list. Some of the features of the collection include FAQ (Frequently Asked Questions) Files, lists of documents held by the Library of Congress in their titles, and archives of the ROOTS-L mailing list. An introduction to this archive is available.
- DearMYRTLE's Daily Genealogy Column includes Genealogy Lessons for beginners and everyone
- SurNames.com includes a primer on how to begin genealogy research
- Geue'logy for WebTV Owners
- Robert Bickham has a list of 26 tips to get you started with genealogy.
- Phil Stringer's Getting Started in Genealogy and Family History is a good introduction to genealogy.
- "Treasure Maps", has an extensive collection of genealogy tutorials on topics such as Getting Started, getting past the "Stone Wall Syndrome," and using the U.S. Federal Census.
- The /pub/genealogy/text directory of the anonymous ftp site ftp.cac.psu.edu contains more guides and help.
- The Journal of Online Genealogy is an excellent free e-zine which focuses on the use of online resources and techniques in genealogy and family history.
- Genealogy On and Offline, with Naturalization Paper examples and Passenger lists on the internet has some tips for beginning genealogists
- Headstone Hunter is a volunteer project to hunt for and take pictures of tombstones
- Serendipity Mystical Discoveries in Genealogy accepts interesting stories of serendipitous discoveries.
- Family Newsletter News, is a newsletter about family newsletters
- Ben Buckner has list of surname frequency and distribution studies
- The Center for Life Stories Preservation covers the importance of recording the stories of living relatives.
- Paper Roots is a weekly roundup of genealogy in the news
- Chip Rowe's Things I Hate and Love About Genealogy discusses the pitfalls and great things about genealogy
- The San Antonio Express-News has an online genealogy column
- Mic Barnette publishes a weekly genealogy column in the Houston Chronicle.
- Suite 101, a guide to the web, has a bi-weekly Genealogy Column
- Genealogical Web Sites Watchdog exposes web sites with misleading or inaccurate information.
- A guide to English Versions of Foreign Given Names
- Information about planning family reunions and a registry are at Family-Reunion.com
- For a bit of humor, read how you can Buy an Ancestor Online
- Genealogy for Beginners
- AncestorNews is a free E-mail genealogy newletter with news, information and tips.
- Your Past Connections is a database of family documents and memorabilia that have been found at auctions, flea markets etc
- GenSuck.com discusses the pitfalls of online genealogy
- Advice about respecting the privacy of living relatives when posting genealogy on the internet
- Center for Life Stories Preservation has tips for writing family stories
- Family Newsletter News

....

The Genealogy Home Page™
Last update 01 February 2002
Register your site or homepage
© 1994-2001 Stephen A. Wood

Stephen A. Wood's *The Genealogy Homepage* **http://www. genhomepage.com/** is excellently done and offers links to a wide range of genealogy related resources, such as this help page.

WHAT TO LOOK FOR <u>EXACTLY</u>

Lila Kobs Hubbard, a family genealogist and research historian has posted an extensive article on getting started in genealogy. It's part of the many excellent resources provided by ROOTS-L on the net. Exactly what ROOTS-L is, and how to access and use it comes later in this book.

Lila's article, "Backward Footprints," is the *faq.starting* recommended by ROOTS-L. The letters *FAQ* stand for *Frequently Asked Questions* in the Unix and internet worlds, and *starting* means beginning. (You figured that one out, right? Sorry.)

In this article (you can retreive it at **ftp://ftp.cac. psu.edu/pub/genealogy/roots-l/faq/faq.starting**), she enumerates exactly the types of information that you'll find useful in constructing family records. We've taken her extremely helpful suggestions and elaborated on them somewhat.

First, the records members of your family might possess, which include but are not limited to the following:

- Bible records
- Books of remembrance
- Certificates, awards, discharges, etc.
- Diaries, printed or manuscript family genealogies
- Employment and societies records
- Family letters, stories and traditions
- Family records
- Photographs
- Wills, deeds, etc.

Next, move on to local records (i.e. those kept by various organizations in the locality in which you or the person being researched lives/lived). If you know the religious preference of the ancestor(s) being researched, don't overlook church records. Many churches have extensive records about marriages, births, deaths, and so forth of their congregations going back many years. Local records include but again are not limited to the following:

- Baptism records (church)
- Birth, death, marriage and divorce records
- Cemetery records and gravestones
- Genealogical or historical societies
- Libraries—many have genealogical information
- Military records, statues, plaques, etc.
- Mortuary records
- Newspaper files (obituary and news items)
- School records and board minutes
- Tax lists
- Town clerk's minutes
- Town histories and historians

Next step up is to the county level. As Lila reminds us, old county boundaries are subject to change! A good atlas is sometimes useful to the family history researcher. County records include but, of course, are not limited to the following:

- Birth and death records
- County census records
- County genealogical and historical societies
- County histories with biographies and genealogy
- Court records
- Deeds
- Hospital and mental institutions records
- Land records
- Marriage licenses / bonds and divorce records
- Military records
- Naturalization records
- Old folks or veterans homes
- Orphans court records
- School records and board minutes
- Tax records
- Wills, administration and guardianships

Next, it's on up to the state level and, yes, in checking local, county, and state records, you are going to run across some duplication and possibly contradictions. Take duplication as confirmation of what you've already determined and keep on researching, and try to resolve the contradictions. Since, over the period of generations, you'll find families often moving back and forth across county and state lines, diligent research at all levels is necessary. State records include but, again, are not limited to:

- Birth and death records
- Census records
- Court records
- Hospital and mental institution records
- Land grants
- Marriage and divorce records
- Military records
- State archives
- State genealogical and historical societies
- Tax lists

From state, we go to the national level. One excellent source of such information is the National Archives, which has branches in a number of cities. There are forms and procedures required in requesting information through the Archives, which you may obtain from the reference sections of many libraries. National records (U.S., that is) include:

- Bounty land warrant records
- Cartographic records (maps and descriptions)
- Census records
- Claims records
- Court records
- Immigration records
- Land records
- Military records
- Miscellaneous records including Social Security
- Naturalization records
- Old soldiers homes records
- Organizational and society records
- Passenger arrival lists
- Passport information
- Pension records
- Records of black Americans
- Records of civilian government employees
- Records of civilians during wartime
- Records of merchant seamen
- Records of native Americans

Nor do we stop here! Thanks to the internet, following your ancestor-line into other countries is now a lot easier. Much the same sort of records detailed above are available in the native countries of your ancestors down to state and county equivalent political divisions, and even towns and villages. We go into the methods of finding these records, or how to request them in later chapters.

WHAT TO DO <u>EXACTLY</u>

The National Genealogical Society (4527 17th Street North Arlington, VA 22207-2399, 703-525-0050) is a leading force nationally in genealogical research and education. They have five basic suggestions for exactly how to begin researching *your* family history. These are published on the internet and we quote them here by the Society's kind indulgence and permission.

1. **Interview Relatives First**: Question older family members. Encourage them to talk about their childhoods and relatives, and do not stop listening when they repeat themselves. They will drop further clues, sooner or later, without realizing it. You must recognize clues and follow up on everything that hints of a family connection, no matter how remote. Consider using a tape recorder and saving the tapes for future generations or your own library. After you have heard their stories, you must verify each fact from some other source, to be sure. Do not let family scandal bother you, but remember that it may embarrass others. You are not responsible for your ancestors. We all have some who did unpleasant things.

2. **Visit Your Library:** Inquire of the librarian what heraldic, historical and genealogical publications are available on paper or microfilm, and consult those that relate to the geographic areas of your interest. You must know something about the settlement (when, by whom and from where) and subsequent history of the county or town in order to know what you might expect to find in research for given time periods. Learn how to use the card catalog. Ask the librarian to suggest or recommend genealogy classes that may be offered by a local college or other adult education facility. Ask about any local, regional, and state genealogical and historical societies; then get in touch with their officers. Ask for the name and address of the state Library and Archives in your state capital; then inquire about its holdings and services. Ask about

cemeteries, any ethnic or religious libraries or archives that may relate to your search, and any collection or compilation of Bible records. Ask about local chapters of any patriotic, royal or other societies for which there are proven lineage membership requirements, such as the Daughters/Sons of the American Revolution.

3. **Visit Your Courthouse:** As you proceed through the foregoing steps you will learn how to ask the right questions, i.e., those calculated to elicit the most productive answers. After you have mastered that technique, visit your local courthouse to find out what is there, even if your ancestors lived elsewhere. The one thing all courthouses have in common is clerks who are busy. They can be enormously helpful. Cultivate them by using their time efficiently. Avoid narratives and convoluted questions. Ask, instead, to see such source records as will, deed and

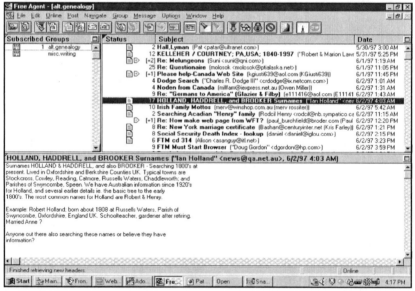

The internet opens a whole new dimension to you for getting help and support from others 24 hours a day! There are dozens of genealogy-related *news groups* where you can both ask and answer questions from other researchers. How to access and use these groups online is covered later in "Resources Available Through the Internet."

marriage books, for example, and inquire as to how they are recorded, arranged and indexed. Read for genealogical clues those that mention the surnames of your interest, including all conceivable spellings. When you encounter conflicting data, ask yourself which variant is more likely to be accurate. Which was recorded nearest the event by the person most likely to know?

4. **Write Letters to Others:** Learning to ask the right questions will help in the correspondence you should undertake with other individuals or societies concerned with the same families or areas, or with foreign embassies in Washington. Enclose a long self-addressed stamped envelope (an SASE to genealogists and others) in every letter you wish to have answered. The recipients will be more willing to reply. Generally, it is better to confine each letter to one specific question, and to tell the recipient what you already know about the subject and what research you have already done. Provide as many dates and places as you can. Thank those who respond and share what you learn with other researchers. Those who share usually benefit most.

5. **Record Your Results Systematically:** Record what you learn, indicating the source for each fact. Do not treat separate families on the same piece of paper, since they should be filed in separate groups. It usually is helpful to use printed family group sheets or pedigree charts and a filing system organized so that you can locate what you have in an ever-expanding collection.

To learn more about these five steps and to continue your pursuit of genealogy, you may wish to purchase *Instructions for Beginners in Genealogy*. This 62-page book will help you get started and develop good record-keeping habits. It is written in a simple, straightforward style and is three-hole punched to carry in a notebook for ready reference. It's available from the Education Division of the National Genealogical Society for $12.00 which includes postage. Order from the Education Division, National Genealogical Society (4527 17th Street North Arlington, VA 22207).

You might be able to find photographs of your ancestors on the internet! Dick Weisiger and Jane Martin offer a web site with over 10,000 old photographs sorted by surname (**http://128.218.113.53/**).

THE IMPORTANCE OF DOCUMENTATION

As we've seen above, tracing family history involves a lot of documents and other materials. You'll want to keep very good records yourself of where you found each such document or other piece of data. There are many reasons for this, the most important of which to you should be the saving of work for you later!

So, the rationale for good documentation includes your possible need later to review or check your sources again (saving yourself work), or someone else might see something in what you've done that gives them a lead on their own research. In this latter instance, the other researcher would find it useful to access your sources. In general, you gotta show where you found the stuff. Write it down.

A common mistake of beginning genealogists is in not considering or underestimating the importance of proper documentation. Please don't make it, yourself. Avoid later trouble by knowing where you got something, and where you can get it again if need be. For example, if information is used from a reference book, keep enough notes so that you could walk back into the library or other place you found the book five or ten years later, locate that same book, and again locate the reference in the book that you used.

When you publish your family history—whether in notebook or regular book form—you'll want the ability to cite your exact sources including each civil registration record used and all the other source material that shows the reader the accuracy of your work and which allows it to be built on in the future.

This includes recording sources in which you found *nothing*. Noting such a negative source could save you or others from following a time-wasting lead in the future.

HAS IT BEEN DONE?

Family history research, especially when it's your own family, can be fun and a satisfying pursuit. It also can be, and often is, tedious and very time consuming. An old cliché says, "don't reinvent the wheel," meaning you don't necessarily have to redo work already done.

In the case of genealogy, one of your first research tasks should be the searching of the many directories published to show who is researching what in family histories. If someone else is already delving into your family lines, check to see if they've published their research yet. Or contact them and trade for or otherwise obtain the information you need.

Such a bonanza of work already done quickly bulks up your family history and saves, perhaps, years of your own digging. *However*, please remember our discussion about documentation earlier. You'll want to make sure the material you get is properly documented so that you can both verify the other researcher's data and/or begin at a particular point in expanding your own research and building on theirs.

Also you'll find many published genealogies, books of pedigrees, and other family history material such as extensive ancestor charts of both famous and even nonfamous families. See if you can link your own family into one of these. Again, you save work—sometimes an incredible amount—and gain a great boost in completing your family history to whatever extent you are aiming toward.

A serious warning here—yeah, again. Just because you find a long pedigree in some dusty old tome that lets you claim descent from, say, King James I of England, don't take that version as absolute gospel (pun, of course, intended—send me a quarter and I'll explain if you didn't get it). Just because the data is published in a book does not mean it's totally correct. (Yep, even this book but we are making every effort to be close!) Instead, consider it a "potentially valuable information." Corroborate the data as much as possible, checking other sources to verify it's accuracy. Only then add it into your own history.

HELP AND SUPPORT FROM OTHERS

Any long and tedious task—from driving across Texas (*really* long and tedious) to constructing a family history—is lots more fun when done with friends. You may be the only member of your family doing genealogical research, but you can safely bet that many, many other people in your area are researching their own families.

So, seek out and join a local genealogical or family history society in your town. You might also consider doing the same with societies in areas where your research is concentrated heavily. For example, if your grandfather moved up from Mobile, Alabama, you'd find lots of support and help from a genealogical society there. If you have relatives from the Asheville,

North Carolina area, I highly recommend the Old Buncombe Genealogical Society. Nice folks!

Your fellow genealogy society members offer you support, tips, and access to useful research materials or already completed family histories that might tie into your own.

Check in your local phone book or with the reference librarian at your town's library or with your equivalent to the Register of Deeds office for your county. The latter two groups, especially, have lots of contacts with genealogical researchers and can point you to them.

LEARN A WIDE RANGE OF DOCUMENTS

In order to make any progress at all, you'll have to learn methods of interpreting a vast array of documentation. There will be hundreds of sources having many kinds of information in as many different formats. You will be using a lot of them to obtain and verify information as you push forward your family history.

You'll look at county records of all sorts from scores of counties, all varying in format. You'll see piles of militia muster rolls, tithe maps, election rolls, military service records, census records, claims records, court records, immigration records, land records, wills, passenger lists, naturalization records, old soldiers homes records, and so on and so on.

As you have no doubt already deduced, none of these documents were produced with your ease or that of any future family history researcher in mind. The papers and ledger books are often scribbled, practically illegible, filled with nonstandard abbreviations and other weird shortcuts. At times, you'll be more detective than researcher, but struggle on through, the end results are worth it.

Treat each new type of document you encounter as a challenge and devise techniques to mine the information it contains. Make copious notes because, sooner or later, you're going to run across another or similar one. *Then*, you'll be prepared.

Harking back to belonging to a genealogical society, maybe a fellow member has found similar records. In such case, his or her helpful tips can save you a respectable amount of time. Also, you'll want to accumulate a small library of useful reference books about genealogical research. All of which helps, but be prepared to see many unusual methods of record keeping—the world is big and the county clerks of ages past most inventive at times.

TYPES OF INFORMATION TO RECORD

Family history ought to be interesting otherwise, why do it? Don't stop with cut and dried facts such as the birthdate, date of marriage, and date of death of an ancestor. Gather, also, information about when he or she lived, what their profession was, and other points of interest that would help you paint a picture with your words of a real human being.

Such true life stories add real fascination to a family history. Include whatever photographs or artwork you can find to make that entry more vivid. Being accurate does not mean ya gotta be dull.

A FAMILY HISTORY QUESTIONNAIRE

Interviewing your immediate family members, such as mother and father, uncles and aunts is a good starting point for getting a lot of fascinating historical information about the family. Below is a suggested format for a questionnaire to be used in interviewing family members. Donna J. Rostetter posted much of this information on the internet in 1993, having abstracted it herself, she

Google™   Advanced Search   Preferences   Search Tips
genealogy   [Google Search]   [I'm Feeling Lucky]

Searched the web for **genealogy**.   Results **1 - 10** of about **8,390,000**. Search took **0.08** seconds

Category: Society > Genealogy > Directories

Cyndi's List of Genealogy Sites on the Internet
... Leat France (311) Updated October 23, 2000. Leaf **Genealogy** in the Media (38)
Television, Radio, Print and the Internet Updated October 24, 2000. ...
Description: Category Index
Category: Society > Genealogy > Directories
www.cyndislist.com/ - Similar pages

Genealogy.com: The Leading Resource for Family History
... here. More. Tips & Tools. HistoryChannel.com. **Genealogy**.com.
News ... a good read. **Genealogy**.com Gems See what ...
www.genealogy.com/ - 38k - Cached - Similar pages

  Genealogy.com: Learn About Genealogy
  ... Learn About **Genealogy** Better family-finding
  skills lead to great family trees ...
  www.genealogy.com/genehelp.html - 7k - Cached - Similar pages
  [More results from www.genealogy.com]

The Genealogy Home Page
Sponsored by Family Tree Maker Online The **Genealogy** Home Page. ... To see these **Genealogy**
pages as one single file see the merged **Genealogy** Home Page. ...
Description: Proudly sponsored by Family Tree Maker Online.
Category: Society > Genealogy > Products and Services
www.genhomepage.com/ - 3k - Cached - Similar pages

Genealogy Online - Gensite
... Since Sun Oct 22 23:01:00 PDT 2000. Rank, Site Name, Hits. 1, FREE **GENEALOGY** RESEARCH
of Birth, Census, Death, Marriage, Veterans, Ship Passenger Lists, 10104. ...
www.genealogy.org/gensite/ - 24k - Cached - Similar pages

  Genealogy Online - Gensite Rootsweb
  ... Since Sun Oct 22 23:01:00 PDT 2000. Rank, Site Name, Hits. 1, FREE **GENEALOGY** RESEARCH
  of Birth, Census, Death, Marriage, Veterans, Ship Passenger Lists, 10141 ...
  Description: Features include events database, Gensite, Genchat, and the GEDCOM Library.
  Category: Society > Genealogy > Products and Services
  www.genealogy.org/ - 26k - Cached - Similar pages
  [More results from www.genealogy.org]

Yahoo! Arts > Humanities > History > Genealogy
... Most Popular Sites: Mathematics **Genealogy** Project - with the goal to list all individuals
who have received a doctorate in mathematics. FamilySearch Internet ...
www.yahoo.com/Arts/Humanities/History/Genealogy/ - 21k - Cached - Similar pages

Journal of Online Genealogy - Promoting the Use of Computers ...
... Who Needs **Genealogy** Conferences? Everybody! Diana Smith reviews the many benefits
of conferences and workshops, and provides some helpful tips about attending ...
Description: Aids the genealogical community in promoting and developing online projects, technologies, and methods...
Category: Society > Genealogy > Magazines and Ezines
www.onlinegenealogy.com/ - 17k - Cached - Similar pages

RAND Genealogy Club
RAND **Genealogy** Club. ... **Genealogy** in the News. Paper Roots: Weekly Round-up of
Genealogy in the News How to Start. Tips for Tracing Your **Genealogy** ...
Description: Forum for RAND employees to discuss **genealogy**.
Category: Regional > North America > ... > Society and Culture > Genealogy > Organizations
www.rand.org/personal/Genea/ - 15k - Cached - Similar pages

Helm's Genealogy Toolbox - Providing the Tools to Research ...
Genealogy Toolbox ... Helm's **Genealogy** Toolbox and **Genealogy** Toolbox is
a trademark and service mark of Matthew L. Helm. ...
Description: This site contains the Journal of Online **Genealogy**, Query Central, Registration Central, GenealogySoftwar...
Category: Society > Genealogy > Resources
www.genealogytoolbox.com/ - 20k - Cached - Similar pages

Gooooooooogle ▶
Result Page: 1 2 3 4 5 6 7 8 9 10   **Next**

genealogy   [Google Search]   Search within results

Try your query on: AltaVista Deja Excite HotBot Infoseek Lycos Yahoo!

Google Web Directory · Cool Jobs · Advertise with Us! · Add Google to your Site · Google in your Language · **All About Google**

©2000 Google

How many genealogy sources are there on the worldwide web? Well, this quick search at **google.com** shows several million! Later in this book, I'll show you how to narrow down your searches.

said, from Virginia Allee's "A Family History Question-naire" in the October, 1978 *Family Heritage Magazine*, and we further adapt it here.

You'll want to set up and save this reasonably simple questionnaire in whatever word processing program you use on your personal computer. Then you'll have the ability of printing out copies when they are needed, either for in-person interviews or for mailing to distant relatives with a request that they fill out and return the question-naire to you. A nice letter saying "please" and including a self-addressed, stamped envelope does wonders in getting your Aunt Flossie to actually fill out the questions and return them.

Basically, the questionnaire itself is a guide that helps you or anyone filling it out record the life experiences of a family member. This data provides important links both backward and forward in the family history.

As you'll see this questionnaire is quite long and may not fit into the type of family history you're doing. If so, just adapt it to your purpose or ignore it. On the other hand, the more data you have in genealogical research, the better. Getting as many of these ques-tionnaires filled out as possible by living relatives will garner you a wealth of clues in following your ancestor lines back into time.

On the top of the questionnaire, put your name and address. Also add a brief statement of who you are and your position in the family. Remember, while your mother and dad probably have at least a vague idea of who you are, this questionnaire will be going to distant cousins who don't, as my daddy used to say, "know you from Adam's housecat." This is especially true if you start adding a lot of collateral relatives—that being those descended through such lines as your grandfather's brother's family or your great grandfather's sister's line.

Remember also to always say "please" and "thank you" in advance.

Okay, here are the categories and questions from which you'll want to construct your questionnaire. There's a lot of typing involved so, to make it easily on you, I am putting up a worldwide web site at **http://abooks.com/genealogy** where you'll be able to just download the file and drop it in your word processor. There's also genealogy news and other interesting things on the site, including links to other genealogy-oriented sites.

Now, the questions and, again, thanks to Virginia Allee and Donna J. Rostetter for coming up with them.

CATEGORIES AND QUESTIONS

Please remember to leave plenty of space between each question so that the relative responding has room to answer in detail.

Parents and Grandparents

1. What are the names of your parents?

2. What were the names of your mother's parents?

3. When and where were they born and where did they live?

4. What did they do for a living?

5. Do you have personal memories of them?

6. What were the names of your father's parents?

7. When and where were they born and where did they live?

8. What did they do for a living?

9. Do you have personal memories of them?

10. Did you know your grandparents well? Please always include names and places where persons lived when known.

11. What do you remember hearing about your great-grandparents?

12. Did you ever meet them?

13. Did your great grandparents, grandparents, or parents

come to the US from a foreign country? Any stories told in your family about the crossing?

14. Do you have any relatives in foreign countries? Please include, if known, their names and what country.

15. What traditions are still practiced in your family?

Childhood

The Family House

1. What type of house did you live in as a child?

2. Other buildings on the same property?

3. If you moved during your childhood, tell where and when and what you can remember of each house and the family circumstances and the reason for the move.

4. In what room did you eat? Kitchen? Dining room?

5. How was your home heated?

6. Did you have a fireplace?

7. What kind of kitchen stove did your parents cook on?

8. What fuel was used?

9. Did you have to buy the fuel or was this a chore, such as cutting wood, with which you had to help?

10. Did you always have electricity? If not, when did you get it?

11. Did you ever use candles or kerosene lamps?

12. Did your family have a cellar? Where did you store food?

13. Where did your family get water? Was it plentiful?

14. What methods were used to conserve water?

Position in Family

1. What was your position in the family? Oldest? Youngest?

2. What were your duties as a small child?

3. Who cooked the meals? Who did the ironing?

4. Did you buy or make your own clothing?

5. When did you learn to cook and who taught you?

6. Did you ever learn to sew? Crochet? Knit? Embroider? And who taught you?

7. Did you ever learn the mechanics of a car and who taught you?

8. Did your family keep in touch with distant family?

9. Did you visit relatives often?

10. How did you get your mail?

11. What do you remember about family pets?

12. Were you especially close to anyone in the family?

13. How did the family spend its evenings?

Family Income and Livihood

1. What did your father do for a living?

2. Did your mother ever work outside of the home?

3. Did you contribute to the family income?

4. When did you get your first job outside of the family?

5. Did your family have a garden?

6. Who did the work on the garden?

7. What kinds of vegetables did you grow?

8. Did your family have fruit trees?

9. Who did the canning?

10. Did you raise chickens?

11. What kind of meat did you eat?

12. Did you keep a cow for milk?

13. Did you make your own butter and cheese?

14. Did anyone in the family sell eggs or butter?

15. If you lived on a farm, what crops were planted?

16. Who did the work? Family? Hired hands?

Days, seasons, and special occasions

1. What did Saturday mean to you?

2. What did Sunday mean to you?

3. Did you attend church on Sunday?

4. Where did you attend church?

5. How did you spend Christmas?

6. What kinds of gifts did you receive at Christmas?

7. Did your family observe Easter?

8. How and where did you observe the Fourth of July?

9. How was your birthday celebrated?

10. What kinds of gifts did you receive on your birthday?

11. Did your family entertain often? When?

12. Did your family attend picnics? Family reunions?
13. What do you remember about them?
14. How did you keep cool in the summer?
15. What did you wear in the winter to keep warm?
16. Do you remember any blizzards or tornadoes or floods?

Friends and Games

1. What did you do for recreation?
2. Did you or your brothers or sisters have any hobbies?
3. Who was your best friend?
4. What did you and your friends do when you got together?
5. Did you and your playmates play any organized games?
6. Did you ever learn to swim?
7. Did you participate in youth organizations?

School

1. Where did you go to school?
2. Did you ever attend a one-room schoolhouse?
3. How did you get to school? If you walked, how far?
4. What do you remember about these walks? Did you walk alone or with friends?
5. Were these walks a hardship in winter?

Transportation and surroundings

1. Describe the size of the town where you lived or shopped.
2. Where did your parents shop?
3. How large or small were the stores?
4. If you lived in a small town or on the farm, did you ever go into the city to shop?
5. What was the largest town you remember visiting when you were young?
6. Did you ever travel on a train while you were young?
7. Did you or your family own a horse and buggy?
8. When did your family acquire its first car? What make? How much did it cost?
9. When did you learn to drive a car?
10. Where did your family go on vacation?

Outlook

1. Whom did you admire most when you were young?
2. When you were small, what did you hope to do when you grew up?

Higher Education and Career

1. What education did you get past high school? Did you study in your adult years?
2. Did your family support, oppose, or encourage you?
3. Who influenced you most and helped you to develop your skills?
4. Would you choose the same career if you had it to do over?

Marriage and Later Life

1. When and where did you meet your husband or wife?
2. How and when did you get engaged?
3. When and where did you marry?
4. Did you go on a honeymoon?
5. Where was your first home?
6. What is your spouse's occupation?
7. Where and when were your children born?
8. Did you or your spouse go into military service?
9. If your husband went into service, what did you do while he was away?
10. What memories do you have of war years?
11. To what organizations have you belonged?
12. Have you been politically active during your lifetime?
13. Which presidents have you voted for?

Philosophy and Outlook

1. Do you have a philosophy of life to share with your descendants?
2. Do you have a favorite philosopher, teacher, or writer who best expresses your philosophy?
3. Do you have religious leanings or strong religious beliefs?
4. In your opinion, which have been the greatest advances or inventions of all?

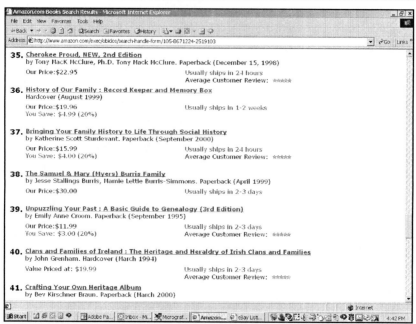

A fast source for genealogy books of all sorts is the huge online bookseller (and more) **http://amazon.com**. Just type in genealogy as a keyword to start.

5. What things have given you the most pleasure or satisfaction?

6. Is there anything that has caused you perpetual concern? What events or trends have disturbed you most in your lifetime?

7. What do you consider to be your greatest accomplishment?

8. What has been your experience in regard to the following?

 a. Answers to prayers?

 b. Necessity and power of love?

 c. Will power as opposed to feelings?

SCOPE

Here is a good place to again address the *scope* or amount of detail that your family history will contain. As we saw just previous in the Family History Questionnaire section, you can *really* get into detail.

Genealogy, also as said before, has a way of hooking

you, and quite pleasantly so. You might have started the research into your family's history with a view to only finding a few of your immediate ancestors just to satisfy a passing curiosity concerning who they were and what they did.

However, from small acorns, large oaks grow as the old adage states. You may very well find, as have many of us, that your project, at some time in the future, swells of its own volition (at least, seemingly so) into a lifelong and exciting pursuit of relatives far removed in time and space. If you put the details down to begin with, and document them properly, you'll be all set if your small project later becomes large. If not, nothing lost and the next person in your family to take up genealogy will thank you for doing such a complete job on the amount you did accomplish.

Also, another thought on thorough documentation. In the press of modern life, it would not be unusual for you to put aside your research, perhaps for years, until again time presents itself for the project. In that case, you'll thank yourself for having the documentation in place which makes it easy to take up your family history research again.

Frankly, I did that after the first edition of this book in 1997, moving on to other projects. This year, I was glad to find my thorough notes, which gave me a jumpstart diving in again on my family research. So, always document what you do.

Another old adage also applies here, "a job worth doing is a job worth doing well." You should set high standards for yourself. Don't scrimp on research, documentation, and the final presentation or publication of your findings. Read books on genealogy research, "talk shop" with your fellow genealogy society members, surf all those wonderful genealogy-related web sites on the internet, keep your genealogy software upgraded, and ever strive to improve your techniques in tracing your family roots.

It all pays off in a well-earned glow of satisfaction!

LDS FAMILY HISTORY CENTERS™

No treatise on the basics of genealogy would be or *could* be complete without mentioning the incredible genealogical resources maintained by and made available to everyone, member or not, by the Church of Jesus Christ of Latter-day Saints (the Mormons).

I am not a member of the LDS church and the fact that the Mormons consider both my own faith, Southern Baptist, and our Jewish brethren to be gentiles, along with most everybody else, really has little to do with the purpose of this book. Nor am I especially offended by it, Mormons have every right to believe whatever they like.

It is, in fact, one of these strongly held Mormon religious tenets that so greatly benefits all of us interested in family history research. Since the 1890s, the LDS church has poured millions upon millions of dollars into genealogical research and has collected many hundreds of millions of pieces of data relating to everyone's ancestors.

Basically stated, members of The Church of Jesus Christ of Latter-day Saints do family history research because they are motivated by love for their deceased family members and desire to serve them. Mormons teach that life does not end at death. When we die, our eternal spirits go to a spirit world, where we continue to learn while we await the Resurrection and Final Judgment.

Members of the LDS church believe that the family can also continue beyond the grave, not just until death and that deceased ancestors can also receive the blessings of being eternally united with

FAMILYSEARCH.
INTERNET GENEALOGY SERVICE

THE CHURCH OF
JESUS CHRIST
OF LATTER-DAY SAINTS

- SEARCH FOR ANCESTORS
- BROWSE CATEGORIES
- COLLABORATE WITH OTHERS
- PRESERVE YOUR GENEALOGY
- ADD A SITE
- ORDER FAMILY HISTORY RESOURCES
- ABOUT THE CHURCH OF JESUS CHRIST OF LATTER-DAY SAINTS
- FEEDBACK
- HELP

Search for Ancestors

You searched for: Jabez Jarvis, Birth/Christening   [refine search]
                    Father: Jabez Jarvis
                    Exact Spelling Off

Results: All Sources (13 matches)

Sources Searched
Matches were found only in the sources listed below. Click on a source to see more matches for that source.

- Ancestral File (1)
- IGI/North America (1)
- Web Sites (11)

1. Jabez JARVIS, JR - Ancestral File
Gender: M Birth/Christening: Abt 1765/1770 <, White Co, Tennessee>

2. Jabez JARVIS - International Genealogical Index/NA
Gender: M Birth: Abt. 1752 Of Possibly, Wilkes, North Carolina

3. Werner Surname Page - Web Sites
Werner Family Werner Family First Generation Johann Adam Werner was born before 1707 in Germany. He married Maria Catharina Sigler in Germany, and their older children's births are recorded in the Evangelische Kirchbuch of Massenbach, Schwaigern, Wuerttemburg, Germany. They immigrated in
[http://cgibin1.erols.com/fmoran/werner.html]

4. Harper Surname Page - Web Sites
Harper Family Harper Family Zephaniah Harper was born somewhere in Maryland and migrated to Rowan Co, NC by Nov 30, 1793, (probably with his father, William) and settled in the Lewisville area then known as the Granville development. The Harper family has a receipt that states in part " ...Nov
[http://www.erols.com/fmoran/harper.html]

5. MEAKER, JARVIS / GERVAIS, DENESHA, EINBODEN GENEALOGY - Web Sites
MEAKER, JARVIS / GERVAIS, DENESHA, EINBODEN GENEALOGY Welcome to the Meaker, Jarvis / Gervais, Denesha, Einboden, Home Page. Jarvis Family Tree Meaker Family Tree Einboden Family Tree Denesha Family Tree Gervais family crest,"Thus Supported It Increases". Unknown Meaker family
[http://freepages.genealogy.rootsweb.com/~somerset/]

6. Find-A-Grave by Location: Pennsylvania - Web Sites
Find-A-Grave by Location: Pennsylvania ');)) if (bN=="Microsoft Internet Explorer') document.write('', // --> > Pennsylvania A Grave Icon ( ) indicates that a photo of the grave is available. Click on the icon or the person's name to view the images. Adams, Earl John "Sparky" b. August 26,
[http://www.findagrave.com/grave/lps.html]

7. Kleinkauf Surname Page - Web Sites
The Kleinkauf Family Genealogy is like looking into the tangled branches of trees, particularly when you are doing a one name study like this one on the KLEINKAUF family. It is also a "journey into time", back into our own personal history. We know where the Kleinkaufs started, Germany, but they
[http://www.geocities.com/Heartland/Acres/6656/]

8. Clark Surname Page - Web Sites
Burgess Clark. Burgess Clark (1763-1851) Abstract of Application for Pension and Bounty Land Warrant for Revolutionary War Service - (W2758 / BLWt 34972-160-55) Burgess CLARK made application on Oct.12, 1832 and stated that he was 69 or 70 years old. He was living in Chatham County, N.C. in
[http://www.tngenweb.org/white/clark.htm]

9. Ziegler Surname Page - Web Sites
ZIEGLER Genealogy ZIEGLER Genealogy Page With the help of my father and my cousins, I am researching the ZIEGLER family history. I am doing this for my self and for my family. If you have questions about my information, or if you think we might be related, please feel visit my Guestbook. The
[http://www.ntwrks.com/~kziegler/ZIEGLER/]

10. Pointer Surname Page - Web Sites
POINTER FAMILY TREE This tree contains the following surnames: BAKER, BLEVINS, BRANSON, CARWILE, COLVIN, DANIEL, FERGUSON, FOWLER, GILMORE, HAMET, HARRIS, HEROD, JAMES, JARVIS, JETT, LEACH, McMANNIS, OUSLEY, OWENS, PHELPS, PHILLIPS, POINTER, ROACH, SIMPSON, SNOW, TACKETT, WALKER, YEATS 1 George
[http://members.tripod.com/~rlbrown/POINTER.HTM]

11. Fmlypage - Web Sites
Fmlypage   Family Search@ www.familysearch.org dss70530@cmsu2.cmsu.edu Ancestry.com@ www.ancestry.com Graphics Courtesy www.cooltext.com www.hoxie.org   Welcome to the Sanders / Jarvis Home Page. We are looking for family connections to several family surnames. Please Click on
[http://cmsu2.cmsu.edu/~dss70530/Pagework/Firstpgs.html]

12. JARVIS / GERVAIS, MEAKER, EINBODEN, DENESHA GENEALOGY - Web Sites
JARVIS / GERVAIS, MEAKER, EINBODEN, DENESHA GENEALOGY Welcome to the Jarvis / Gervais, Meaker, Einboden, Denesha Home Page Jarvis Family Tree Meaker Family Tree Ancestral File Email Paul Jarvis jarp@idirect.com Gervais family crest,"Thus Supported It Increases". Unknown Meaker
[http://webhome.idirect.com/~jarp/]

13. Jarvis Surname Page - Web Sites
Jarvis Family Home Page The Jarvis Family & Other Relatives Over 200 Families and their Descendants You Can Now Reach This Site By Just Typing Jarvis-NC or Holder-NC Search this site for Thanks for stopping in and visiting our home page. My name is Faye Jarvis Moran and genealogy is my
[http://www.erols.com/fmoran/]

Return to top of page

11

One exciting thing that has happened since the first edition of this book came out in 1997 is that some of the vast LDS genealogical holdings are now searchable online. Go to **http://familysearch.com**. I visited them above to get an illustration and got distracted because of finding some information on my Jarvis ancestors. Yep, researching your family history on the web is always exciting.

their families. Even those ancestors who died before the Church was founded in the early 1800s.

For this purpose, LDS church members make covenants in temples on behalf of their ancestors, who may accept these covenants, if they so choose, in the spirit world. Of course, in able to make covenants on behalf of their ancestors, those ancestors must first be identified. The Church of Jesus Christ of Latter-day Saints has gathered genealogical records from all over the world. These records are available at the Family History Library in Salt Lake City, Utah, and at Family History Centers™ throughout the world.

Because of security concerns, this vast wealth of family history data is not all yet available online, but it is through the many Family History Centers. If you live in the U.S. or Canada, there is almost certainly a Center within moderately reasonable driving distance. Worldwide, Centers exist in many countries. And, of course, vast amounts of LDS genealogy data is now available for searching on **http://familysearch.com**.

Why get so excited over Mormon genealogical resources? Well, the list below should give you an inkling of just how incredible vast they are:

The Family History Department of the Church of Jesus Christ of Latter-day Saints *each year* researches and catalogs approximately *100 million new pages* of historical documents. In an average year this is about 70,000 new microfilms, 25,000 microfiche, and 12,000 books of additional family research records added to their already astronomically vast holdings.

This *universe* of original records dates from medieval times to the present, and is constantly being updated.

In size the Church holds over 1.9 million rolls of microfilmed records, equivalent to something like 6 million written volumes. There are also almost 400,000 microfiche available. These records include data from governments, churches of many denominations, various organizations, and individual contributions. (*Microfilm* are rolls of film where each frame is a recorded document, *microfiche* are sheets of film with rows and columns of documents—both require special readers that enlarge the document enough so that it may be read.)

As might be expected, the Church's Family History Library has a lot of information pertaining to the United States, something like 600,000 rolls of microfiche pertaining to all 50 states. Included in this marvelous mass of data are over 100,000 rolls of federal records from more than 2,400 archives, county courthouses, and many other types of record repositories. To only a slightly smaller degree, this wondrous wealth of genealogical raw material extends across international boundaries, including records from Canada, Great Britain, and many countries in Europe proper.

The above is just a brief, very brief, hint of what the Family History Library has. At our publishing company, we get regular orders from the Family History Library for our books about genealogy. (We a growing list of genealogy titles. Check **http://abooks.com/genealogy**. Or request a list at 828-255-8719, voice or fax, or write us at Alexander Books, 65 Macedonia Rd., Alexander NC 28701 or email *sales@abooks.com*.)

Now, for something even more wonderful about the Family History Library's extensive holdings! Almost all of the data described above is available to you for only nominal rental fees. This data could save you many years of hard research and cut thousand of miles from your travel time.

The only real restrictions on your use of the Family History Library's holdings is that the material you want must be requested in person at a Family History Center and must be used in the Center. Microfilm rolls are returned to Salt Lake City when you are finished with them but all microfiche stays at the Family History Center which ordered them.

This all is a very nice service the LDS church provides and you need have no fear of religious proselytizing in making use of these services. While the Mormons do send out missionaries and would like you to consider joining them, this quest for religious conversion is not done either at the Family History Library or at Family History Centers. You may use those facilities without fear or obligation. Just say, "thank you," to the nice folks that make it all possible.

As an aside—and this really has little to with genealogy, it's just somewhat amusing. We live way back up in the Blue Ridge Mountains of Western North Carolina. Up in "these here hills," we only get two kinds of missionaries—Mormons and Jehovah's Witnesses. I'll say this for the polite young men on bicycles, dressed in crisp white shirts with neatly knotted ties, they are a much less scaggly lot than the Witnesses. Of course we don't listen much to either group, but that's *our* privilege.

Yet, again, we must say a hearty "Thank you!" to the Church of Jesus Christ of Latter-day Saints for all the invaluable genealogical resources they make available. Below is a list of Family History Centers in the United States and Canada. (Remember areas codes are changing rapidly—check for new ones if you don't get through.)

UNITED STATES
State. City. Telephone Number
Alabama. Montgomery. 334-269-9041
Alaska. Anchorage. 907-277-8433
Arizona. Mesa. 602-964-1200
Arkansas. Rogers. 501-636-8090
California. Los Angeles. 310-474-2202
California. Oakland. 510-531-3905
Colorado. Colorado Springs. 719-634-0572
Connecticut. Bloomfield. 203-242-1607

Delaware. Wilmington. 302-654-1911
Florida. Plantation (near Miami). 954-472-0524
Florida. Tampa. 813-971-2869
Georgia. Roswell. 770-594-1706
Hawaii. Laie. 808-293-2133
Idaho. Idaho Falls. 208-524-5291
Illinois. Wilmette. 847-251-9818
Indiana. Bloomington. 812-333-0050
Iowa. Davenport. 319-386-7547
Kansas. Wichita. 316-683-2951
Kentucky. Lexington. 606-269-2722
Louisiana. Metairie (near New Orleans). 504-885-3936
Maine. Bangor. 207-942-7310
Maryland. Kensington. 301-587-0042
Michigan. Bloomfield Hills (near Detroit). 810-647-5671
Mississippi. Clinton (near Jackson). 601-924-2686
Missouri. Frontenac (near St. Louis). 314-993-2328
Montana. Helena. 406-443-0713
Nebraska. Papillion. 402-339-0461
Nevada. Las Vegas. 702-382-9695
New Jersey. Morristown (near Newark). 201-539-5362
New Mexico. Albuquerque. 505-266-4867
New York. New York City. 212-873-1690
North Carolina. Charlotte. 704-535-0238
North Dakota. Bismark. 701-222-2794
Ohio. Reynoldsburg (near Columbus). 614-866-7686
Oklahoma. Oklahoma City. 405-721-8455
Oregon. Portland. 503-235-9090
Pennsylvania. Broomall (near Philadelphia). 610-356-8507
South Carolina. Charleston. 803-766-6017
South Dakota. Rosebud. 605-747-2128
Tennessee. Madison (near Nashville). 615-859-6926
Texas. Pasadena. 713-487-3623
Utah. Salt Lake City. 801-240-2331
Virginia. Falls Church. 703-256-5518
Washington. Tacoma. 206-564-1103
West Virginia. Charleston. 304-984-9333
Wisconsin. Hales Corners (near Milwaukee). 414-425-4182

CANADA
 Province. City. Telephone Number
Ontario. Kitchner. 519-741-9591
Quebec. Montreal. 514-523-6131
Alberta. Calgary. 403-571-3700
British Columbia. Burnaby. 604-299-8656
Manitoba. Winnipeg. 204-261-4271

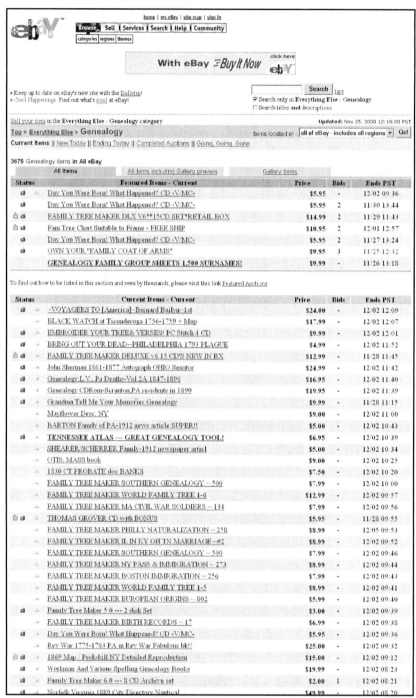

The largest online auction, eBAY (**http://www.ebay.com**) has thousands of genealogy related items for sale at any one time. It's a great resource.

WARM UP YOUR COMPUTERS

We could fill this whole book with the basics of genealogy. In fact, having written as much as I have in this chapter, I feel kinda like this has become the case. It's not, however, and we move on now to computerized genealogy, then on to the wide open cyberspaces of the internet.

I do believe, however, that this chapter adequately introduces you to the wonders of genealogy while still showing that our learning process is never over. The better you become at genealogy, the faster and easier your family history research goes.

Never stop learning; always be open to new techniques. In fact, once we get out onto the internet, I'll give you many places that cater to both beginning and advanced genealogists, and which offer you all sorts of references on the nitty and the gritty of this most fulfilling hobby of ours.

RECOMMENDED READING

One final offering for this chapter on the basics of genealogy is the recommended reading list below (courtesy of the National Genealogical Society). Many of these books may be found at your local library and all are excellent references in answering questions about how to get started in family history research, where to go, what to do when you get there, and how to record your findings.

Bentley, Elizabeth Petty. *County Courthouse Book*. Baltimore: Genealogical Publishing Co., 1990.

The Genealogist's Address Book: 1992-93 Edition. Baltimore: Genealogical Publishing Co., 1992.

Crandall, Ralph. *Shaking Your Family Tree*: A Basic Guide to Tracing Your Family's Genealogy. Camden, Maine: Yankee Books, 1986.

Croom, Emily Anne. *Unpuzzling Your Past: A Basic Guide to Genealogy*. White Hall, Va.: Betterway Publishers, 1983.

Doane, Gilbert H. and James B. Bell. *Searching for Your Ancestors: The How and Why of Genealogy*. 6th ed. Minneapolis: University of Minnesota Press, 1992.

Dollarhide, William. *Managing a Genealogical Project*. Rev. ed. Baltimore: Genealogical Publishing Co., 1991.

Eichholz, Alice, ed. *Ancestry's Red Book: American State, County & Town Sources*. Rev. ed. Salt Lake City: Ancestry, 1992.

Everton, George B., Sr. *The Handy Book for Genealogists*. 8th rev. ed. Logan, Utah: Everton Publishers, 1991.

Greenwood, Val D. *The Researcher's Guide to American Genealogy*. 2nd ed. Baltimore: Genealogical Publishing Co., 1990.

Kemp, Thomas J. *International Vital Records Handbook*. Baltimore: Genealogical Publishing Co., 1990.

Lackey, Richard S. *Cite Your Sources*. 1980. Reprint. Jackson: University of Mississippi, 1985.

Meyer, Mary K. *Meyer's Directory of Genealogical Societies in the U.S. and Canada*. 9th ed. Mt. Airy, Md., 1992.

Pence, Richard A., ed. *Computer Genealogy: A Guide to Research through High Technology*. Rev. ed. Salt Lake City: Ancestry, 1991.

Rubincam, Milton. *Pitfalls in Genealogical Research*. Salt Lake City: Ancestry, 1987.

Stryker-Rodda, Harriett. *How to Climb Your Family Tree*. Reprint. Baltimore: Genealogical Publishing Co., 1987.

Szucs, Loretto Dennis and Sandra Hargreaves Luebking. *The Archives: A Guide to the National Archives Field Branches*. Salt Lake City: Ancestry, 1988.

U.S. Department of Health and Human Services. *Where to Write for Vital Records: Births, Deaths, Marriages, and Divorces*. Publication No. (PHS) 93-1142. Hyattsville, Md., 1993.

GENEALOGY VIA THE INTERNET

TRACING YOUR FAMILY ROOTS QUICKLY AND EASILY

PART III:

GENEALOGY SOFTWARE

In this section we look at some of the many fine programs available for assisting you in computerized genealogy.

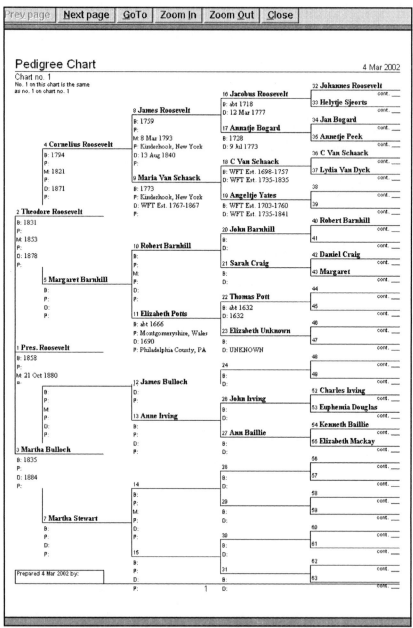

The advantages of computerized genealogy include an easy method of managing literally thousands of your family relationships with automatic calulation of kinship and records showing visual representations (making your research a great deal easier). The above report is a pedigree chart generated by *Family Origins*. It shows the ancestors of President Teddy "speak softly but carry a big stick" Roosevelt.

COMPUTERIZED GENEALOGY

First, some quick background and explanations; then we'll look at a number of actual genealogy programs and how they work.

The marriage of genealogy and personal computers was made in heaven, but still strikes many people as a very unlikely one. The contrasts are stark.

Genealogy is of the past; proud family traditions and history stretching back into the dim mists of time. It is pursued in musty but elegant old courthouses. Or in the silent sanctity of hallowed cemeteries with weathered headstones mustered in precise rows like soldiers of marble guarding your ancestors' last earthly remains. It is old books and vast ledgers in the spidery, almost indecipherable hand of some long-dead county clerk. Yellowed newspaper clippings and faded old family photographs. Dusty boxes in attics, long unopened, and the memories of elderly relatives, often still green and fresh as distant years were in the spring of their being.

Computers, on the other hand, are not even of the present but rather the shiny future. They are technology incarnate; fast, colorful, blinking lights and scrolling images briefly glimpsed, not always comprehended.

Often perceived as new, frightening and powerful; ruling our lives in barely understood but ever more pervasive ways. A sign of the new millenium of which even computers seemed fearful, refusing acceptance of the year 2000 via the infamous Millenium Bug. That turned out—thanks to a lot of money and technical effort being thrown at it—not to have been the problem it could have been. But this is just one more example of how computers now permeate all our lives.

The truth, of course, lies between the old perceptions of genealogy and computers. Genealogy is more alive than fusty old records; computers far simpler and far more *helpful* than one first thinks.

Even the dread Millenium problem (which fizzled) is nothing more than human shortsightedness of a few programmers back in the fifties and sixties, programming in two instead of four digits for the yeardate. This simple oversight cost us all a few billion dollars to fix. However, other than perhaps a bit of tax increase and raised rates from such entities as insurance companies as they pass their costs on to the consumer in the time accepted if not honored method, you probably noted little effect. Personal computers change so rapidly that you perhaps had upgraded at least twice or three times from your first computer to the year 2000 anyway. The new computers sold today, do not have the millenium problem. Yes, they no doubt have other problems, but that will always be true, and we'll live with those bugs and triumph, just as we have everything heretofore.

In short, computers are both here to stay and incredibly helpful when used for tedious tasks such as family history research record keeping. So helpful, in fact, that you'll agree—once the initial shock of learning the computer wears off—there is no other logical way of doing genealogy. Computers just make it too easy, removing drudge, increasing accuracy, and saving

Scottish Genealogy Society

CEUD MILE FAILTE

TO VIEW THIS SITE AT ITS BEST PLEASE SET YOUR MONITORS RESOLUTION TO 800 X 600 PIXELS

The Scottish Genealogy Society was founded in Edinburgh on 30 May 1953 by a group
of historians and genealogists.
The aims of the Society are to promote research into Scottish family history and
to undertake the collection, exchange and publication of material relating to genealogy.
In accordance with the wishes of the original members, the Society remains academic and consultative
and does not engage itself professionally in record searching.
Since the Society does not engage itself professionally in record searching, it
has established a Library & Family History Centre, non members may become
day members at a charge of £5 UK per day,
subject to availability of space.
At present, printed books, manuscripts, periodicals, journals, microfilm and microfiche are collected.
The Society always welcomes gifts of the material mentioned above, and they should be sent to

The Scottish Genealogy Society,
15 Victoria Terrace,
Edinburgh. EH1 2JL,
Scotland

The Society has a sales list of over 300 titles which is regularly augmented

click on one of the buttons below to browse through our site

library	subscriptions	books

For those with the blood of Scots (Hoot, mon!) in their veins, the site of the Scottish Genealogy Society at **http:// www.scotsgenealogy.com** will be of interest.

unbelievable amounts of time. Augment the personal computer's mighty power with that of the internet and other online services and ... ah ... it's like a miracle!

Once you get there—using a computer proficiently, that is—you'll never want to go back and will always wonder how you got along without your own personal computer.

COMPUTERS OVERCOMING CONTROVERSY

Back in the late seventies, the personal computer—long before it came into the acceptance it enjoys today—was applied to genealogy by a hardy few. The lack of memory and storage space as well as the relatively slow speed of those early computers required major dedication in learning and using.

Yet the promise was there and some began adopting the computer into genealogical research, writing their own programs where none existed. Slowly, ever so slowly, support grew. With the introduction of the IBM Personal Computer—the now classic "XT"—in 1982, the personal computer revolution had truly arrived.

An explosion in software (computer programs) for the personal computer came into being and is still expanding like that primordial cloud of universe-creating gas favored by those proponents of the Big Bang Theory. All of which is not to say that computers have been easily accepted into the world of genealogy—far from it. Only over the last 10 years has a sometimes grudging acceptance been wrung from those genealogists who preferred older, manual methods.

Richard A. Pence, writing over a decade ago in the November, 1989 *Monitor* (a publication of the Capital PC User Group) put it very succinctly when discussing the use of personal computers in genealogy.

"To others," Mr. Pence wrote, "especially those who

have worked long and hard to raise the professionalism and quality of genealogical research far above hearsay and guesswork, it was the devil's own invention."

Richard continued, however, by stating that the aptitudes of the computer to store and organize large amounts of data were a plus. As was the machine's willingness and talent in doing repetitive tasks such as those necessary for generating the traditional and widely understood genealogical forms like ancestor charts.

So the debate has raged between "genealogical scholars" and "genealogical computerists." The scholars, again according to Richard Pence, were convinced that the use of personal computers would "flood the world with machine-generated pedigrees that are dubiously researched and poorly documented." What the scholars saw as "a mountain of 'trash genealogy.'"

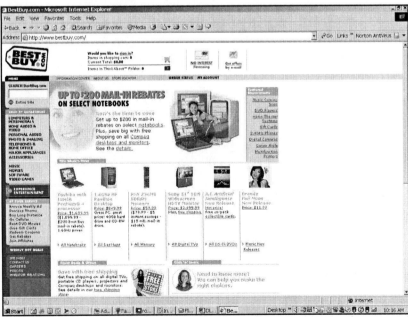

Large computer retailers like Best Buy make owning the latest and greatest computer hardware and software *cheap*. In the case of Best Buy, you can purchase either through one of their stores on via their website. (**http://bestbuy.com**)

Whereas computer users looked upon computerized genealogy in a far kinder light. They would, he wrote, see the personal computer as a wondrous new research and record-keeping tool, plunging headlong into the new technological age "spurred by dreams of on-line access to such staple research sources as U.S. census records or even a gigantic *linked* database of *the family of man*." That latter, by the way, is being worked on by several groups on the internet. One such program is the World Family Tree project sponsored by the publisher of *Family Tree Maker*. We'll look at it in more detail later in this chaper.

For additional information on the topic of old versus new, the saga of technology's impact on genealogy, we recommend Richard Pence's book, *Computer Genealogy: A Guide to Research Through High Technology*, Rev. ed. Salt Lake City: Ancestry, 1991.

The truth, as ever, lies in between both extremes. Since Pence wrote—only a few short years ago in 1989—an incredible amount of change has occurred. Two primary factors have pushed computerized genealogy from being something you either did or you hated, to a thing whose time has not only come but which you can't afford *not* to do. If you want to achieve a great family history in some reasonable amount of time, computerized genealogy is your *only* answer, and a very good one, indeed.

COMPUTERIZED GENEALOGY HERE TO STAY

Those two primary factors in computerized genealogy's coming of age are, of course, Microsoft Windows and especially Windows 95 and all its more recent versions like XP and Windows 2000—discussed in Chapter 6—and the main subject of this book as related to genealogy, the *internet* itself. Windows made the personal computer truly usable for everyone, and the internet provides the medium through which fast and accurate genealogical research literally worldwide is merely a *local* phone call away.

Again, I emphasize that you should either buy or upgrade to a computer running a Pentium chip (or equivalent) and the latest version of Windows.

The reasons are overwhelmingly favorable for doing so. The main one is the internet and the worldwide web. The newest Windows operating system—Windows XP— is designed to work with the internet. It makes getting on the net far easier and less convoluted than machines operating under earlier versions of Windows, DOS, or other operating systems.

Also, all the new and powerful software is now written for Windows 95 and beyound or at least optimized for those operating systems. Many new programs—especially the more powerful ones—no longer will run at all in older versions of Windows.

Technology has marched on, as well. The new, fast, powerful computers you need cost less than the old clunker you might currently have that's simply not up to the job any more.

As I write this, I just bought a new Pentium 1.8 gigahertz computer from our local Best Buy store for only $1499. It came with CD-ROM drive, a DVD *recorder*, speakers, a tower case, Windows XP already installed, and everything else I needed except a monitor (which I already had). Monitors are always "sold extra" it seems. Of course, the way computer prices are dropping, that price will seem high by the time this book sees print. It's truly wonderful!

Still, the point being whether you buy a computer on the net or from your local Office Depot or Circuit City or other large electronics retailer; the new machines are cheap, have blazing speed, and make your family history research a joy.

I do apologize to those enthusiasts, lovers, proponents, aficionados, and boosters of older tech machines such as the Apple Macintosh or Atari, as well as to those running earlier versions of Windows or plain old Microsoft DOS. Those computers all had their day and I loved them then. Alas, events move onward. The desktop computer market is currently dominated by Microsoft and the internet is more easily accessible with Windows 95. So let us go with the flow and enjoy it.

Now, we'll move on and see how genealogy software actually works. Then we'll take a look at the packages currently available out there.

HOW COMPUTERIZED GENEALOGY WORKS

The bestselling family history research software is *Family Tree Maker*™ by Genealogy.com (a division of A&E Television Networks. There are numerous other good genealogy programs also, and we'll elaborate on those later in the following chapter. However—since *Family Tree Maker* is the most popular—it serves quite nicely as our example in showing you exactly how computerized genealogy works.

VERSIONS OF *Family Tree Maker*™

The really good news is that most software—like the computers these packages run on—are truly inexpensive. *Family Tree Maker*, or *FTM* for short, is available in several computer-yummy flavors. The Version 9.0 for Windows upgrade is a mere $29.95, and comes on CD-ROM with a 90 day satisfaction guaranteed warranty is for those who already have an older version of the software.

Visit the site **http://familytreemaker.com/ ftmvers.html** for more information on the *Family TreeMaker*9.0 upgrade and the company's other genealogical related products and services.

The system requirements for all of the current ver-

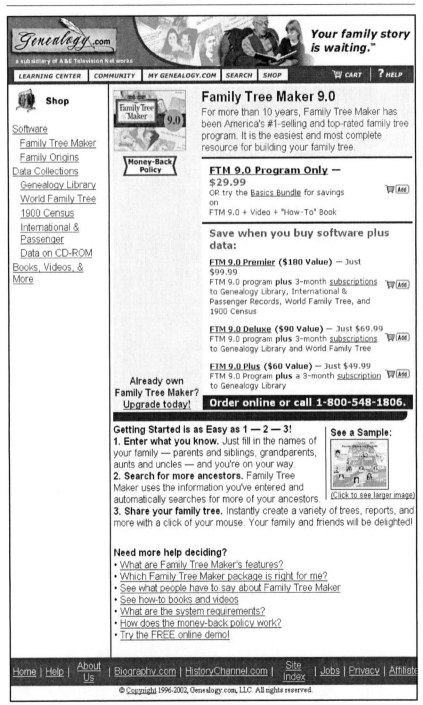

The latest versions of *Family Tree Maker* are detailed at **http://familytreemaker.com/ftmvers.html**.

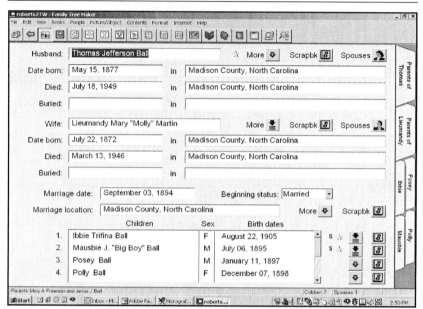

A screen from Family Tree Maker 9.0 showing how FTM keeps track of family data. This screen is from my personal family tree and shows my maternal grandparents, "Big Tom" and Molly Ball. By the way, if your tree ties into mine, please get in contact and we'll trade info!

sions of *Family Tree Maker* are: A 2X CD-ROM Drive; Microsoft Windows 95 or 98 or higher; Pentium 90 (Pentium 166 recommended); 16 MB RAM (32 MB RAM recommended); VGA display running in at least 256 colors; mouse; and 100 MB free hard disk space (50 MB free HD space after install). 50 MB of program files will be copied to your hard drive; the rest of the data, including the FamilyFinder Index, will remain on the CD-ROMs to be accessed during program use. *Family Tree Maker* 9.0 will read files from all previous versions of *Family Tree Maker*, although Version 3.0 and earlier versions will not be able to open files created or modified in *Family Tree Maker* 9.0 unless converted to GEDCOM. Please note that *Family Tree Maker* 9.0 is a 32-bit application and will not run under Windows 3.1 or earlier; Windows 95, 98, ME, or higher is is required (I run it on a Windows 2000 workstation). Also, you need a modem and internet access (for connecting to *Family Tree Maker* Online); video capture board and sound board (for video or audio clips); scanner (for digitizing graphic images), digital camera. As with all Windows programs, a faster processor, more RAM and more free disk space will enhance performance.

CD-ROMs, to continue, are wonderful! An awesome amount of information resides on these small disks of plastic. The acronym stands for *Compact Disc Read Only Memory*. This is an efficient and cheap method of storing large amounts of data on a very small item; to wit, those little round platters that have supplanted the old LP 33 1/3 record albums. Remember those? Now that's a blast from the past!

The only difference between music CDs and CD-ROMs is the format in which the data is recorded. In fact, both music and computer data can be on the same disc. Additionally, most computers today can also play music CDs, giving you some mellow accompaniment as you work. Versions of Windows from Windows 95 and up, for example, will automatically detect music CDs and plays them while still allowing you to do your regular work.

Here's yet another reason for upgrading your computer: most computers today include a sound card, speakers, and a CD-ROM drive.

The CD has the capacity of containing a huge amount of computer data in this very small package. A CD-ROM holds about 600 million bytes of information, where a byte is equivalent to one letter or number. A bit of quick math tells us this is approximately *100 million words* or around *200,000 typed pages of data, single-spaced*! All easily and quickly searched for specific items.

That's a bunch, all right. So it should be mighty obvious that a lot of genealogical data could be crammed onto just one CD-ROM.

Programs require little room on CD-ROMs, otherwise they could not fit into the working memory of your computer in order to run. So the vast majority of the space on the CD-Roms included with *Family Tree Maker* is useful data for the family history researcher.

It's a nice thing to garner extensive family data and even nicer to share the results. After all, if you do possibly years of work in researching your family history, don't keep it to yourself. Publish in some manner, be it books or the internet or both. Share your wealth of information with others. If they are interested in your data, most

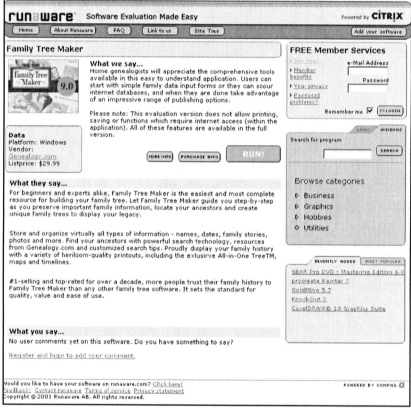

Try before you buy! In conjunction with Runaware, Genealogy.com offers a free online demo of Family Tree Maker that will allow you to see and test drive many of its features without having to actually install the program on your computer. Access this test drive at **http://www.runaware.com/action=show_app?c_app_id=3323**.

likely they are distant relatives. Always be nice to your kinsfolk. That's what family is all about.

FEATURES OF COMPUTERIZED GENEALOGY

Family Tree Maker is America's best-selling family tree program. The program is easy-to-use, but comprehensive so that you won't outgrow it. Just enter a few family names and facts, and then instantly produce a wide variety of beautiful trees, reports, and even complete *books.*

Of course, you should and must realize that a lot of time and work goes into finding and entering the necessary family records before these "instant" reports occur. That said, I also can tell you that any computerized genealogy program—be it *Family Tree Maker* or any other—is well worth the minimal investment. Genealogy software in conjunction with the internet turns an arduous task into one both less arduous and a great deal more enjoyable.

ORGANIZATION

Family history research, at it's most basic, is the collection of a *lot* of *stuff.* Piles of photocopies or Xeroxes of old records. Tons of scribbled handwritten notes reflecting the gleaning of this or that piece of information from the yellowed pages of some huge old tome jealously guarded by a county clerk in the Nowhere County, Alabama courthouse. And more, and more, and piles, and stacks, and cardboard boxes, and file folders, and... Well, you begin to see the problem.

How the heck do you find something in this great haystack of your family records. After awhile, they all start looking much the same. As some great and wise person once said, "the best place to hide a needle is in a haystack of its own kind."

That's where computerized genealogy jumps into stardom! You'll easily have the capacity to organize names, dates, facts, photos, and archive records of all sorts for near instant retrieval. The computer alphabetizes and performs other types of sorting automatically. It also allows you to construct all sort of reports based on the information you've collected, and to print your family trees using the data parameters you specify. Just being able to find whether you have or do not have a particular piece of information will save you hours upon hours time after time.

Family Tree Maker, in specific, can handle all kinds of information for about two million of your relatives. That should take care of your immediate family and mine.

As the descriptions of FTM's features on the FTM web site points out, this includes anything from basic names, dates, and places to more personal information. For example, FTM stores pages of notes, such as stories, favorite jokes, and recipes; nicknames and special titles; height, weight and medical information; addresses and phone numbers; information about special family relationships, such as adoptions, divorces, and re-marriages; and other quick facts and dates, such as graduation, baptism, and burial. In addition, you can introduce multimedia (i.e. sound, music, pictures, etc.) elements into your family records by placing video clips, audio clips, and even scanned documents into *Family Tree Maker*'s Scrapbooks.

PRINTING REPORTS

No matter how useful a computerized genealogy program may be in assisting you, the basic concept behind the collection of any data is the ability to share it. This is still primarily done via paper, although many family historians now make their results available on the internet as well.

Family Tree Maker excels in formatting and printing out attractive and versatile reports of your family data in several different styles. These styles include:

- Ancestor and Descendent trees in ten styles, with your choice of contents and size.
- Genealogy reports, such as Register, NGS Quarterly, and Ahnentafel, automatically create narrative family histories, complete with names, dates, notes, sources, and more. [*NGS* is the National Genealogical Society 4527 17th Street North Arlington, VA 22207-2399]. The word *ahnentafel* is from the German and is a century-old genealogical term referring to a method of numbering generations. For example, you'd be 1, your father 2, mother 3, paternal grandfather 4, paternal grandmother 5, maternal grandfather 6, maternal grandmother 7, and so on and so on, all giving a framework of reference to a common

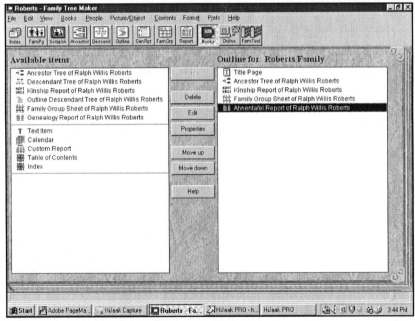

Once you have your family research completed, formatting and printing out your data in book form is just a matter of "dragging and dropping" the components you want into the book. Then print it. Writing your genealogy book will be a lot easier than this one is for me, but we're having fun so far, I hope.

point—in this case, you.)

- Kinship reports showing how individuals in your file are related.
- LDS (Church of Jesus Christ of Latter-Day Saints) reports with standard formats and ordinances.
- Birthday and anniversary calendars.
- Custom reports listing medical history, longevity, and more.
- Family Group sheets and individual fact sheets.
- Multimedia Scrapbook images.
- Mailing labels, name tags, stickers, and more.

CREATE MULTIMEDIA FAMILY ALBUMS

Family Tree Maker takes you beyond just a dry recording of names and the records associated with them, it lets you actually create a more living history. FTM's Scrapbooks feature preserves your family's true character—the sights, sounds, and stories that go beyond just names and dates. You can include photos, video and audio clips, and even scanned images. Scrapbooks accept Kodak Photo CD pictures, TIF files, BMP files and other common file formats. And, once you've placed everything you want into a Scrapbook, you can impress your family by creating multimedia "slide shows," where each item in a Scrapbook is displayed sequentially for the number of seconds that you choose. You can also print Scrapbook albums, choosing how many images are on each page, the style and color of the text and borders, and whether or not to include page numbers.

FAMILYFINDER™ INDEX OF 250 MILLION NAMES

The FamilyFinder™ Index already described earlier as being included on the CD-ROMS that come with all editions of *Family Tree Maker* gives you an amazing head start for finding ancestors. It lists the names of more than 250 million people who appear in centuries of state and federal records. While the actual records are far too vast

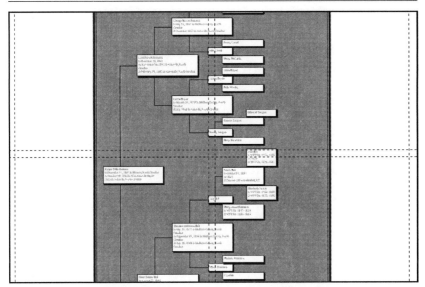

An example of a paginated report. This descendant tree requires four pages to print out (as shown by the dotted lines) but may easily be pieced together and taped to make a single and rather elegant chart. Use good quality colored paper and frame or mat them for wonderful wall decorations or gifts to relatives.

to be included on a single CD, FamilyFinder does tell you exactly where to find more information about each person in the list. It references dozens of sources from around the country, including U.S. census records indexes (1790-1880), selected marriage records indexes (1600-1950), collections of family trees and family histories, and Social Security death records. Think of the FamilyFinder Index as a guide that tells you which Family Archive CDs contain information that you need, removing the guesswork.

The latest version of the FamilyFinder Index also may be used at the very extensive FTM web site (**http://www.familytreemaker.com**). It is available for anyone's use there, but provided as stated also on CD-ROM versions of *Family Tree Maker* for faster searching (especially advantageous if you have a slow modem) and to minimize online connect time.

VIEW AND SEARCH OVER 80 FAMILY ARCHIVE CDS

If you have a CD-ROM drive, you can use *Family Tree Maker* to look for family information on Family Archive CDs. These CDs give specific dates, places, and other details on people who appear in centuries of state, federal, World Family Tree, and other records. All you need to know is a relative's approximate last name, and the FamilyFinder Index will tell you exactly which Family Archive CD has more information. This way, you can quickly make progress right from your own computer. However—when searching this or any of the many online databases—the more exact information you can give, the better. Otherwise, you get 100,000 results instead of a more manageable 10 or 20.

"SOURCES" DATABASE

Keeping an organized record of your information sources is one of the cornerstones of genealogy. I emphasized this point considerably in Chapter 7 of this book. It allows you and future generations to follow your exact research steps in case some of the information is ever called into question. To keep track of the sources you've used in your family history research (such as family Bibles, wedding albums, or government records), *Family Tree Maker* has a sophisticated system that tracks all your sources in detail.

Each source, Genealogy.com says in the literature describing *Family Tree Maker*, has its own notecard-style screen where you list the source's title, author, reliability, and other details. You only need to record each source once—then, whenever you include information from it in your Family File, you can "point" to its listing in your Master Sources database. Of course, you're not limited to just one source for each piece of

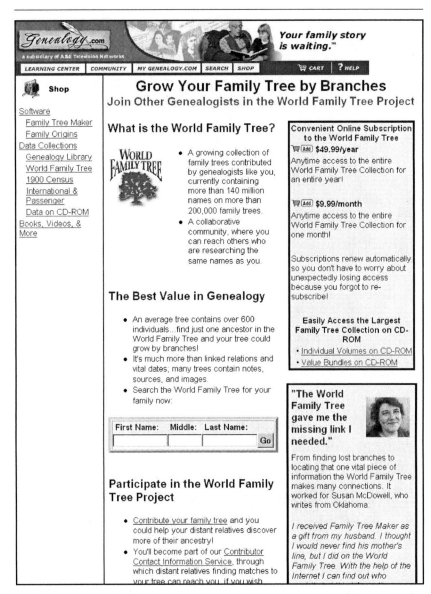

Full details on the World Family Tree project may be found on the worldwide web at **http://familytreemaker.com/wfttop.html**.

information (such as a name, date, or location)—you can list as many sources as you have. This helps you resolve confusion or faulty data at later dates.

What the savvy designers of FTM have done with this feature in particular and the entire program in general is construct it to benefit from the two huge advantages of doing genealogy on a computer via the internet (and which is what this book is all about). The first, of course, being the personal computer's awesome strength in recording and sorting facts, and to report those facts according to whatever criteria you specify. The second, naturally, is communications via a phone line into the worldwide vastness of the internet. The large *Family Tree Maker* site (again, **http://familytreemaker.com**) covers the second part of FTM's overall design by providing you access to tons of useful information and family research data.

The main (index) web page at **http://familytreemaker.com** allows you to start a seach immediately.

In Family Tree Maker 9.0, the little typewriter on the main tool bar accesses the Publishing Center, as shown above.

EASILY CREATE PROFESSIONAL-QUALITY BOOKS

The Family Book feature of *Family Tree Maker* is yet another powerful tool; in this instance, to publish your completed research, or just your research to date. The feature combines your choice of printouts—such as Ancestor trees, Family Group Sheets, Kinship reports, and narrative Genealogy reports—and assembles them into one continuous document. A physical book may then be printed from the document and bound between covers. You may do this yourself with the help of a quick copy place, or have a printer produce an actual conventional book from your data—paperback or hardback.

You can include page numbers, a list of source citations, and more. *Family Tree Maker* automatically generates a Table of Contents and an Index that shows all the pages where each individual appears. Just drag and drop the printouts you want to include. It's that easy!

Family Books can also include free-form text pages, so you can record heart-warming stories that go beyond the names and dates. And you can bring your stories to life by inserting pictures! It's like having a word processor right inside *Family Tree Maker*. Now you can create a lasting record of all those special times—anniversary parties, vacations, holidays, reunions—to preserve the true character and spirit of your family.

Once you've selected the trees, reports, and stories to include in your book, Genealogy.com continues, one click of the "Print" command puts it all together. Better yet, you're not limited to just one style of Family Book. You can design several different Family Books and specify what to include in each. Whenever you want, you can edit the contents of existing Family Books or create more new Family Books.

Turning Family Books into real books that meet all publishing legalities and have colorful covers, by the way, is both easy and inexpensive. You have the option of printing a very low numbers of books that still look like the books sold in bookstores. In fact—since they meet all the publishing requirements, you *can* sell them in bookstores! We do that at my publishing company, Alexander Books. You may contact us via email (*sales@abooks.com*) or on the web at **http://abooks.com** or call 1-828-252-9515 voice or fax 1-828-255-8719.

GENEALOGY AND NARRATIVE FAMILY HISTORIES

When it's time to print your family information, Register (descendant ordered), NGS Quarterly (descendant ordered), and Ahnentafel (ancestor ordered)

Descendants of Thomas Jefferson Ball

Generation No. 1

1. THOMAS JEFFERSON[16] BALL *(JERIUS JAY[15], NOAH[14], JOEL[13], WILLIAM[12], DANIEL[11], DANIEL[10], EDWARD[9], RICHARD[8], COLONEL WILLIAM[7], WILLIAM[6], JOHN[5], JOHN PARIS[4], WILLIAM[3], ROBERT[2], WILLIAM[1])* was born May 15, 1877 in Madison County, North Carolina, and died July 18, 1949 in Madison County, North Carolina. He married LIEUMANDY MARY "MOLLY" MARTIN September 03, 1894 in Madison County, North Carolina, daughter of HUMPHREY MARTIN and NORA CORRELL. She was born July 22, 1872 in Madison County, North Carolina, and died March 13, 1946 in Madison County, North Carolina.

Children of THOMAS BALL and LIEUMANDY MARTIN are:

    i.   IBBIE TRIFINA[17] BALL, b. August 22, 1905, Little Pine Creek, Madison County, NC (Source: (1) Broderbund Family Archive #110, Vol. 2, Ed. 5, Social Security Death Index: U.S., Date of Import: Jun 27, 1997, Internal Ref. #1.112.5.57373.168, (2) Broderbund Family Archive #110, Vol. 2, Ed. 7, Social Security Death Index: U.S., Date of Import: Jan 26, 2000, Internal Ref. #1.112.7.78786.169); d. August 16, 1994, Asheville, North Carolina; m. CARL FRANCIS ROBERTS, November 20, 1941, Asheville, North Carolina; b. December 18, 1903, Little Pine Creek, Madison County, NC (Source: Broderbund Family Archive #110, Vol. 2, Ed. 5, Social Security Death Index: U.S., Date of Import: Jun 27, 1997, Internal Ref. #1.112.5.57238.31); d. February 08, 1982, Alexander, North Carolina.

A portion of a Genealogy Report generated by *Family Tree Maker* in a narrative style. This one shows data about my maternal grandparents and my mother.

reports are the recognized way to publish family information in text format (as opposed to chart format). Writing one of these reports by hand would take several hours. Instead, *Family Tree Maker* can create them for you instantly—complete with your choice of fonts, layouts, and information.

FTM takes names, dates, notes, sources, and other information in your family file, and automatically weaves them into a narrative story. You'll read about each generation in real sentences instead of just bare facts. Use them in your family books, or attach them to your user home page to share your family history with others.

PAGINATED FAMILY TREES

For trees larger than one page, *Family Tree Maker* can neatly split your tree onto as many standard-size pages as it takes, labeling each split with the page number where that branch is continued. With "Paginated Trees," boxes are never cut in half on page breaks. Each person's entire box is printed on a given page, and (if necessary) reprinted in connection with generations on later pages.

STEP-BY-STEP GENEALOGY "HOW-TO" GUIDE

This computerized "How-To" Guide is your expert

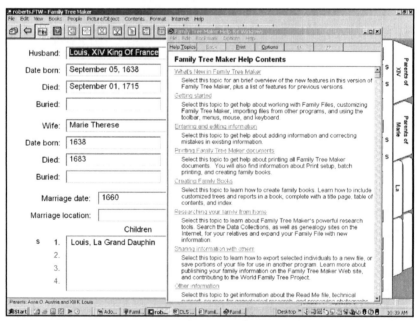

Family Tree Maker provides popup Help screens as a handy aid in answering questions while you use the software.

Family Tree Maker's Outline Descendant Tree offers yet another powerful way of looking at your family data.

family history companion. It tells you how to start, whom to contact, what to ask, and more. Topics range from doing overseas research to interpreting centuries-old handwriting. Built-in form letters and address directories make requesting official county records simple. The "How-To" Guide is also available online right there on *Family Tree Maker* Online. But it's handy to have an extra copy of it on your *Family Tree Maker* CD-ROM for quick reference.

SHARE AND EXTEND YOUR FAMILY TREE

Family Tree Maker Online is the gathering site for family history enthusiasts, and it's only a mouse click away. With over one million copies sold, *Family Tree Maker*'s customers form a vast community across the U.S. and overseas. A growing number of these customers use the Internet and gather at *Family Tree Maker* Online. By joining them there, you can personally benefit from the shared experience and knowledge of the community. That's because *Family Tree Maker* Online gives you and your fellow family history enthusiasts many ways to share family information directly with one another. Some of your fellow visitors may even be tracing the same family lines that you are!

FREE ONLINE GOODIES

Family Tree Maker now includes three new resources as you join the thousands of daily *Family Tree Maker* Online visitors and explore your family history online. Classified ads give you a quick way to see if someone has the information you're looking for.

You can also create a User home page in minutes and publicize your family research for other enthusiasts who share your interests.

Genealogy message boards give you a tremendous

opportunity to tap into the collective experience of other *Family Tree Maker* Online visitors.

WORLD FAMILY TREE

Genealogy.com is inviting all *Family Tree Maker* customers to participate in a remarkable genealogical opportunity—the World Family Tree Project. With over 2,000,000 copies sold, *Family Tree Maker* has been used by people just like you to collect information about hundreds of thousands of families. Over five years ago, in response to many requests, Genealogy.com invested in the equipment and know-how needed to compile all of those submitted family trees into a massive database of family information covering more than 140 millions name in over 200,000 family trees.

With your participation, the World Family Tree could become the largest genealogical database in existence! As they collect family trees, they make them available on CD-ROM at affordable prices. They are also exploring other ways to give you access to the family trees, such as an on-line service.

Imagine uncovering generations of new information about your family without even leaving your computer— you'll be able to do that by finding just one shared ancestor among the millions of records available.

I can tell you that the above happened to me personally. After finding one name that tied into my own family tree, suddenly my tree expanded by generations and over a hundred previously unknown relatives were added in little more than a blink of an eye. Nice!

What are the benefits of sharing your family tree?

Millions upon millions of linked names is the main advantage—you could increase the size of your tree by accessing the files of others who share your ancestry. When you find a common ancestor in the World Family

Genealogy.com
a subsidiary of A&E Television Networks

Your family story is waiting.™

| LEARNING CENTER | COMMUNITY | MY GENEALOGY.COM | SEARCH | SHOP | 🛒 CART | ? HELP |

Shop

Genealogy Data Online and on CD
Create Your Personal Library from 325 Jam-Packed Titles

Software
  Family Tree Maker
  Family Origins
Data Collections
  Genealogy Library
  World Family Tree
  1900 Census
  International &

What Are Data Sets?

• Information-rich, indexed records that may be helpful to your family research. The collection includes marriage and census information, actual family trees, and much, much more. You'll find records on

Search Data on CD-ROM...

By Name:

First name:

Middle:

Last name: Go!

FTM now offers 325 CDs with genealogy data Find our more information about it at **http://www.genealogy.com/cdhome.html**.

Tree, you can easily attach the newfound branches to your own Family File.

Also, by sharing your work, you safely store your research—protecting your family history data from loss or damage. Your family tree will be part of a readily-accessible database, to be archived at the Library of Congress in Washington, D.C.

You help other genealogists, as well—by allowing access to your family tree, you may help others increase the size of their family trees.

And you preserve your labor and findings for future generations—your family history data will be preserved so that your descendants can access it.

Most genealogists don't ever feel that their work is done, but we assure you that your family tree is valuable to other researchers, no matter how large or small, complete or incomplete.

Whether you have just begun your family tree or you are looking to add more branches, submitting your family tree immediately is important to the creation of the World Family Tree. You can always send additions or changes to Genealogy.com at a later date. They will regularly modify the database and make updated versions available.

AVAILABLE SOFTWARE

Not even Genealogy.com—whose program we used as an example in the preceding chapter—would say that *Family Tree Maker* is the only computerized genealogy software worth your consideration. And while I'm honest enough to give you my preference for that particular program (it being what I've chosen for my personal use), there are other good packages on the market.

Let me modify the above statement a bit. In 1997, when I wrote the First Edition of this book, yes, I used FTM exclusively. As my research efforts have now added over 100,000 relatives since that time, I've found other programs come in handy, as well. So now, in 2002, I still used the latest version of FTM (9.0 as this is written) as my primary respository of names. But I also use other software for various purposes, since no one program can do it all. For example, Family Origins does much better on relationship reports (finding a common ancestor and the kinship between any two people in your database). It also formats books more elegantly, an important consideration to a publisher.

So, always keep your eye on new software coming out. In the interests of presenting you with a complete picture, the remainder of this chapter describes those other packages and tells you where you can obtain more information about them using, of course, the internet itself.

FINDING THE RIGHT PROGRAM FOR YOU

The best place to buy the program of your choice is—you guessed it—on the internet! There are several good purveyors of genealogy books and programs on the net (including my own company at **http:// abooks.com/genealogy**).

Family Tree Maker may be purchased directly from the FTM web site at **http://familytreemaker.com**.

For a wide selection of both books and software— including a good many of the ones mentioned in this chapter—**Amazon.com**'s hard to beat. This huge internet retailer sells a lot more than books, they carry most of the better genealogy software packages at a discount. Go to the main web page (**amazon.com**), select *Software* on the Search form at the upper left, then type in *genealogy* as the keyword.

Now, on to those other packages! While I prefer genealogical software that runs on Windows—for all those reasons listed in Chapter 1—other programs are also covered.

Additionally, I have limited the programs described in the following pages to those whose publishers have web sites so that obtaining additional information is easy for you. This book, after all, is entitled ***Genealogy via the Internet***, so the programs recommended must all be supported on the net itself, allowing you easy access in obtaining more information in the process of making an intelligent decision as to which is the best for you.

By no means do I claim to present a complete overview of all packages available—there are just too many for any

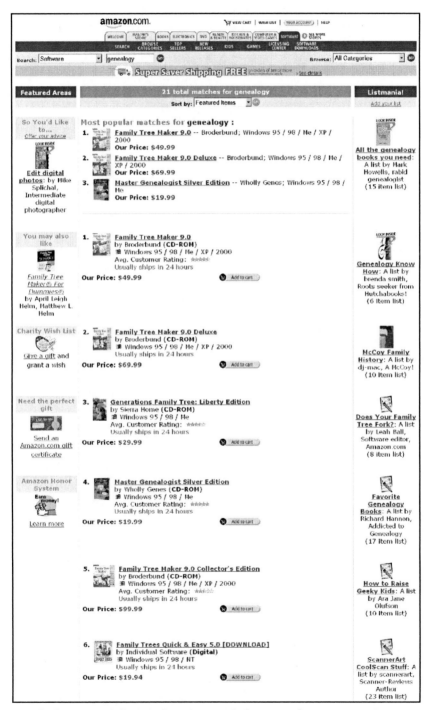

For deals on genealogy software, search for *genealogy* at **amazon.com**.

one book to cover. What I've done is select some of the more popular and/or ones in my opinion being worthy of your consideration (in no particular order).

Prices, availability, and version numbers, of course, are current as of this writing (March, 2002) and subject to change, as they say, without notice.

ANCESTRY FAMILY TREE V 9.0.2

(version 9.0.2)
from Ancestory.com, **http://ancestry.com**
FREE!

Let's start with a *free* family data manager, Ancestry.com's newly released Ancestry Family Tree. Ancestry.com (their address on the web is... shucks, you guessed it already, **ancestry.com**) enjoys the status being the largest "for pay" family research site on the

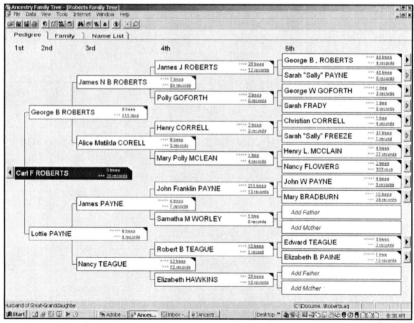

Ancestry Family Tree's Pedigree view shows you a tree view of your family data. Note next to each names are links that take you to more data online at **ancestry.com** (you'll need a paid subscription to access this additional information but it can really enhance your research).

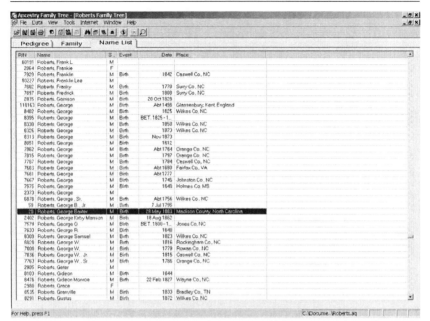

Ancestry Family Tree's List view shows a well-formatted list of people in your family research database by name. Clicking on a name takes you to a more detailed view of data about that particular individual.

world wide web. Since this company's revenue comes mostly from selling subscriptions, this "free" genealogy software does have links attached (see screen dump on facing page) tying you into **ancestry.com** online data, for which you'll need a paid subscription to access.

Why would you want to pay for genealogy data when so much of it's free on the internet, and that's what this book emphasizes?

It all depends what stage you're at in your research. For broad stroke construction, such as looking for lines that take you back to royalty and pulling in a thousand relatives a month, free sites such as my avowed favorite, **http://worldconnect.rootsweb.com**, is the way to go. And, in fact, Ancestry has now taken over sponsorship of **rootsweb.com** but, again, rootsweb remains free, even if you access it through Ancestry's site.

But once your initial building is over (the broad strokes), or you did not find the data you needed on the free sites, a subscription to Ancestry's site helps fill in the holes and provides access to source documents which prove all those thousands of entries in your database. I subscribe myself as needed. In fact, I'm in the process of renewing now just so I can further refine some of my current data.

But, back to Ancestry Family Tree, now that you've been reminded of that basic philosophy—TINSTAAFL (there is no such thing as a free lunch).

AFT can be down loaded directly from ancestry.com (see the link on the leftside of the entry page to the website) and installs in seconds. It runs on all versions of Windows from 95 up. I use it on my Windows 2000 workstation and it runs blazingly fast.

AFT allows you to automatically search more than 1.2 billion names at **ancestry.com** to find the best matches for trees and records for each person in your family tree. You can also use it in publishing your family tree online to share publicly or privately. It also make downloading existing family tree files from the web easy, and lets you collaborate with other genealogists through Ancestry's Online Family Tree and Ancestry World Tree.

This software does what you expect computerized genealogy to do. It affords you an easy method of adding and editing individual data within a family tree. It includes features for merging multiple files into one family tree. You can have notes and sources for each individual in a tree, and print genealogy reports in multiple formats. Adding photos and other media associated—such as voice recordings or video clips—is also possible for each individual. Plus, you can generate HTML pages of your family tree to publish online.

In short, I've found AFT a worthy addition in my collection of genealogical research tools. If you are just starting out, you may want it as your primary software.

REUNION FOR MACINTOSH V7.0

(available for both Macintosh and Windows!)
Leister Productions, **http://www.leisterpro.com**.
$99.00

Reunion, while available for Windows is a genealogy software program—a "family tree program" reads the Reunion official website—for the Macintosh. So if you have one of Apple's snazzy babies, Reunion is a must consideration in selecting computerized genealogy software.

Reunion, as the website at **http://www.leisterpro. com** also reports, received the highest rating for genealogy software in MacWorld, MacAddict, and Mac Home Journal magazines.

Reunion helps you to document, store, and display information about your family—your ancestors, descen-

dants, cousins, etc. It records names, dates, places, facts, plenty of notes, sources of information, pictures, sounds, and videos. It shows family relationships in an elegant, graphic form—people and families are linked in an easy-to-understand fashion.

Reunion makes it easy to publish your family tree information — even if you want to share it on the Web. You can automatically create common genealogy reports, charts, and forms, as well as birthday calendars, mailing lists, questionnaires, indexes, and other lists. Reunion even calculates relationships, ages, life expectancies, and statistics.

Reunion also creates large, high-resolution, graphic charts allowing complete on-screen editing of boxes, lines, fonts, and colors. Wall charts are one of its specialties. A great choice for the Mac user!

BROTHER'S KEEPER FOR WINDOWS

("try before you buy" *shareware* v6.0)
John Steed, **http://ourworld.compuserve.com/
homepages/brothers_keeper/**
$45 (if you register the program)

Brother's Keeper is a Windows genealogy shareware program that will help you organize your family history information and let you print a large variety of charts and reports. BK5 works with Windows 3.1 or up with 8 megs RAM or more. BK6 works with Windows 95, 98, ME, NT, 2000, XP. There is no charge to download BK to try it out.

Brother's Keeper is a set of programs to help you organize your family tree information and which allows you to print the information in several different ways. You can easily print ancestor charts, family group sheets, alphabetical name lists, descendant trees, and customized reports. You are allowed to try the shareware version for 30 days free. It then costs you $45 to register Brother's Keeper for Windows. Documentation is sent to you after registration.

Shareware is an excellent way to evaluate programs before making an investment. Again, you get to try before you buy! Download (i.e. copy via the internet) the trial version program at the web address above.

The Brother's Keeper website at **http://ourworld.compuserve.com/
homepages/brothers_keeper/** lets you download and try it for free.

FAMILY ORIGINS V10.0

Genealogy.com
http://familyorigins.com/
$29.95 (program only)

Family Origins comes, now, also from Genealogy.com, the publishers of Family Tree Maker. A lot of consolidation currently goes on in the genealogy field, like in many others. Origins—when I did the previous edition of this book—was owned by Parsons Software, but has since been acquired and added into the growing Genealogy.com offering of family research products and services.

Why have two of the leading genealogy software packages owned by one company and competing against each other? The answer, no doubt, makes good business sense. What I know and can tell you is that FTM and Origins take different approaches to managing your family history database. Again, I use FTM as my primary manager, but I also have bought and find Family Origins (now in release 10.0) very useful, especially in the area of reports. I love how it does relationship reports and formats books.

The main advantage Family Origins enjoys is a reputation for simplicity of use. The way it presents data on the screen just makes better sense to many people, especially the pedigree (tree) view. I, for one, certainly wish FTM included that facility! So check out the Origins website (**http://familyorigins.com/**)—this program certainly deserves serious consideration.

If you are just getting started researching your family's history, the process using Family Origns (as described on the official website) is simple. Just start filling in the blanks with names, dates, and facts about family members that you already know. Family Origins helps you expand your research with valuable tools, such as the FamilyFinder® Report, which searches the Internet and over 300 CD-ROMs to give you more information on your ancestors, and letter writing templates that make it easier to request records from agencies. Family Origins even lets you keep track of your research with To-Do Lists and Correspondence Logs. Once the information is in there, you're just a click away from creating amazing family trees, reports and charts that your family will admire and cherish through the years. Great for all family history enthusiasts, Family Origins offers superior LDS capabilities, such as full compatibility with PAF® and TempleReady™ for Windows, which continue to make it the most complete genealogy resource for LDS members.

Origins' Visual Photo Tree report generates beautiful charts in color!

THE MASTER GENEALOGIST FOR WINDOWS V 4.0

Wholly Genes Inc.,
http://www.whollygenes.com/tmg.htm
$59.00 for Silver edition, $99.00 for Gold edition

Now for what I like to call an "expert friendly" program and one worth taking a serious look at if you take genealogy seriously. The Master Genealogist (TMG) is billed as being *the* complete family history project manager. It offers more features and power than most of the so-called "popular" software packages. Of course, it also costs a bit more but the old adage of "you get what you pay for" holds and TMG gives you a *lot* for your money.

Who is The Master Genealogist best suited for? Two types of people—serious genealogists (or, again, those who take genealogy seriously) and people like myself who find the broad sweep of history, the interrelationship of humanity as shown through full genealogy

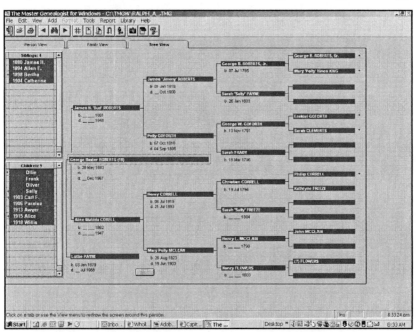

TMG's Tree view provides a lot of information on one screen.

more interesting than strict ancestor genealogy but still want all the power a computer can give in maintaining a genealogical database.

In my case, I've used Family Treemaker since the early nineties. I know it best and have used it in this book quite a bit in showing you how computerized genealogy works. I'm comfortable in it and to wean me away from that familiarity and resulting ease of use takes some doing, but TMG, to be frank, *is* doing it. While beginners can use TMG from the first day a family research project is started, its many advantages may not be obvious until your database has grown along with your expertise in genealogy. Once that happens, you begin hitting limitations in the other programs that TMG does not suffer. So look at TMG closely, you might like what you see (again, the website is at **http://www.whollygenes.com/tmg.htm**).

The Master Genealogist, as described on their website) is the complete family history project manager for Windows. As this official site points out, whether you are a weekend hobbyist or a professional researcher, TMG comes with everything you need to:

- manage volumes of research data, photos, and sources.
- organize a research trip, including "To Do" lists, reference material, charts, and forms.
- track your correspondence and expenses.
- be the hit of a family reunion!
- ... or publish a book, complete with table of contents, footnotes, multiple indexes, and bibliography!

The Master Genealogist is limited only by your imagination. If you are disappointed with the limits of other family history software, then you need look no further! TMG supports an unlimited number of:

- freeform text
- photographs
- sources
- citations

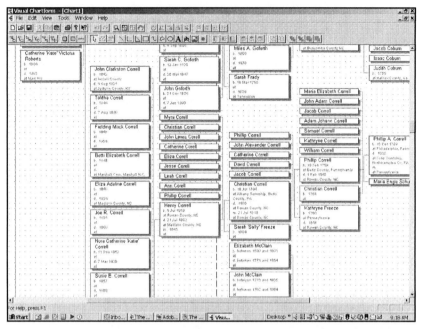

TMG, using a program included called Visual Chartform, can generate files that you can send off and have beautiful wall charts printed from (up to 3' by 30').

- repositories
- independent projects
- people
- events per person
- names per person
- relationships
- user-defined events
- user-defined flags

And most data-entry fields are of unlimited length - so there's no need for awkward abbreviations!

Direct import of following formats and versions are supported (i.e., without GEDCOM):

- Ancestral Quest™
- Ancestral Quest™ BACKUP
- Brothers Keeper v5.x™
- Everyone's Family Tree™
- Family Gathering™
- Family Gathering™ BACKUP
- Family Origins™ v4,5,6,7,8,9

- Family Roots™
- Family Tree Maker™ v3,4,5,6,7,8
- My Family™ v2.x
- Personal Ancestral File™ v2.x
- Personal Ancestral File™ BACKUP v2.x
- Personal Ancestral File™ v3.x, 4.x
- Roots III™
- Roots IV™
- Roots IV™ BACKUP™
- Roots V™
- Roots V™ BACKUP
- The Master Genealogist™ v1,2,3
- The Master Genealogist™ BACKUP v1,2,3
- Ultimate Family Tree™ (*.PRO)
- Ultimate Family Tree™ BACKUP (*.SQZ)
- Visual Roots™ (*.PRO)
- Visual Roots BACKUP™ (*.SQZ)

(GEDCOM imports are also supported for users of other programs that are not directly supported.)

When you upgrade to TMG, you can import your data directly (i.e., without GEDCOM) from a long list of other genealogy programs using the built-in GenBridge™ technology.

While TMG will also import data through GEDCOM v4.0 or v5.5, the direct import modules generally produce much better results and are strongly recommended.

TMG was designed by experienced genealogists who understand and prepare you for common research problems, including:

- conflicting data
- uncertain dates
- adoptions
- unwed parents
- "Old Style" dates
- disproven data
- contradictory sources
- spelling changes
- multiple lines of descent
- extra-long place names
- missing data
- sensitive data

Special features not found in traditional genealogy software make it easy to:

- pursue theories
- establish parent or child candidates
- record any type of event (including LDS events)
- record all of the evidence, not just your conclusions
- integrate historical timelines
- trace medical conditions
- document witnesses and other non-primary roles
- search for Soundex or true phonetic matches
- search by married name or spelling changes
- conduct Boolean (and/or) searches

So I recommend TMG if you want powerful software with room for expansion. A quick analogy. Most of the comsumer genealogy packages are like minivans—easy to drive and park, good for picking up groceries. TMG's more like a big Volvo diesel 18-wheeler—it can haul tons for long distances without getting out of breath. Check it out for the power.

Visit **www.whollygenes.com/products.htm** for more about TMG.

ANCESTRAL QUEST V 3.0

Incline Software, LC
http://www.ancquest.com/
$37.95

The Ancestral Quest website describes its software as the easiest to use and most versatile genealogy program on the market. "Its format," they say, "is perfect for the beginner and yet powerful enough for the most advanced genealogist. Easy data entry, keyboard shortcuts, super-fast mouse navigation, and excellent sourcing capabilities are just some of the software's wonderful features."

In my look at Ancestral Quest, I found the above to be true, so you might consider looking at this package. It's about the same level as FTM or Family Origins yet with some unique features.

Incline, the company that publishes Ancestral Quest, helped The Church of Jesus Christ of Latter-day Saints

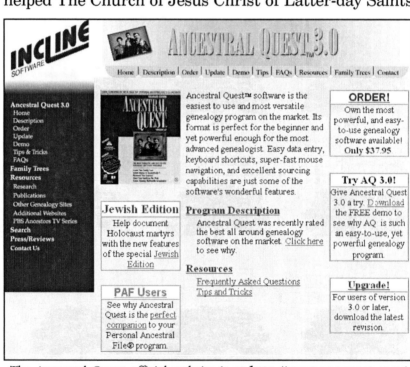

The Ancestral Quest official website is at **http://www.ancquest.com/**

develop its Windows version of Personal Ancestral File® (PAF). So they can claim, with credibility that Ancestral Quest (including programs derived from Ancestral Quest), has become the most widely used genealogy software program in the world.

Ancestral Quest 3.0, Incline stresses, is the ONLY complete genealogy program that is compatible with the database used by Personal Ancestral File® (PAF), both versions 3.0 and 4.0. What this means to a user of PAF is that you can use both your PAF program, developed by the Church of Jesus Christ of Latter-day Saints, and Ancestral Quest 3.0 to work on your data files. You can treat PAF 3 or PAF 4 as an add-on to AQ 3, or you can treat AQ 3 as an add-on to PAF 3 or PAF 4. An important consideration for those of you belonging to the Mormon church and doing genealogy as part of that religion.

One of the unique offerings of Ancestral Quest is a special Jewish version. It is, says Incline, a collaborative effort between the Simon Wiesenthal Center, Avotaynu, Ancestry.com, Risk International and The Hope Foundation (under whose name Ancestral Quest was being promoted at the time) and was initiated to help descendants of Holocaust victims determine whether any assets of their ancestors had been confiscated by the Nazi state, and to help them recover these assets. The project was called the Living Heirs project. A special Jewish version of Ancestral Quest was commissioned as part of this effort.

In Spring of 2001, Incline Software enhanced this Jewish Edition of Ancestral Quest to also include a Page of Testimony feature. This feature allows Jews to record information required on the Page of Testimony along with the other genealogical information that Ancestral Quest allows one to collect. A Page of Testimony can then be printed and sent to Yad Vashem's Hall of Names for inclusion in their records.

AGES! V 1.21

Jörn Daub EDV-Beratung
http://www.gensoftsb.com/agesftd.htm
$35.00 US, 35 Euros

The Ages! genealogy package is published by Jörn Daub EDV-Beratung in Germany. As one would expect from a European program, it has strong language support—offering currently English, German, Spanish, Italian, Greek, Czech, Ukrainian, Dutch, Polish, Russian, French, and Portuguese.

Another advantage of this finally crafted German entry in the genealogical software sweepstakes concerns its ability of editing GEDCOM files directly. Most family research programs either use a proprietary format or server as front ends to this or that database management program (FoxBase, DBase, Access, etc.). This is why the GEDCOM standard was developed, to serve as a means of exchanging data between all these widely variant programs.

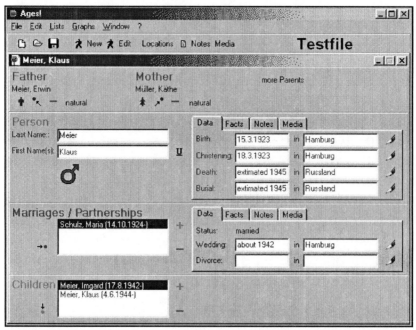

Ages! edits GEDCOM files directly and supports several languages.

By operating directly on the GEDCOM file, Ages! cuts out one big step in the import and export of data.

So, if you need language support not offered in most software, or like the concept of direct editing of GEDCOMs, Ages! awaits you.

BEHOLD V1.0

Louis Kessler
http://www.lkessler.com/behold/
shareware, price not yet announced

Behold has not been beheld yet—it's still in development. Yet, I feel it worth keeping an eye on for two reasons: the development shows interesting concepts on how your family research data is viewed and is addressing the problem of reports in an innovative manner. "Behold is built around its innovative Everything Report," the developer writes, "this report puts all your data in front of you where you can see it in a clear and organized manner. Its many useful index views, explorer-like contents, and extensive use of hyperlinks and modern navigational tools make it easy to move around. It has complete GEDCOM compliance meaning that every bit of your family data is available."

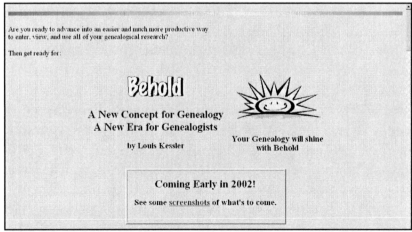

Check the Behold website for progress of this interesting software.

The SierraHome website provides more information about Generations.

GENERATIONS DELUXE DVD-ROM

SierraHome
http://sierrahome.com/products/
$49.95

"Generations® Deluxe DVD-ROM™ steps into the future of genealogy," reports the publisher's website. "A single DVD-ROM allows full access to the entire Generations program without constantly changing CDs, and allows you to carry all of your data with you wherever you go. Generations Deluxe DVD-ROM gives you the most customizable and comprehensive charting capabilities available, plus over 350 million names and resources to begin your search. It contains a free 3-billion name search from a professional genealogist, exclusive multimedia tutorials on genealogy research, one free year in the Heritage Quest Research Club, automatic web authoring, and a Create-a-Family CD wizard to help you store all of your important genealogy information." Worth a look!

LEGACY V 3.0

Millennia Corporation
http://legacyfamilytree.com/
free!

Yes, you read it correctly! Legacy Family Tree 3.0, the most comprehensive and easy-to-use family history software is now free for the taking (and I certainly grabbed my copy). This is the entire program. Nothing has been held back. No restrictions. Everything is there. From world-class merging, search and replace, and spell checking to powerful research logs, reports and sources, Legacy overpowers the competition with an unbeatable feature list.

Of course, Millennia exists to make money, so they offer several very good add-ons to the basic Legacy package that enchance your family research. These add-ons include the Deluxe version of Legacy with many more features for $19.95 (download) or $24.95 (disk), a companion program for your Palm or other PDA, and so forth. Check the site.

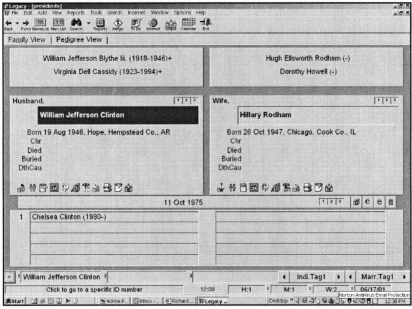

How the free Legacy 3.0 looks on the author's screen.

PAF (PERSONAL ANCESTRY FILE) V 5.1

The Church of Jesus Christ of Latter-Day Saints
http://familysearch.org
download free

Personal Ancestral File 5.1 (Build 5.1.12) is a new Windows®-based version of one of the most widely used genealogical management programs for home computers. The new software program can be downloaded free from the Internet. PAF 5.1 does not provide genealogical data. Instead, it helps users organize their family history records. It can produce, either on screen or on paper, family histories, pedigree charts, family group records, and other reports to help users in their search for missing ancestors. Download it free at **http://familysearch.org**.

This version includes changes to the individual record to accommodate the wide variety of naming conventions used throughout the world. This version will convert PAF 3.0 and 4.0 data files to its improved file format. PAF 5.1 will be available on compact disc in the future.

If you are Mormon, this is the software to rely on for meeting Temple requirements for the baptisim and sealing of your ancestors.

PAF 5.1 is an extensive family history manager that is free.

CUMBERLAND FAMILY TREE FOR WINDOWS

Cumberland Family Software
http://cf-software.com
$45.00

Here's another package that I personally own and use and which also shows promise. Cumberland Family Tree is a powerful second generation genealogy program with many features, multi-lingual, and easy-to-use. Language support includes the following languages: Afrikaans, Danish, Dutch, Finnish, French, German (Austria), German (Standard), Hungarian, Italian, Norwegian (Bokmål), Norwegian (Nynorsk), Polish, Portuguese (Brazil), Portuguese (Standard), Slovak, Slovenian, Spanish, and Swedish.

The software—as described on the official website at **http://cf-software.com**—automatically links names as they are added to the database. You are allowed to include 250 events per person, multiple marriages, scanned photos and documents, sources, stories and more. Printed reports provide over 31 different formats. *You can even create your very own indexed family history book!*

The major concept of Cumberland Family Tree for Windows centers around creating your very own Family History Book (although the program still maintains the capability of printing individual reports). The body of your book will likely consist of the unique "Story" reports, which have the capability of taking your dry data—such as dates and places—and structuring them into a delightful readable form. By allowing you to add up to 250 events in a person's life and attaching notes to those events you can easily create a full and complete biography on each individual in the database! Imagine showing ALL major events of a person's life in this fashion: births, church ordinances, schooling, addresses, immigrations, marriages, occupations, travels, awards, deaths, burials and any other life event you could think of!

In addition, you can easily document your data with source notes which can be end-noted when printing the story reports. The Indexed Book will keep track of all  individuals as you create the book and at the end show an index of every individual in the book—plus you can print the source notes which will have been footnoted througout the book.

And if you think the Indexed Book is a wonderful idea, imagine what it will be like when you add photographs and scanned documents! A wide variety of Photo reports can also be generated: pedigree charts with photos, descendant charts with photos, family groups charts and even a photo album. Definitely software you might like.

OTHER SOFTWARE AND DATA

This chapter has only touched the surface of all the wonderful and useful programs out there as I've only presented the more interesting ones. Later in this book you'll find listings of other software and data resources. Indeed the nicest thing about the internet and the worldwide web is the total ease with which you are able to find such resources.

A bit later we'll learn about *search engines* (services for searching the net employing key words or phrases). For now, I'll just give you a quick example. Using the **google.com** search engine, I did a search for "genealogy software" and found—in .06 seconds according to Google—over *four hundred thousand* references! Yes, plenty of software out there for you, which is why you need a book like this one to help you narrow your choices down a some.

Now, ride on with me as we venture bravely out onto the Information Superhighway. I'll drive at first, but you'll soon take over at the wheel.

GENEALOGY VIA THE INTERNET

TRACING YOUR FAMILY ROOTS QUICKLY AND EASILY

PART IV:

OUT THERE ON THE INTERNET

The internet is far more than just the world wide web. In this section, we look at its many resources.

"Describing the Internet as the Network of Networks is like calling the Space Shuttle, a thing that flies."
—John Lester

When I took office, only high energy physicists had ever heard of what is called the Worldwide Web.... Now even my cat has its own page.
—former president Bill Clinton

"Wow! They've got the internet on computers now!"
— Homer Simpson, "The Simpsons"

10

HOOKING UP WITH THE WORLD

What's the largest, longest, widest highway system in the world? The BMW *und* Mercedes-in-a-blur faster-than-light German *autobahn*? *Nein!*

The Russian road network from St. Petersburg in the European west across eight time zones of President Reagan's broken "Evil Empire" to the frozen, hungry wolf-haunted tundra of Siberia in Asia's limitless northern wastes? *Nyet*, comrade!

Hmmm. Well, what about that endless system of American Interstates? Like I-40 stretching from Wilmington, North Carolina on the east coast all the way across the forever-long vastness of this great land to the Pacific-washed shores of sunny California? Nope! You ain't got it right yet, pard!

Okay, okay. Maybe you do—yelling "Internet! Internet!" like that. I hear you, and ... yes, now you unquestionably do have it correct to the farthest, most insignificant decimal place at the very edge of infinity (and that's *close*).

The "Information Super Highway," you see, drapes across space like some vast ethereal fishnet with planet Earth as the catch of the day. Each of the thousands upon thousands of places where strands intersect has a computer crouching there, fielding and passing along signals to other computers all around the world. Every computer, using the net, can talk to every other computer, even those continents away.

These computers are called *servers*. If you connect your personal computer to a server, then you are also connected to the network of all those other thousands of computers by the ultra high speed lines and other connections (such as satellites) comprising the strands of this great net. Any location where strands of this net cross, there you can go too!

Refining our analogy a bit more, think of this huge net as a unimaginably extensive grid of city streets in cyberspace (that virtual and alternate reality comprising the internet—a truly fun vacation destination). Turn left on Elm, go four blocks, take a right on Main, down two blocks, and you've reached the library. Back up four blocks, turn right onto Transatlantic Boulevard, go straight 3,000 miles. Bingo, you are in London.

Of course the Information Highway is not all straight and wide. Often there are twisty turns and narrow alley shortcuts in achieving your destination. Still—like a city

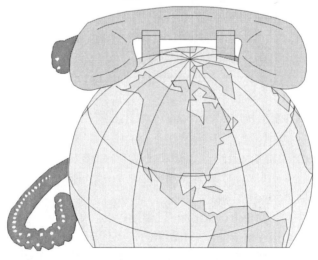

Modems keep getting fancier and faster, connecting you to the world.

in our more commmon everyday reality—you can get there sooner or later ... *If* you have a car.

MODEMS

Analogies of the Information Superhighway and likening your personal desktop computer to a car traveling on it possess great popularity with writers of books and articles about computers. This is no less true with me. Such simplifications, while not exact, speed your visualization and enjoyment of using the internet and the worldwide web that is only one part—albeit the most visible—of it.

If your computer is a car, then your *modem* is the wheels of that car. A modem is a device that is most

 commonly used in connecting two computers via a telephone line. In the case of your connection to the internet, it puts your computer in communication with one of those servers on that vast network of cyberspace "streets."

The modem remains the most common way of connecting to the internet, albeit other, faster ways like cable and DSL (Digital Subscriber Lines) continue making inroads.

Modem is an acronym for MOdulator-DEModulator. In brief, it converts the digital signals in which computers think into analog ones which are transmittable over regular telephone lines. A number of standards exist for speed, error-correction, and the way data is sent over the phone line. (The nice thing about standards, as the old saw goes, is that there are *so many* of them.)

The major modem parameter that should interest you is its maximum *baud rate*, or the fastest possible speed of data transmission. The faster, the better in achieving a connection to the internet that doesn't force you to sit and wait forever while, for example, pictures load from the worldwide web. The modem box pictured on the previous page denotes a speed of 33,600 baud (how speed is measured is explained below), and that's pretty obsolete these days. As improvements in modems occur, you'll find yourself upgrading to a faster one from time to time.

Technology, you see, changes fast in relationship both to the internet and computers in general. It's like a dog's life, where one year in real time supposedly equals seven or eight to the dog. A dog that's ten years old is really about seventy or so in equivalent age to a human. Poor old hound can barely move, and that's even truer when it comes to modems. A two-year-old modem is about ready for replacement. That old dog just don't hunt no more, as we say in these parts.

Modem speed (baud rate) is measured in what is approximately equivalent to characters transmitted or received per second. I say *approximately* because these "characters" are really *bytes* of information. A byte is a spurt of computer data usually comprised of eight *bits* in modem communications. A bit is just a string of ones and zeros, such as *10010110*. This is the *binary* or *base two* system in which all computers think. A byte, then, could be a letter, a number, or just an eight-bit part of a photograph or other graphic element.

Luckily you don't have to know squat about all that except for the fact the baud rate of a modem is just about equal to moving that many characters per second over the phone lines. You need to understand that speed is not exact but is rather the fastest speed of transfer under perfect conditions. Conditions, naturally, are never perfect. The number of other people using the server computer to which you've called in, noise on the line, whatever else your computer might

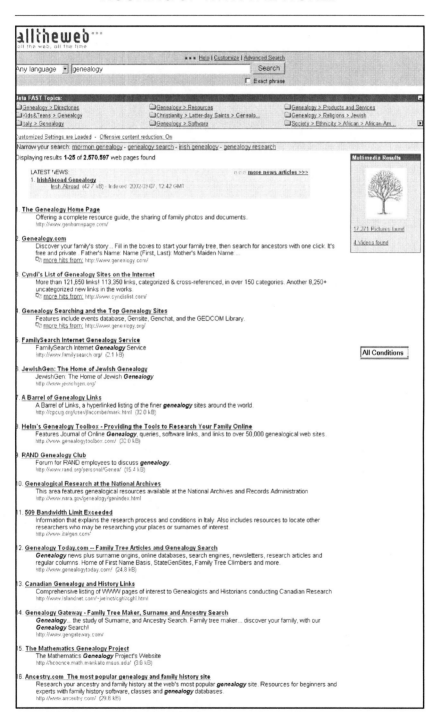

A search using the keyword *genealogy* on the web seach engine at **alltheweb.com** yields over 2.5 million results. Always plenty there!

be doing, all tend to degrade speed in greater or lesser amounts.

Back around 1994, the standard modem speed was 14,400 baud. Then it went to 28,800—which is pretty much the minimum useful rate when surfing the worldwide web; otherwise, waiting for graphics to load simply takes too long. Around 1996, the standard speed jumped to 33,600 baud, with many "experts" claiming we had reached the absolute limit a digital to analog modem could be pushed to. And, of course, in 1997, those experts wiped pie (crow, I believe) from their faces as the 56,000 baud modems arrive. However, five years later—in 2002—as I write this, modem speeds are still restricted to 56K. That technical limit on dial-up lines has yet to be broken. But, of course, there are other methods of making fast connections—cable and DSL being the two most easily accessible. We have a DSL line here, it's wonderful. Forget 56K, we connect at minimum some 10 times faster.

Basically, however, all you really need to know is "faster is better." Most new computers you buy off the shelves as this is being written (March, 2002) come standard with internal 56K baud modems.

If your computer has a slower modem—especially if it has a 14,400—upgrading is easy and cheap. You have two choices—*internal*, which is a board that plugs inside your computer (replacing the modem already there, if one is), and *external*, which plugs into a serial port on the back of your computer. You can even buy an external modem and use it without ever opening your computer's case and removing the old modem. Just reconfigure the computer for the new modem according to the instructions that come with it.

The bottom line about modems then—since practically all computers now come with a modem included and already installed—is speed. Just ask the salesperson how fast that puppy is. If he or she says "33,600" or faster than that, nod sagely. The salesperson will think you know your stuff and maybe give you a better deal. In this case, at least, you *will* know your stuff.

The only installation you need worry about is the actual hooking of a telephone line into the computer. This is accomplished in exactly the same manner as you connect a fax machine or telephone answering device into the phone line. Usually instructions and a wire with *modular jacks* (those little "demiflodgets" that click into places where phones hook up) are included along with pictorial instructions. It's truly easy.

Shortly we'll look at how you find a local telephone number to call other computers, and how by so doing, you can zoom your personal computer "car" out onto the Information Superhighway. First, you need just a smattering more knowledge.

COMMUNICATIONS SOFTWARE

If modems may be likened to the wheels for your "car" that travels the highways and byways of the

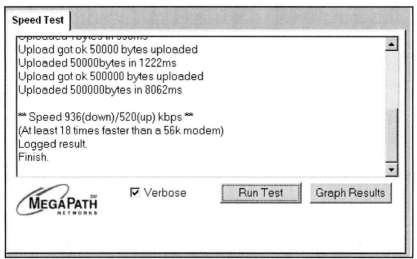

A DSL (Digital Subscriber Line) gives you much faster internet connections than regular phone service. Above, my current connection.

internet, the communications program is the air inflating the tires.

A communications program tells the modem how to connect with a remote computer, feeds it commands and other data in the proper format, and translates the results so that you, the operator, understand and find whatever is being fed "down" from the server computer useful. (Sending information to a server computer is called *uploading*, receiving data into your computer is *downloading*.)

In the past, you'd need a whole book just to adequately inform yourself about modems and communications software. With other types of computers than those running Windows (any version from 95 and up, which includes 95, 98, ME, NT, XP, and 2000—Mr. Gates does lots of Windows) you still need a book. Using the current version of Windows—for all the reasons detailed in Chapter 6—getting out onto the internet via your modem is much, much easier.

Again, new computers almost invariably come with modems built in. Just as invariably—these days—some version of Windows, already installed, is included as well.

Right there you have everything needed except an account from an *internet service provider* (ISP) to get on the internet. The ISP is the company with a (hopefully) local phone number to a server computer. You pay a certain amount per month for access—the going rate currently being about $19.95 for unlimited access (i.e. as many hours as you care to surf the net for one low monthly rate).

There is no need to buy a special communications program. All is included in Windows. In fact, you'll probably never even need know that Dial-Up Networking is the feature of Windows making your connection to the worldwide web possible.

I could engage here in a lengthy explanation of how

Dial-Up Networking works but that is, as already alluded to, unnecessary. Because, usually, when you sign up for internet access with an ISP who covers your local phone exchange, they (here's that word again) almost invariably these days give you a disk that configures your computer for you, making it easy to access their online service.

More about finding the right ISP for you in the next chapters but—to make a long story short—look in your phone book's Yellow Pages.

Dial-Up Networking connects your computer to the planetary network that is the internet. Well, actually it is now more than a planetary network since the Mars Rover has been sending its vacation pictures back to Earth and so many millions of us have been looking at them via the internet.

Anyway, just connecting is not enough, you still need some program which lets you actually see the pictures, read the colorful text, hear the music, enjoy the animations, and all the rest that is the glory of the worldwide web. (With the Mars Rover now, we gonna have to start calling it something like the "solar system-wide web.)

The communications program just described above is called a *browser*. Browsers work in conjunction with Dial-Up Networking, providing the actual images and sounds you see on the screen and hear from your speakers.

There are numerous browsers for sale; the biggest selling one currently being Netscape's. However—just as Dial-Up Networking comes as part of Windows—so now, too, does Internet Explorer. This browser is Microsoft's free offering to help you enjoy the web. Not only is it *free* (a price even us poor writers can afford) but, in my somewhat educated and long-experienced opinion, it is also the best available. I recommend it.

Compared to years past, yeah, getting on the internet is *real* easy these days.

Which is why—also compared to those years past—there are tens of millions more people using the internet today, including you and me!

As Charles Fort once wrote about unexplained phenomena—and in specific about why certain technologies seem to become universal all at once—when it comes time to railroad, people build railroads.

Right now, they're building Information Superhighways like you wouldn't believe.

It's downright wonderful.

I'm sure my 8th great grandfather William Ball (who died in 1681 in Middlesex County, Virginia) would have been even more considerably amazed. But I found him, you see, via the internet. And a lot of other relatives both in between and beyond!

TELEPHONE LINE BOTTOM LINE

Hooking your computer to the world using the telephone line is incredibly simple. Most computers now come out of the box *internet-ready*.

Got dial tone on your modem? Got the engine revving on your "virtual car?" Okay, dokey! Let's venture out onto the wide open roads of the internet.

You drive now. Okay?

It's called "surfing" the net, dude!

11

ONLINE SERVICES
AND BULLETIN BOARDS

H ave you ever seen one of those wondrous old silver screen movies from the thirties and forties where a transition in time is shown by days going by in the blink of an eye? Where newspaper headlines change like shuffling a deck of cards?

That, my friend, describes the internet today. A year is like unto a day, and days fleet-footedly fly by each second. What was "state of the art" in the morning becomes laughably antiquated in the early afternoon.

All of which is by way of introduction to stating that we won't be spending a lot of time in this book discussing online services and electronic bulletin board services (BBS). They were great in their day. I certainly spent many years enjoying them, including eight years of service on the Delphi network running the Writers Group.

Alas, times have moved onward. The internet has superceded all of the above. Not that the net is all that new, it actually predated all the online services and the BBS wave of the 1980s. The internet was always superior in concept, scope, and service to all the rest.

It wasn't until the early 1990s when the introduction of the worldwide web and various technological advances forced the internet from the province of academia and the military. The net—over the loud but geneally ignored screams of longtime users—became commercialized and made available to the masses.

A longtime *netizen* (or net citizen), I personally was of two minds about this vast sea change in the internet. Yet—while huge abuses of the net exist—overall it has become larger and even more wonderful.

As that great philosopher Bob Dylan put into song, "The times, they are a changin'."

I love it now, this new internet—for even with all its warts and abuses, there is nothing else in this universe quite so useful for the gathering and exchange of information. But... back to online services and bulletin boards.

BULLETIN BOARD SERVICES

Bulletin Board Services—often referred to as BBSes—came about during the 1980s along with the personal computer. In fact, most of the early BBSes were nothing more than a single personal computer in someone's bedroom or basement.

Special software allowed the computer to answer the phone and provide such services as messaging and file uploads/downloads. The name *electronic bulletin board* originated because this messaging service was not unlike the posting of actual written messages in the "real" world on a cork board using thumbtacks.

Many specialized boards sprung up over the years devoted to a particular interest. Genealogy boards soared in popularity as more and more people began tracing their family histories. Genealogy BBSes were a wonderful resource for those of us looking for information on this or that long-lost relative to fill in a blank on the old family tree.

As technology improved, BBSes became more and more sophisticated (remember, the trend of technical improvements in the computer world is really fast-paced and all this happened in a very short time). BBSes soon existed with several incoming phones lines, allowing users to chat among themselves, and with *connections* to other BBSes!

Most BBSes—the genealogical ones no exception— began as local in scope. Soon, in part simply because the technology now allowed it—boards begin exchanging messages, files, and electronic mail with other boards. In other words, the local BBSes joined into *networks*.

The most common of these networks in the 1980s was *Fidonet*. You must keep in mind that this was all happening before the internet became publicly accessible—some alternate method was needed for the exchange of mail and other information country wide and even world wide.

Two visionary programmers—Ken Kaplan and Tom Jennings (living the width of the U.S. apart) came up with the original Fidonet software. Their idea was to give local

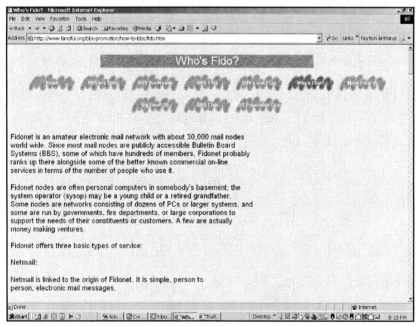

A good place for learning more about FidoNet and BBSes in general is **http://www.fanciful.org/bbs-promotion/how-to-bbs/fido.htm**.

BBS operators software that would "fetch" update data from other boards late at night when long distance rates were cheap. This software was a concoction of other programs—"really a mongel" someone tagged it. Thus, the name Fidonet was coined.

Fidonet worked through *interest groups*. If, for example, a BBS was oriented to genealogy, the board would call one or more other computers each night and download genealogy interest groups. The data would consist of messages and files for those interested in family history research. A user would sign onto the board the next day, see a particular message from someone states away requesting or asking for information. He or she could then post a reply to that message. The next night, the message would go out to another computer and soon wind up posted on the BBS where the first message originated.

Fidonet worked well and is still in existence (yep, even today in 2002). Covering it, however, is beyond the scope of this book (it is entitled, I remind you, *Genealogy via the Internet*). However—remember also technology changes—and many BBSes are now accessible on the internet.

For years, BBSes have also exchanged messages via the *Usenet*. The Usenet developed as part of the internet itself, and is discussed in the next chapter.

So, BBSes live on, thanks to the internet.

A good book that does cover bulletin boards and online services is *Genealogy Online* by Elizabeth Powell Crowe (McGraw-Hill, 1996). We, however, will stick to the internet specifically in this book.

ONLINE SERVICES

The temptation exists (and some writers succumb) to describe *online services* as super bulletin boards. After all, they allow users from all over the United States and, indeed, all over the world to call a local number and connect just like the service was a local BBS. They offer messaging and files—just like local boards, albeit usually in far greater quantities and scope.

The major online services (those left in business) include America Online (AOL), CompuServe, Prodigy, and the Microsoft Network (MSN). For more information on a particular online service, consult the appropriate websites (**http://www.aol.com**, **http://www.compuserve.com**, **http://www.prodigy.com**, and **http://www.msn.com**).

Some of these online services, like Delphi and Prodigy, no longer offer much in the way of dial-in services but still exist as strictly internet entities. Others—yes, we're talking about AOL—have been incredibly successful and bought up a few toys... things like Time-Warner and so forth.

Yet, while online services are similar in appearance to super BBSes, the concept is really 180 degrees opposite. The local BBSes with Fidonet and Usenet, so it turns out, had the right idea, *inter*networking.

Online services concentrate all their offerings into one set of big computers at a specific location. If those computers break down, or get overwhelmed with people calling in, it becomes useless for at least a period of time.

The problems users of AOL experienced in 1996 and '97 are a good example, and were much played up in the popular media. Going to a $19.95 per month flat rate resulted in more people calling in than their equipment could handle. Frustrating delays, electronic mail turning turtle-slow, and more caused AOL much grief, loss of customers, and bad public relations. Of course, that's ancient history now, in AOL's case, and they continue to be fantastically successful.

BBSes, spread out in thousand of locations, are not affected by such problems. If one goes down, only a few local callers might notice, no one else is much affected.

The internet is like the BBS system multiplied by tens or hundreds of thousands of times in scope. With this vast grouping of computers that (as some florid writer purple-prosed earlier in this book "drapes across space like some vast ethereal fishnet with planet Earth as the catch of the day") downtime seldom happens.

In fact, the last time the internet came anywhere close to being totally closed down was in 1988 when Robert Tappan Morris, Jr. unleashed a "worm" (as opposed to a computer virus) that wreaked havoc throughout cyberspace, shutting down many important government and academic computers by essentially filling up their working memories. This was before most people even knew the internet existed, although it was huge even then.

By sheer luck (to be less than modest for a moment) I had just published the first U.S. book on computer viruses. As one of the "experts of the moment" I got to be on NBC "Nightly News" the day after the attack explaining what had happened. That's my little niche in computer history. Not that it keeps me from having to take the trash out every Monday or relieves me of the necessity of writing books for a living (obviously, as witness this one).

But neither Mr. Morris nor the many so-called hackers who roam the net from time to time are much of an overall threat. The internet—like that estimable and admirable Energizer Bunny—just keeps right on drumming along.

Basically online services are not as dependable as the internet, or even BBS networks like Fidonet. They all now provide you access to the net, but are still acting

AOL offers information about their online services at **aol.com**.

The MSN main page at **www.msn.com** links you to more information about software giant Microsoft's online service.

as a buffer between you and what is really the net. Most of the "extras" they offer you can easily find out on the net itself. And buying your service directly from an internet service provider (ISP) is generally cheaper while providing faster, more reliable operation. Still, the big boys, lik,e AOL offer a lot of added value with their service.

But, just exactly how do you get onto the internet and run barefoot through all those green, green files other than using an online service as a gateway?

Glad you asked.

That's up next!

12

THE INTERNET:

HOW TO GET ON, HOW TO USE

Here's a variant on the game we played at the start of Chapter 10. Can you name the largest computer network in the world? This is an easy enough little amusement to engage in since you have perhaps hundreds of thousands of chances to come up with the right name—or at least of guessing *a* right name.

The answer, naturally enough, is the *internet*—an often anarchic collection of connections comprising many hundreds of thousands of local-area networks (LANs) located all over the world, all tied together by several wide-area networks (WANs) or, in internet parlance, *backbones*—a backbone being ultra high speed data lines or satellite links.

Because the internet is made up of many, many subnets, I use lower case in referring both to it and to that very visible subpart of the internet, the world wide web. I know this goes against current usage but, hey, this is *my* book<g>*, both as author and publisher, so please indulge me.

No one knows for sure, but some experts claim that the internet—this multitude of interconnected networks of computers—has as many as 50 million users and continues to grow like crazy. Hundreds of colleges and universities worldwide are connected to the network, as are government agencies of many countries, and all sorts of commercial companies, institutions of all types (schools, churches, associations, clubs, etc.),

---

*You'll often see the characters <g> used in email and in online chats, one of many internet shortcuts—it simply means *grin*.

and private individuals. Because the network ties together so many researchers, it is also one of the most important computer networks in the world, in addition to being by several orders of magnitude the largest.

The internet is what the "worm" launched by Robert Morris, Jr. in November of 1988 shut down for a night by overloading some 6,000 very important governmental and academic research computers. This caused a good deal of concern, a lot of attention by the mass media, and tightening of security procedures, but the internet remains open and essentially free to everyone who can obtain access. Although Morris' worm was not really a computer virus, it was this attack that brought computer viruses to the attention of the public and made them a household term.

WHERE IT CAME FROM

The internet is perhaps the only military project in history that got totally out of hand and turned out to enhance the greater good. It was started by the U.S. Defense Department's Advanced Research Project Administration in 1969 as an experiment in interconnecting regional networks— using the names ARPANET for the more general portion, and MILNET for the military subnet. Other government agencies joined their computers to it—including NASA and the Department of Energy. Since much research was done at universities, school systems began appearing on the network.

The National Science Foundation (NSF), another U.S. government agency, came into the picture, funding high speed connections between research centers here and abroad. Through the 1980s, the internet grew steadily, spreading across oceans and losing its American governmental control by simply outgrowing it. NSF funded some of the internet "backbones" (at least until recently) in the United States, and commercial companies others, but it's safe to say now that no one owns or controls the network. It simply exists—there for the use of anyone who can access it.

Who pays for all this? Each institution, agency, or company pays for its own equipment and for any lines necessary to connect to the internet. NSF, similar agencies in various other

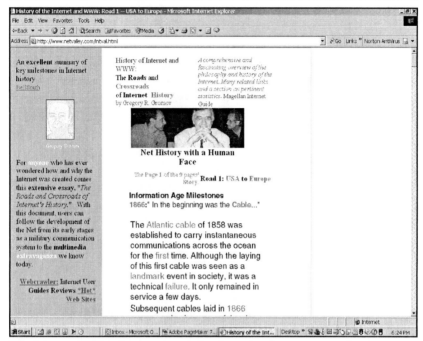

The history of the internet may be found, of course, on the internet. Check out **http://www.netvalley.com/intval.html**

countries, and increasingly companies in the commercial sector pay for the backbones to connect the many thousands of subnets together.

There are few restrictions except peer pressure not to abuse the net. A nebulous code of conduct known as *netiquette* or net etiquette spells out a lot of what is acceptable and what is not.

A phenomena known as "flames" will let you know when you cross the line. These are nasty e-mail messages from a myriad of people in varying degrees of impoliteness letting you know exactly what you did wrong. Outspokenness and a nonreluctance to lambast those you disagree with are certainly not rare traits on the internet, that's for sure!

ACCESS

Access to the internet in one form or another is easy to obtain. If your school or company is on the internet, and you have an account on their computer system, you may already be on the internet, or can get on by simply asking your system administrator to assign you internet privileges. This way, you get the world for free!

Should you not be associated with an institution or firm whose computers are hooked up to the net, it is still easy enough to get on the internet. Many avenues are available to you. One is to find a local college or university that would be willing to grant you an account on their computers in return for your contribution of service to that institution, or to the internet and the world community in general.

A more likely option is to sign up with a commercial service offering access to a server computer with internet connections. These companies are called *Internet Service Providers* (ISPs). After our discussion about online services in Chapter 11, you should not confuse the big online services like AOL and CompuServe with a ISP. There are very important differences.

An online service is basically trying to sell you what's on their computer system. Access to the internet (or at least the web portion of it) is offered now by all of them because that's what the public demands. However, with the online folks, putting you out onto the internet is an "add on" value, not their primary product—which is, again, selling you what's on their system.

While the online services do offer vast amounts of files and other information in attractive formats, you can get all of what they have and ever so much *more* out on the net itself without putting a sometimes very slow and expensive buffer between yourself and the real net.

An ISP, on the other hand, sells just one service, a fast connection to the internet. And *that*, my friend, is what ya do need!

ISPs come in many sizes and flavors. They range in size from large national companies providing you with local access numbers—like Earthlink (**http://www.earthlink.net/**), AT&T Worldnet, Sprint, MCI, and others—to small (sometimes just one computer but a bunch of modems) owned by an entrepreneur servicing only your town.

Occasionally a worthy nonprofit group will band together and satisfy the internet access needs of a particular region. Here in Western North Carolina (home to the Great Smoky Mountains), we have the Mountain Area Information Network

Mountain Area Information Network
The Community Network for Western North Carolina

m@in

Where We Live
Community Links
Business Links
Web Market
Mountain Voices
About MAIN
Join MAIN
Volunteer
Support MAIN
Calendar
Classifieds
Film Reviews
Book Reviews
Weather
Web Mail
Contact Us
Help & Virus Info
Search the Web

County Sites [go]

Search MAIN: [____] Find

Comments about this Web site?
webmaster@main.nc.us

Technical question?
help@main.nc.us

Question about your MAIN account?
accounts@main.nc.us

Interested in volunteering?
volunteer@main.nc.us

Need brochures?
brochures@main.nc.us

Tell a friend about m@in

What's Happening in WNC:
03/10/2002

◆ Today - "Spring Returns to the Mountains" Exhibit

◆ Today - THE EROICA TRIO - Diana Wortham Theatre at Pack Place

◆ Today - Blue Ridge Banjo and Fiddle Concert

◆ Today - Cinderella - North Carolina Dance Theatre

A Look Ahead:

◆ 03/11 - Tony Walton Lecture at Warren-Wilson

◆ 03/11 - "Spring Returns to the Mountains" Exhibit

◆ 03/11 - Empty Bowl Dinner Benefit in Waynesville

Community Calendar | Submit an Event

Spotlight on:

THE MERCHANTS OF COOL

Small Business Resource EXPO
Tools & Tips for Doing Business on the Internet

Community Network News:

◆ 03/08 - new WNC coffeehouse in USA Today top 10

◆ 03/08 - new Lack of snow could fuel spring fires in WNC

◆ 03/08 - new 1999 speeding case triggered DMV probe

◆ 03/08 - new Blue Ridge won't name resigned doctors

◆ 03/07 - Opinion: Wal-Mart Warriors

◆ 03/07 - "Buy Local" campaign goes national

◆ 03/07 - Woodfin flap reveals DMV probe

◆ Citizen-Times story

◆ 03/07 - WNC hosts recycling conference

◆ 03/07 - Five doctors quit Blue Ridge health clinic

◆ 03/06 - Helms: Views on AIDS

Mountain Web Cam

Southern Mountains
TONIGHT
LO:21°F
Clear

Extended Forecast

School Closings   Road Conditions

Local Media by county

Regional [go]

Media Contacts for Nonprofits

Regional News:

ASHEVILLE CITIZEN-TIMES
VOICE OF THE MOUNTAINS

Crowded race
◆ for senate is starting to sort out

Documents
◆ show DMV in region troubled

Leak of SBI
◆ report tied to Woodfin remains mystery

◆ Lions rack up big win

WNC needs
◆ health-care workers

Mountain Xpress
mountainx.com

Folk icon's
◆ influence still warm in today's activists

Woodfin: Small
◆ town scandal or the tip of the iceberg?

Rumors of band's demise
◆ have been greatly

If you find Western North Carolina of interest, check out MAIN's homepage at **http://main.nc.us**

(MAIN). More information on MAIN resides at **http://www.main.nc.us**. They are nice folks bringing the light of the internet into the dark mountain hollows of Appalachia. MAIN is my own access point into the net, and I thank Wally Bowen and the other MAIN staffers muchly for their fine service.

As to the best access for *you*, as earlier I again recommend consulting your local phone book's yellow pages. About $19.95 a month for unlimited time is the going rate. Exercise some care in finding a reliable ISP that you can stay with, or you'll be changing your e-mail address and making yourself a bit harder to find for friends and fellow family history researchers.

Another source would be any of the major computer magazines sold on your local newsstand. Lots of national ISPs advertise in those.

Or, best of all, just ask your friends already on the internet. Chances are they've already tried one or more services before settling on a good one. Find out which that is and save yourself a lot of trouble.

TYPES OF INTERNET ACCESS

How do you know which internet service provider is for you? A little introduction as to types of access is in order. ISPs generally provide a range of services which vary in the extent of internet access, speed of data transmission, and cost.

Companies often require high speed, dedicated modes of connecting to the internet but, as a private individual, one of the four basic methods listed below will fill your needs.

SHELL ACCOUNT

A shell account is usually the least expensive way to access the internet. It also requires the most computer and internet knowledge since you log into a Unix operating system based computer. This type of account gives you a command line prompt, like the old DOS computers but a lot more powerful. You then use text-based programs running on the remote computer (server) to access *ftp* (file transfer protocol), *e-mail* (electronic mail), and other text-based services. You *do not* get the pictures, sound, and animation of the worldwide web.

Of course, not much in the way of equipment at your end

```
198.168.0.40 (113x39)
File  Edit  Options  Help
Trying 198.168.0.40...
Connected to 198.168.0.40.

Red Hat Linux release 7.2 (Enigma)
Kernel 2.4.7-10 on an i586
login: ralph
Password:
Last login: Sun Mar 10 18:57:15 from 198.168.0.35
[ralph@beauregard ralph]$ ls /usr/bin
[                    gsnd              msg2qm
411toppm             gsoelim           msgchk
4odb_clean           gtbl              msgcmp
4odb_clear           gtkasp2php        msgcomm
4odb_create          gtk-config        msgfmt
4odb_destroy         gtroff            msghack
4odb_dig             gtv               msgmerge
4odb_grant           gunzip            msgunfmt
4odb_metadig         gusload           msh
4odb_odmsdump        gzexe             mtrace
4odb_odmsload        gzip              mtvtoppm
4rdf                 h2ph              mutt
4xslt                h2xs              muttbug
a2p                  halt              name-clien
a2ps                 head              namei
aclocal              HEAD              ncftp
actmerge             hexdump           ncftpbatch
actsync              hinotes           ncftpbookm
actsyncd             hipstopgm         ncftpget
addDbDomDocument     hltest            ncftpls
adddebug             host              ncftpput
addftinfo            hostid            neat
addr2line            hoststat          neqn
addresses            hpcdtoppm         netscape
afmtodit             hpftodit          netscape-c
alarmd               htdb_dump         newaliases
ali                  htdb_load         newgrp
anno                 htdb_stat         new-object
anytopnm             htdig             news2mail
apacheconf           htdigest          news.daily
apm                  htdump            newsrequeu
Start    [icons]        Inbox - ...   Adobe P...   EarthLin...
```

A shell account often requires knowledge of the Unix or Linux operating system—used by many of the underlying controllers of the internet. Above is the shell account I have on one of our inhouse Linux servers for maintaining my company's various web sites. Unless you need such programmer type "command line" access, a shell account is probably not your best bet.

is called for, either. A modem and a terminal (or a PC running a terminal emulator) does the job. Aside from the *terminal emulator* (a simple communications program), no other software is needed since everything else runs on the remote machine.

If all you are going to do is read and send e-mail and send or receive an occasional file, this is probably a good way to go. But, again, it requires the most knowledge on your part and you can do the least on the internet with this type of access. For those who maintain actual web pages on the net, a shell account is a necessity for quick editing and other mainte-nance chores.

For general usage, however, you should pass if offered only a shell account (although shell accounts are harder to come by these days, mostly due to security concerns).

INTERNET GATEWAY

As we saw in the last chapter, the big online services like Compuserve and AOL, also offer *internet gateway services*. This is nothing more than providing you with a sometimes cluttered pathway through their system out onto the "real" net. For all the reasons already given here and in preceding chapters, I suggest that the internet gateway approach is not the way to fly either. Why pay for stuff you don't want or need?

SINGLE USER SLIP/PPP ACCOUNT

SLIP (serial line internet protocol) or PPP (point-to-point protocol) service usually provides you complete internet access at a reasonable rate. Using SLIP/PPP, you can run any combination of internet activities on your own com-puter. These might include (all at once) an electronic mail program such as Eudora, a browser like Microsoft Internet Explorer, a *telnet* program (which lets you do all the stuff described for a shell account previous), video conferencing software, a ftp (file transfer protocol) program, and much more. All at *once*! Simultaneously, even.

I belabor the above point because so many people miss the sheer power of the internet and run only one application at a time. It's a *network*, folks. You can and should be doing more than one thing at a time.

A most wondrous source for all kinds of these internet applications is Dave Central (**http://www.davecentral.com**). Dave always has hundreds of programs for instant download, many of which are *freeware* (no charge for using), or *shareware* (try it out for free, pay only if you decide to keep). There are also many commercial programs there that now let you download and try them out before buying also check out **http://shareware.com.**

So ... a SLIP/PPP account is the best of the methods described in this chapter, and the type you want. And you want it for $19.95 a month or less, for full access.

"SURFER" OR "CRUISER" ACCOUNTS

Okay, admittedly SLIP/PPP accounts are somewhat sophisticated for some people. These folks either fail to comprehend the vast power such a connection gives, or just don't want to go to all the trouble of properly configuring the various pieces of software which must operate together to take full advantage of this power.

Many ISPs attempt to simplify SLIP/PPP accounts by providing disks or CD-ROMs that have proprietary SLIP/PPP connection programs. This eliminates the need for the customer to deal with SLIP/PPP configuration issues. You just pop the disk into your computer and it does all the setup.

The drawback to these accounts is that you lock yourself into whatever programming the ISP has done. This can be a major, major, *major* disadvantage to you! As I've pointed out several times already, the technology of the internet changes far faster than "real" time. There is always a new browser coming out with fantastic new features, and you may want to latch onto it.(Keep mixing it up, Microsoft and Netscape, we love your browser war!)

If you are locked into some proprietary software given you by a local ISP who might not be able to upgrade it as fast as the net changes, this can become irritating to you. Or even one of the big national providers—such as AT&T Worldnet with their own versions of the major browsers—might not give you the full freedom on the net you'll no doubt come to expect and want. Or at least be slow in giving you the very latest version.

So I do recommend you find a full SLIP/PPP account, even if you also need to find a friendly computer expert that will help you get all the configuration done. The end result is the reward of more freedom and power in using the internet and the worldwide web.

BUT GET ON ANYWAY YOU CAN

As I have indeed said many times already, internet technology changes rapidly. There are other ways of obtaining internet access than those we've discussed in this chapter. WebTV, for example, lets you surf the internet without a computer by using your television set. Libraries and even providers of rental office services offer temporary access to the net.

Pat, my lovely wife, and I attended a trade show for the vending industry recently (we also have a small vending company). Several companies were offering *internet vending machines*, i.e. equipment that would allow people access to the internet just by using their credit card to activate a computer. They could then use it for whatever length of time they had purchased.

Then, too, a proliferation of internet cafés now exist, where you can quaff cappuccino and check your email at the same time.

Electronic commerce and the internet is the hot wave of opportunity at the moment. I guarantee you that as this is being written and, yes, even as you read it that thousands of entrepreneurs out there are thinking feverishly about the net. These guys and gals want desperately to come up with ways of getting you and me and Uncle Ferd on the net in such an easy and convenient manner that we will all rush to pour profits into their coffers. Some of them will succeed.

Therefore, I say to you, get on the net anyway you can. Additional ways of net access than the ones above already exist. The bottom line being that whether you're doing genealogical research or a thousand other things, the net's the place for you ... and me ... and old Uncle Ferd.

So—now that you're on the internet—what about the worldwide web?

It's all coming in the next chapter.

13

THE WORLD WIDE WEB

The internet—that grand cyberspace compendium of connected computers—has existed for about 30 years. Why *now* the sudden surge in popularity? Why now flock we millions upon millions in high baud rate exuberance out onto the Information Superhighway? Why now—after all this time—has such universality come to the internet?

The answer, my friend (to paraphrase the great Bob Dylan once more) is blowing in the wind of technology. A wind that has become more gale force these days than the calmer, slower zephyr of past decades. Yet—if you rig your sails for these higher winds—you'll scud along with nicely taut rigging at awesome speed over an ocean of information ... and the fishing is ever so good; whether it be family research or any other fact-laden feast. You cast your nets so widely to capture fat, juicy, delicious bits of this information or that. (Do information fish swim in *schools*? I think so.)

Technology brings us ever-faster, ever-cheaper computers and the modems with which we cruise about cyberspace. It's now the easiest thing in the world to connect up *to the world*. Yet—as glorious as the internet was and is—if blasting along these information highways was not simple and rewarding, most of us would not make the trip over and over and over as we now—in our many tens of millions—do.

The primary mechanism that makes all of the above of such ease is called the *world wide web*. By the mere click of a mouse, we can peruse millions upon millions of brightly colored pages, full of sound and music and pictures that move. By so doing, we find information of all sorts far faster and in much greater detail than our hometown library can offer.

The world wide web makes it possible.

WHAT IS THE WEB?

Understanding and using the world wide web requires us to comprehend first of all what it *is not*. Luckily, what the web *is not* just happens to be something we as family historians are intimately familiar with, *trees*.

A family "tree," as we know begins with one person and "branches" out with each generation, doubling the number of persons in each level. A descendant tree starts with some ancestor and comes forward though time. An ancestor tree starts with a person such as perhaps you and goes backwards through generations, but all are *trees*.

Most computers—including your personal computer—are organized in exactly the same manner.

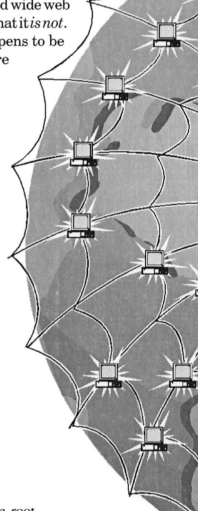

```
\  (Root Directory)
  ANTIQUES          AUCTIONS
                    POTTERY
  ARTICLES
  AUTO3RD
  AUTOGRAP          PRICE          TURNIN
  BERSERK
  BOOKS
  COKECOOK
  ERWIN
  EXCUR
  FAN
  GARBO
  LARRY
  LEOWHITE
  LETTERS
  PEOPLE
  PROJECTS          PEOPLEBK
  RALPHS
  SALES
  SCRIPTS
  SF
  SPORTSBK
  SPRINT
  VETERANS
  WESTERN
```

Computer file systems are like trees with a root directory and the other directories branching out in the manner of trunks and branches on a real tree. Actual files are equivalent to leaves on a real tree. Learning this basic fact makes computers really easy to use, but the structure has limitations.

The World's Web

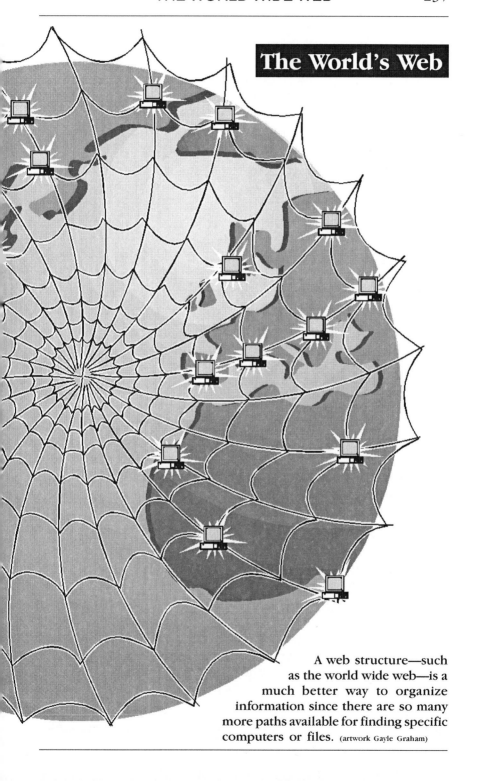

A web structure—such as the world wide web—is a much better way to organize information since there are so many more paths available for finding specific computers or files. (artwork Gayle Graham)

The way files (programs and data) are stored is in the form of a tree. See how easy computers are! I've seen people use computers in great frustration for years because they did not grasp this simple basic fact that makes finding and using stuff so beautifully uncomplicated. If you don't understand it, learn it! You'll take much of the pain out of computing.

Anyway, all computers—yours, mine, and all those big mudsuckers on the internet—*all of them* have a *root* directory at the top (equivalent to your **C:** directory on a DOS or Windows-based machine). Below or above (however you want to look at it—just like descendant and ancestor trees) are directories (branches) containing information. These directories have subdirectories which can have more subdirectories (more branches), and so on and so on.

This method of organization is also often likened to a file cabinet, and even directories on Windows machines are now called *folders*. When you think about it, though, a file cabinet is *also like a tree*. Drawers are branches; folders in drawers yet more branches; and folders within folders, and the sheets of paper in each yet more branches.

On your personal computer, the directory or folder tree structure is a godsend. Looking for programs or information in this manner quickly routes you in the right direction. If you do not understand this "tree" concept as it relates to your personal computer, you might as well go bash your head on the wall—either way, you're gonna have headaches.

But—while directory trees are great on personal computers—on the larger server machines making up the internet, the complexity becomes horrendous. Think of thousands upon thousands of computers all having sometimes widely varying types of directory trees. Forget head bashing, here's your headache! You're swinging from tree to tree through a vast jungle searching for just one little leaf—some particular piece of information tiny and hidden in that vast jungle. Yep, you got only two chances, as mixing old clichés goes—fat and slim.

Sure—there are ways of power inquiries on the internet. We'll look at search programs like *archie* and navigation menus called *gophers* ("go-fers") in the next chapter.

We can, however, describe finding anything by this method in one word—*slow*. A better way was needed and was created.

Back around the start of this decade various visionaries decided the information available on the internet should be easier to find and use. They said—and rightly so—that instead of all these tree structures with so many "dead ends," a "web" would be far better (and so it is). Each document you find should point beyond itself to other resources that are related or otherwise useful.

In a tree structure, if you come to the end of a branch (a "dead end"), you often must return to the nearest junction of branches to find and follow a new, perhaps more productive path. A web is like the fishnet analogy we used for server connections—albeit we are talking about *web pages* now and not computers. Strands crisscross all over the place, and it is far simpler to change strands and hie off in new directions.

Part of the fun of research—be it genealogical or otherwise—is on the interesting stuff you find on the way to finding stuff!

The web was originally developed at CERN (European Center for Nuclear Research). CERN is located in Geneva, Switzerland and is an institution specializing in high-energy physics research. The web was originally meant to promote sharing of research materials and serve as a mode of collaboration between scientists worldwide.

CERN generously made the web available to everyone and, by so doing, sparked the internet revolution we all are enjoying today. Thanks, CERN!

HYPERTEXT

Hypertext is not nervous writing. Instead, *hypertext* is a word coined by the renowned visionary and freethinker Ted Nelson in the mid-1960s to describe text not meant for sequential reading. Today, this has become the underlying concept of the world wide web. Documents are electronically *linked* to other documents, sounds, graphics, or anything else that might help clarify a thought or provide additional information on a specific subject.

Pursuing these *hyperlinks* (by just moving the arrow on the screen and clicking your mouse button) takes you from document to document, perhaps presenting you with con-

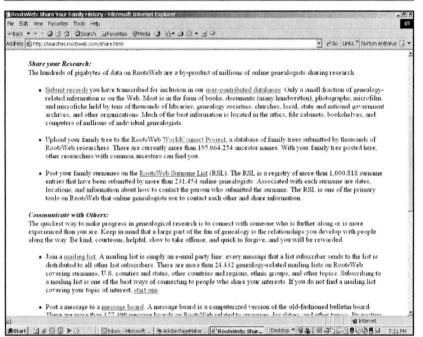

An example of hyertext (text with embedded links that lead you to associated information) is this article about how to share your family research at **http://searches.rootsweb.com/share.html**). Clicking on any of the underlined words or phrases in the article sends you to the web page containing that source. Hypertext is wonderful for informative articles, turning text from the flat two-dimensions of printed material into multidimensional, interactive sources of learning that are both fun and easy.

cepts and information that might not have occurred if you had read only the parent document.

Here's an example. What if in reading this book you came across one of my favorite words, *paronmasia*. If it was not explained in the text, you'd have to stop reading, find a dictionary, and look it up. (It means, by the way, a play on words, a *pun*.)

In a hypertext system, you would instead click on the word itself and receive an explanation, links to other web sites containing puns, and/or other information helping you grasp the concept. These links do not happen by accident, but require much programming by the web page creator.

Hypertext is what makes the web of such great value. If you find genealogical data useful in your research on a particular page on the web, chances are links from that page will lead you onwards in finding other useful facts.

A hypertext link in regular text usually appears as an underlined word or phrase in a different color from other text. The color might be anything, but often is blue. Just move the arrow over the hyperlink and click your mouse button. The link then sends you to the new page or a new location on the current page.

BROWSERS

To access the worldwide web and see all the pretty pictures, read the text, and what not, you need a computer program called a *browser*. A browser works in conjunction with your computer's communications program, such as the Windows dial-up networking described earlier.

Somewhere around 85 to 90 percent of people surfing the worldwide web today use browers from one of two sources—Netscape or Microsoft. The Netscape Communicator software, for a brief time years ago, was the most popular but

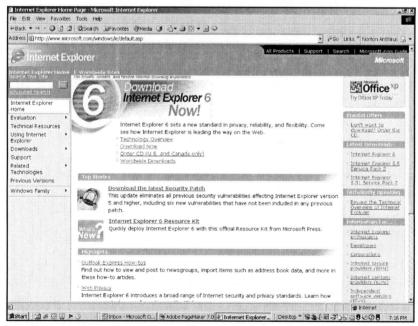

Find out more about Microsoft's Internet Explorer and how to get it free at **http://www.microsoft.com/ie**.

its status long since was rapidly eroded by the new leader, Microsoft's Internet Explorer, now in its version 6.0 release.

We recommend Internet Explorer for a number of reasons. First, it's tightly integrated with Windows and will actually became an integral part of Windows starting in 1998 (and thereby hangs an ongoing legal dispute between Microsoft, the federal government, and several states. But the price of this browser is also right—it's free!

Chances are—if you at present have Windows or buy a new computer in the near future—Explorer is on your computer already or will be on the new one.

More information on Microsoft's Internet Explorer may be found at **http://www.microsoft.com/ie**. Netscape's site is **http://www.netscape.com**.

NAVIGATING THE WEB

No doubt by this time you've either browsed the web yourself or seen it in action on a friend's computer or during one of the many times it gets shown on news programs these days. If so, you're already familiar with how one goes from page to page on the web. That's called *surfing*!

Web pages—as described above in the section on hypertext—present you with *links* or *hyperlinks* (either term is correct). Move the arrow (called a *cursor*) on the screen over the link by moving your mouse. Then click the mouse's button, which activates the link and loads a new page or sends your browser to a new location on the current page.

We described underlined words or phrases in the previous section (often in blue) as being links. Also, however, graphics (pictures, icons, buttons of various types, etc.) may be links as well. Sometimes a blue or other color border around a picture or other graphic indicates the presence of a link. Otherwise, you can just move the arrow around over the page. In Internet Explorer, the arrow changes to a little hand with a pointing finger to indicate that you've now selected a link. Click the mouse button and this link will be activated.

When you get right down to it, there are really only two basic ways of navigating on the world wide web—clicking on a link and, thus, have your browser find the page for you, or knowing and typing in the actual address of the page (the URL) as defined in the following section. The URL addresses are what we have been giving you for every internet resouce shown or mentioned in this book, such as **http://www.abooks.com** for the homepage of this book's publisher (please feel free to visit it).

THE UNIFORM RESOURCE LOCATOR (URL)

The *Uniform Resource Locator* is one of those many terms associated with the internet and its world wide web that you can promptly forget the meaning of but should remember its acronym, *URL*. URLs are the actual addresses of pages on the net, the information that points your browser to the page you want to retrieve. For example, if I tell you to point your browser at **http://**

| Address | 🔘 | http://www.abooks.com/genealogy | ▼ |

Type URLs into the address box on your browser's screen. Exactness is *everything!*

abooks.com/genealogy, type in that address while connected to the internet with your browser active, and you'll see my main page regarding this book.

All web pages—and there are tens if not hundreds of millions by now—all have a specific URL. We won't do a treatise on URLs, but here are the very basics. Each URL is comprised of four elements: the protocol, the hostname, the port, and the path (or the page name). In most cases, you'll only be concerned with three (excluding the *port*, which is not often used manually for *http* addresses but handled automatically by the server computer depending on the type of connect request).

The first part of an URL (such as *http*) is the *protocol*. This tells your computer how to connect to the machine being addressed. The *http* protocol is the *Hypertext Transfer Protocol*, or web pages in general (forget the full name, just remember that *http* means web pages). Other protocols include *mail* (electronic mail), *ftp* (file transfer protocol), and *gopher* (a "go-fer" menu).

Following http in a typical web address is a colon (:) and two slashes (//). These are called separators, and are needed to help the communicating computers properly translate the requested address into terms they comprehend.

Following the slashes, as in **http://abooks.com/geneal-
ogy**, is the *hostname*. The hostname (in this case *abooks.com*)
specifies which computer on the internet to contact. Many,
many hostnames include the letters *www*, which means (you
guessed it) world wide web. In the case of *abooks.com*, which
happens to be the server computer for my publishing company,
Alexander Books, you may use either *www.abooks.com* or just
abooks.com as the host name. But a lot of computers are not
programmed with such latitude—always enter URLs exactly in
the syntax you are given. Preciseness is always critical when
talking to computers.

The *path* tells in which directory the requested page is
located. Using **http://abooks.com/genealogy** as an example,
again (and please visit us), the slash (/) and word *genealogy*
following the hostname tells the computer you want a page
located in the *genealogy* subdirectory. No page name is given,
so the *default* page that you are shown is the index or main page.
If you were to type **http://abooks.com/genealogy/
pagetwo.html**, you would instead get the second page in that
directory, assuming there is one by that name. Web pages are
files with extensions such as *.html* or *.htm* or *.shmtl* and other
variations. The letters *html*, by the way (another forgettable)
stand for hypertext markup language, the basic web programming language at this time.

FINDING A HOSTNAME

Your browser examines a URL (whether you've typed it in
or generated it by simply clicking on a link) in order to find the
requested hostname and connect with that server computer. It
first converts the descriptive hostname (such as *abooks.com*)
into an internet address (in this case, 208.159.130.67, a real
location on the net).

All internet addresses are part of an addressing scheme
known as the Domain Naming System, or DNS. The actual
internet address is referred to as a computer's *dns number*.

Once your browser has obtained the correct *dns number*—
which it does by automatically requesting information over the
net that resolves the descriptive name of the computer to an
address number, it is ready to connect.

The process of connecting and actually bringing up the page in your browser so that you may view it—although occurring in mere seconds—is a lengthy and highly technical process. That, of course, is beyond the scope of this book. Still, we can say the process works darn well and you'll come to love the web and all of its myriad sources of family history research data.

FINDING STUFF ON THE WEB

There are several ways of finding things on the web. Following links is one; albeit lengthy. Another are the many directories giving you URLs for specific pages and/or sites on the net. This book includes tons of those for you.

But directories get out of date and just groping about in the dark following links—while often very interesting—takes a good deal of time. If you are looking for pages relating to one topic of interest, a *search engine* is your best bet. Search engines use programs called *robots* or *spiders* to constantly search and index pages on the network.

You use a search engine by entering a topic and obtaining a list of links. Click on an interesting sounding link and your browser shows you that page.

An example of a search engine is HOTBOT. A *bot* is a robot, or automatic program that continuously indexes the web. Connect to this engine at **http://www.hotbot.com**.

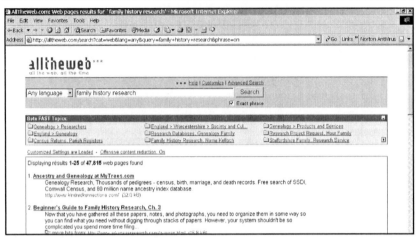

A search for *family history research* on **alltheweb.com** returns 47,815 hits. Use the *help* feature of search engines and learn methods of narrowing down your search to a more focused result.

You'll want to read the help text at the various search engines to learn ways of narrowing down your search. Just entering the word *genealogy*, for example, could give you literally hundreds of thousands or even millions of pages. That's a bit more than you can handily check.

A good starting point for search engines is **http://search.com**. This site has links connecting to several of the major engines. Other good places are **http://yahoo.com**, **http://www.altavista.com**, **http://lycos.com**, and **http://hotbot.com**, and **http://alltheweb.com**.

There are thousands of search engines on the net, many keeping track of specialized topics. Use a search engine to search for (yes) search engines to wrinkle these out.

SCOPE OF THE WEB

There are hundreds of millions of pages right now all over the world available to you on the world wide web. Certainly hundreds of thousands are useful to the family research historian to varying degrees.

The best way to learn the web is to surf the web. So rev up your computer and roar out there! It fascinating; it's fun! It even helps you find your long-lost great-great-great grandpa.

Now, on to some of the many other resources on the net.

14

OTHER RESOURCES AVAILABLE ON THE INTERNET

Okay, okay—in Chapter 12 I told you a shell account was probably a bad idea; that you needed some version of a SLIP/PPP account for your internet access. Naturally most of the other resources available on the internet (the subject of this chapter)—with the notable exception of electronic mail—were designed for access from the Unix prompt. Or, in other words, these resources were set up assuming the user *has* a *shell account.* That is, the type of access where you can see the Unix command line that is usually hidden way down under worldwide web pages and do all sorts of neat computer gobble-degook involving long, esoteric Unix commands such as *getstats -sr "/oscar/meterboss/*" -a > oscarstats; cat oscarstats | mail -s stats oscar@meterboss.com &*. (Which, by the way, is an actual command I used on our internet server computer for a few years in generating a statistics reports for one of our web site clients—Teramar Technologies in El Paso, Texas.)

You most likely don't want to type in commands like *getstats -sr "/oscar/meterboss/*" -a > oscarstats; cat oscarstats | mail -s stats oscar@meterboss.com &,* but chances are you would like the capability of using the internet resources in this chapter that were designed for use from the command prompt (i.e. a shell account). But ... yeah ... I said you don't need a *shell* account. This being my book, of course I'm right. For all of the "shell account" activities following, I'll show you easy ways of doing them while connected to the net via your trusty and highly recommended SLIP/PPP account. So, forget the shell account except to know that in the old days (i.e. before SLIP/PPP) ya needed it. Today, you don't.

As we'll see also in the pages following, once you've established a dial-up networking connection to the internet, it easy to literally do 14 things all at the same time. For example, you could be getting your *e-mail* (electronic mail), downloading a new program, using a search engine to look for records pertaining to your family history, and carrying on a conversation with a friend two states away *all at once*.

It is wonderful and doggone cotton pickin' *productive*.

And that is one of the secrets of why people get hooked on the internet and world wide web—you can do so very, very much, and a lot of it simultaneously, even.

I refer you back to Chapter 12's "Single User SLIP/PPP Account" (page 232). The concept of *networking* is so incredibly important to your enjoyment and "power use" of the internet that it bears pounding upon again.

Write it on a note and tape it to your computer monitor if you must.

> I CAN DO MORE THAN ONE THING AT A
> TIME ON THE INTERNET!

Good. You'll love it!

Again, nothing I show you in this chapter requires a shell account today, even though all of them did originally.

BASIC NAVIGATION

As we've already seen, by using a modem and your personal computer, you can dial into a larger computer (a *server* computer), then go out on the internet to almost anywhere in the world. Most computers on the internet are Unix-based, so a *minimal* knowledge of that operating system will help you to navigate along the network from computer to computer, from country to country, and especially in using most of the special internet resources covered in this chapter. Not to worry, however—there's really not a lot of knowledge required to take full advantage of everything here.

To access these other resources, you'll need two additional

programs. These programs used to be Unix prompt commands (and still are for shell accounts). On a Windows 95 (soon to be Windows 98) computer, these little programs (actually more utilities than full-fledged software) are included as part of the operating system (i.e. you already got 'em!).

We speak here of *telnet* (a terminal emulation program) and *ftp* (a file transfer protocol program).

TELNET

The *telnet* utility gives you full access to any computer that you know the internet address of (and thousands are published on the net and easily found). However, you must have a valid username and password to log on, or know a public account. For example, in accessing many university or college systems, the username *library* will let anyone access the university library's card catalog.

To use the included *telnet* utility while running Windows 95, 98, ME, XT, or later you should

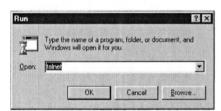

first be connected to the internet via your SLIP/PPP account. Then, simply click on the **Start** menu on the bottom left of your computer's screen, then select **Run**. In the dialog box, just type **telnet** in the space titled **Open** (see figure above) and hit your **Enter** key. The **telnet** window appears. Click on **Help** for details on how to use the program.

If you use telnet to any extent at all—and with so many resources available using this method, I encourage you to learn it—you'll probably soon become dissatisfied with the limitations of the telnet utility included with Windows. I suggest you check **http://www.davecentral.com**. Dave always has an extensive selection of the latest internet programs. You can pick a more sophisticated *telnet* program, or find both free and shareware programs in many other categories as well. I, personally, like CommNet's *telnet*.

As already indicated, some minimal knowledge of Unix commands is helpful. If you already know DOS, you'll understand Unix operations a little more readily—DOS is, in essence, a limited (very) subset of Unix. Below are just about all of the Unix commands you'll ever need in navigating a Unix server computer.

For more information on how to use these commands, just type **man <name of command>** at the Unix prompt. The *man* (manual) command gives you usually very detailed explanations of what the command does and all the many ways in which it may be used. Unix help facilites are not the wimpy brief sketches found on Windows these days, but full-blown highly exact and informative, albeit technically sophisticated, discussions.

SIMPLE UNIX COMMANDS

cp   Similar to DOS *copy* command. Copies a file to a new location or a new filename.

ls   Similar to the DOS *dir* command. Displays a list of the files and subdirectories of the current directory.

mkdir   Similar to the DOS *md* command. Makes a new directory underneath the current directory.

mv   Combines features of the DOS *move* and *rename* commands. Moves a file to new location, or renames it by moving it to a new name.

pwd   Shows the name of the directory you're in.

rm   Much the same as the DOS *del* command (and should be used just as cautiously!). Removes, or deletes, the specified file.

rmdir   Similar to the DOS *rd* command. Removes (deletes) an empty directory.

So, if you have an account on a server computer, you can use *telnet* to access it from anywhere in the universe via the internet and operate just like you were using a terminal in the same building as the computer. However, it is exceptionally unlikely that any of us will achieve valid *telnet* accounts on the many hundreds of thousands of server computers worldwide,

The CommNet telnet screen.

and even less likely that we could remember all the associated usernames and passwords.

There must be another way to access and retrieve data and other information from remote computers. There is.

FTP

Since the internet exists primarily to encourage and facilitate the free exchange of information, most computer systems will allow you access even though *you don't have an account on that computer* by use of the *ftp* command. To access a computer in another city, state, or country that is on the internet, **type ftp <internet address>.** Once connection is indicated, type the word *anonymous* and, if asked, your username on the system that ties you into the net. Often you are requested to use your e-mail address as a password.

If the computer allows public access, you can now use Unix commands such as *ls* to list the files in the current directory and *cd* to change directories. Most systems with public access have a /**pub** directory with subdirectories below containing programs and data files that you can transfer to your home system (using the *get* command—which is a ftp command, not a Unix one, meaning *ftp* has to be running before you can "get" a file). Since internet connections are very fast, you can "get" files megabytes in length in only a couple of minutes or so. Alas, if you've dialed into your internet gateway at 28,800 baud, it might take you hours to get those same files across town and into your personal computer.

Like telnet, ftp is included with Windows but more advanced versions are yours for the downloading at program sites on the web such as **http://www.davecentral.com** and **http://www.shareware.com**.

There are thousands upon thousands of computers at leading universities and other research facilities all over the world hooked to the internet. Most of these allow some sort of public access, meaning there are literally millions of programs and data files that you can download into your own computer.

But, how do you find files you might want to download by *ftp*? Our buddy *archie* can help.

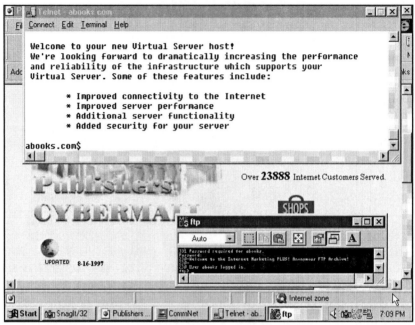

Just to emphasize once more that you can do many things at once on the internet, the above screen shows my browser (background) pointing to **http://abooks.com** (old site design, it looks much better these days), the Windows-included *telnet* utility connected to my server at **abooks.com**, and the included Windows *ftp* utility also connected to **abooks.com**. This example shows only three simultaneous tasks being run on the same phone connection, but you can perform a good many more! Again, please always remember you can do more than one thing at a time on the internet, then you will begin taking advantage of it's wonderful *power*.

ARCHIE

Let's say you have a personal computer running Windows, and you want to find Windows-related programs useful to your home system. You could spend a century or so visiting all those thousands of huge computer systems, both here and across the big shining waters. A far better solution is to call our buddy "archie," who came into being originally up at McGill University in Montreal, Quebec. The archie service was conceived and implemented by Alan Emtage, Peter Deutsch, and Bill Heelan. The entire Internet is in their debt.

The *archie* command works because of computers connected to the internet which keep track of programs and other files on those thousands of computers across the world. You tell Archie the subject you want (online help is always available), and Archie will give you a list of the machines having matching files, their internet addresses, and which directory you will find the files in. To talk with *archie*, just type **archie** at the Unix command prompt.

```
abooks.com$ archie
Usage: archie [-acelorstvLU] [-m hits] [-N level] string
        -a : list matches as Alex filenames
        -c : case sensitive substring search
        -e : exact string match (default)
        -r : regular expression search
        -s : case insensitive substring search
        -l : list one match per line
        -t : sort inverted by date
   -m hits : specifies maximum number of hits to return (default 95)
-o filename : specifies file to store results in
   -h host : specifies server host
        -L : list known servers and current default
  -N level : specifies query niceness level (0-35765)
```

Typing just **archie** returns its basic arguments.

(See the "Telnet" section above on how to get one of those babies.) If nothing happens, it means that the server computer does not have *archie* installed. Most, however, do—this being one of the standard programs long available on the net.

Old Archie can be your best friend for finding other resources on the internet. Otherwise, you may never find the files you want. Just don't confuse the concept of Archie with that of search engines—Archie is a search service from the Unix command prompt (reached via a telnet utility) while search engines like Yahoo, Excite, Hotbot, *et al*, are all to be found on the worldwide web.

For lots more on what the *archie* command can find and how it works, just type **man archie** at the Unix prompt.

And, of course—just like with *telnet* and *ftp*, there are ways of having Archie without the hassle of getting to a Unix command prompt. Got to **http://www.davecentral.com** and do a search for "archie." Ol' Dave has several programs that will do Archie functions for you while running Windows. I personally like WSArchie.

GOPHERS

The *gopher* program is, again, one of those designed originally to be available from the Unix command prompt. Remember that for the first 20-plus years of its life, the internet did not have all those pretty graphical elements that make the world wide web so easy to use. The net, instead, was character-based and the Unix command prompt the only way of navigating. As wonderful as the world wide might be and is, these activities from the

Unix command prompt are still the most powerful. However, admittedly, not everyone wants to take the trouble to learn the esoterics needed in taking advantage of these resources. Anyway, that's why *telnet, ftp, archie, gopher,* and other such commands were developed—i.e. to make navagation easier.

The Gopher concept was developed by folks at the University of Minnesota, and the Mother of All Gophers still resides on their system. The definition of "gopher," as given in the gopher help screen is amusing and informative:

> **gopher**: Any of various short tailed, burrowing mammals of the family *Geomyidae*, of North America. 2. (Amer. colloq.) Native or inhabitant of Minnesota: the Gopher State. 3. (Amer. colloq.) One who runs errands, does odd-jobs, fetches or delivers documents for office staff. 4. (computer tech.) Software following a simple protocol for tunneling through a TCP/IP internet.

The internet gopher, as the help screen goes on to tell us, is a *distributed document delivery service.* It allows users access to various types of information residing on multiple computers in a seamless fashion. In other words, users can access information from all over the world without having to know a specific machine name or how to log on to that machine. By simply selecting an item on a menu, that information is retrieved for you.

Finding and using a Gopher is well worth the time and effort. They allow you access to many resources not yet on the world wide web. A prime example of this happens to be library card catalogs. Thousands of university and other types of libraries all over the world have searchable card catalogs on line that are accessible via *gopher*, but no other way.

To find out if your internet service provider (that old ISP) gives access to a gopher, use a *telnet* utility to bring up the Unix command prompt and type **gopher**. If a numbered menu appears, you have access. Otherwise, you'll have to find another server computer offering *gopher*.

Or—if you want to avoid the Unix command prompt entirely (many do)—simply do a search for "gopher" on the world wide web (on Alta Vista, you'll get about 1.5 million hits!). You'll find lots of Gophers are accessible from the web itself. To see what a gopher is like, try the Youngstown Free Net Gopher at **http://yfn.ysu.edu**.

Now, let's move on from navigating the internet to some major resources used in a different way. With these resources (the ones following), you can use your browser and forget about Unix and command prompts.

USENET

The *Usenet* is not the internet, but parts of it overlap, everyone gets the same *news*, and *e-mail* or electronic mail can be exchanged between users on both networks.

Usenet is a collection of computers, also worldwide, which exchange large packets of information consisting of electronic mail and that most wonderful of institutions (on both networks) *news*.

The major difference between the two networks (or actually collections of many subnets) is that the internet is an interactive network—i.e. you actually log onto and operate the remote computer. On Usenet, only information is sent from computer to computer, showing up on your Usenet system to be read or used. There is no real time connection where you can do directory listings on the remote computer, or run its programs as you can on the internet.

Usenet was started in 1979 by two graduate students at Duke University in North Carolina (Tom Truscott and Jim Ellis). The first connection was to Duke's arch rival, the University of North Carolina in nearby Chapel Hill. From there, Usenet spread out to also cover the world.

Access to either network is worthwhile. If you have your own home Unix system, a Usenet connection so that you get news is a very nice thing to have. Or just use the facilities provided by your ISP.

NEWS

Ah, now for the real fun part, *news*. News, which is on both networks, is the world's largest (by far) electronic bulletin board. There are literally hundreds of *news groups* on every topic under the sun, including Suns (a leading manufacturer of workstations—you'll often encounter them as server computers on the net).

News groups	
alt.genealogy	
fido.belg.fra.genealogy	
fido.eur.genealogy	
fido.ger.genealogy	
othernet.fidonet.aus.genealogy	
othernet.fidonet.eu.genealogy	
othernet.fidonet.i&uk.genealogy	
othernet.fidonet.nz.genealogy	
soc.genealogy.african	
soc.genealogy.australia+nz	
soc.genealogy.benelux	
soc.genealogy.computing	
soc.genealogy.french	
soc.genealogy.german	
soc.genealogy.hispanic	
soc.genealogy.jewish	
soc.genealogy.marketplace	
soc.genealogy.medieval	
soc.genealogy.methods	
soc.genealogy.misc	
soc.genealogy.nordic	
soc.genealogy.slavic	
soc.genealogy.surnames	
soc.genealogy.uk+ireland	
soc.genealogy.west-indies	

Some of the Usenet genealogy-oriented news groups available to you.

News has been variously described as "the most fun you can have with a computer terminal" and even "the most fun you can have with your clothes on." You can communicate with people of similar or even wildly dissimilar interests, and exchange information with the world.

Be warned, news is not only exceptionally useful, it is also addictive. Few of us oldtimers on the internet or Usenet could survive without our wonderful daily fix of news.

ELECTRONIC MAIL

You'll make a lot of friends out there in the electronic

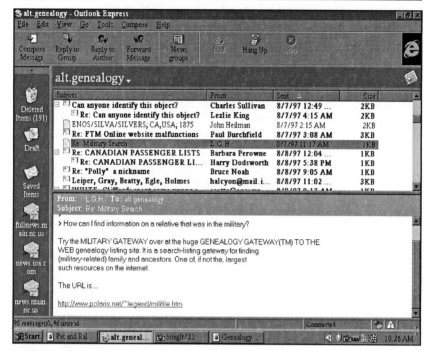

News groups provide you with many helpful tips. For example, in this alt.genealogy message, the poster gives a hyperlink to a web site that specializes in military research for the genealogist. Read news regularly; it truly helps in both finding ways of obtaining data and in meeting people with similar interests to yours.

universe. Both the internet and Usenet give you the excellent medium of electronic mail to keep in touch. Sending a message to a friend in Denmark is not only free, but it arrives sometimes only moments after you send it (depending on how the network routes it).

The easiest way to use electronic mail these days is by using the mail program built into your web browsing program. Again, we highly recommend Microsoft's Internet Explorer. The mail and news reading program included with Internet Explorer 6.0 is Outlook Express.

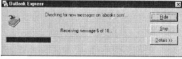

Outlook Express receiving

It's a humdinger and should fill your needs.

If you prefer a separate mail progam, check out Eudora. It's available almost everywhere.

I'm not going to spend a great deal of time or space here

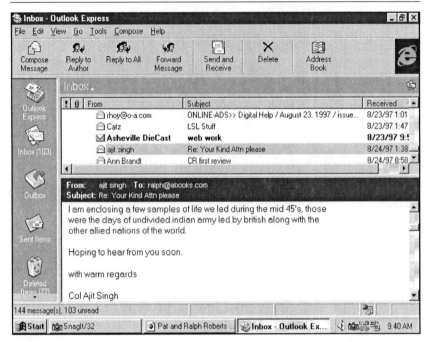

Reading and replying to your electronic mail is easy using the programs like Outlook Express, included free with Microsoft's Internet Explorer (which, itself, is free—certainly an affordable price).

discussing electronic mail. Usually this is one of the first things you learn and use on connecting to the internet, it opens up a world of personal interconnectiveness to you.

CONCLUSION

Alas, space and the purpose of this book precludes a fuller discussion of the internet and Usenet—one would need a series of very, very large books to do the subject justice. However, this should introduce you to the electronic universe out there. It should also whet your appetite to travel in the wondrous realms of cyberspace along the silver strands of the internet and Usenet, and to use the many other available resources than just the ones found on the world wide web.

Now, on to learning all about getting and exchanging data not online, then we'll move on to the final section of this book, in which I show you how to rapidly find your relatives.

15

GETTING AND EXCHANGING DATA NOT ONLINE

Getting and exchanging family research data not online essentially covers everything *except* the internet. In Chapter 7 we discussed the many, many ways of finding information about your ancestors other than online—the old way, if you will, of doing things. Dusty and musty old courthouses, books, other records of all sorts, and so on.

The thrust of this book, of course, is how you circumvent much of the hassle of the old methods and shorten the otherwise lengthy and arduous tasks of constructing your own family tree. Instead of visiting courthouses in person, we travel in realms of cyberspace via the internet. In lieu of riffling through endless stacks of old record books and scribbling notes, or ruining our eyes in the dim waver of some library's microfiche reader, we surf the net and pull down already completed trees that tie into ours from places like the World Family Tree project sponsored by Family Tree Maker.

My personal philosophy in all matters might be likened unto that of those cowboys in the old wild and woolly West—if they couldn't do it from their horse, they didn't do it.

If I can't do it on the computer, I don't do it.

Both philosophies concerning *modus operandi*—horses and computers—have some drawbacks. One does have to get down off the horse occasionally, if only to more conveniently answer the call of nature. And Miss Kitty sure don't allow no horses in her saloon.

Which is to say, the internet is not your complete answer

to genealogy, just a very helpful tool. There remain a few things best accomplished out of the saddle.

Again, Chapter7 gives you a good founding in what these task are, but I will elaborate a bit more in this chapter about one which ties in very well with computer and internet technology in general, the CD-ROM (and, increasingly, the DVD).

We gave examples earlier of the vast amount of data that a CD-ROM so easily can hold—i.e. about 600 million bytes of information, where a byte is equivalent to one letter or number. This is approximately *100 million words* or around *200,000 typed pages of data, single-spaced*! (And DVDs can hold 4.3 gigabytes!)

And CD-ROMs are *cheap*!

So CD-ROMs definitely fit within the spirit of this book—that being the ease and wonder of computerized genealogy and the awesome augmentation offered by the internet.

Bottomline—if you can't find what you need somewhere on internet, chances are you'll find a CD-ROM *on the internet* that you can order and thereby obtain the information you seek. It's certainly the next best thing. Most of the major genealogy software packages today come with CD-Rom databases, along with offers for the purchase of even more. Check the major sites like **ancestory.com**, **familytreemaker.com**, and so forth for the thousands now available.

LAST BUT NOT LEAST

Let's not forget the very best way of getting data not online—that of receiving files from friends or relatives. The next chapter—"Making Friends Online" is also important in helping you find sources of additional information.

If a friend or other person willing to trade data with you has the same program as you do (i.e. such as Family Tree Maker), then it's easy to take a file from them and add it to your own files. Otherwise, take some time to learn the standard file exchange formats, especially GEDCOM. Most of the major genealogy programs will export to this format, and import GEDCOM-formatted files.

More about GEDCOMs coming up in the next section.

GENEALOGY VIA THE INTERNET

TRACING YOUR FAMILY ROOTS QUICKLY AND EASILY

PART V:

FINDING AND ADDING HUNDREDS OF RELATIVES A NIGHT!

This final section gets down to the nitty-gritty, wholesale genealogy! You shows you how to find and add cousins literally by the dozens.

The world communications net, the all-involving linkage of electric circuitry, will grow and become more sensitive. It will also develop new modes of feedback so that communication can become dialogue instead of monologue. It will breach the wall between 'in' and 'out' of school. It will join all people everywhere. When this has happened, we may at last realize that our place of learning is the world itself, the entire planet we live on.

—Marshall McLuhan and George B. Leonard
Look Magazine, 1962

16

MAKING FRIENDS ONLINE

Regardless of how much information I give you in this book, or whatever I might have left out, it's still just a brief introduction. A starting point, if you will, into that great limitless, ever-growing, totally awesome and wonderful expanse of cyber reality, the internet.

While this book focuses mainly on using the internet for family history research, you no doubt have many other interests in your life. Be those interests as many as the grains of sand in the Mohave Desert, the Sahara, and the Gobi all totaled together. Or greater than the multitude of stars—millions upon millions in blazing glory—(and all of that is a *lot*). Still you'll find plenty of infomation about each and probably *every* subject you look for on the internet.

It's that big.

It's that wonderful.

And, yep, it can be that confusing!

So—despite the incredibly lucid prose of this book and those tons of others purporting to explain the internet, the world wide web, and many allied subjects—you'll have a good many questions on a continuing basis.

One way of answering those questions and learning to manipulate the web and the net is simple experimentation. Play around on the web as much as you can. It soon becomes more familiar, and many of your questions are answered in the context of browsing. That is, in looking for something else, you run across the answer to a question you had yesterday, or last week.

A good deal of the internet's true utility in general is—like wandering through a good library—the things you find on the way to looking up something else. And the internet is fantastically larger than any library you are likely to encounter, and it's all right there in that little magic box on your desktop, your personal computer.

MAKING FRIENDS

"But..." you are saying to yourself, "I'm not going to understand all this stuff right off."

Well, that is certainly true enough. The internet is more of a chunk than any of us can digest in one sitting. That's why friends as so important. You need the solace and helpfulness of others who are doing or have done what you're trying to do on the net.

Your circle of friends locally may or may not possess that kind of expertise. However, with something around 50 million people already on the internet worldwide and that number growing rapidly, chances are you can find a friendly expert in just about any field of endeavor.

How do you find them?

Below are some starting points.

USENET NEWS GROUPS

We discussed the Usenet news groups in Chapter 8. There is no better source for rapidly finding a lot of people interested and active in any one specific subject than news groups.

For example, there are dozens of news groups specializing in various topics related to genealogy and family history. You use a piece of software called a *news reader* to subscribe to, read, and even post your own questions and answers. The two most popular internet browsers—Internet Explorer and Netscape—include both mail and news reader programs. Also sources like **http://www.davecentral.com** let you download other programs that might even more closely fit your needs.

People who *post* to news groups (place messages for others to read) usually include their electronic mail addresses. You can either send a message directly to them, or post a *reply* to the news group that everyone can read.

Mailing Lists | Usenet Newsgroups | Telnet Sites | Gopher Sites | Web and other sites | Email sites

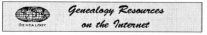

USENET NEWSGROUPS

URL: http://www.rootsweb.com/~jfuller/gen_use.html

Last update: November 10, 2000 by John Fuller, johnf14246@aol.com

Register Resource | Update Resource | Report a Broken Link

Please note that you will not be able to access newsgroups which your local site does not carry. The number of articles displayed may be limited by the browser or site, and posting to the group may or may not be enabled. Also, many of these newsgroups have gatewayed mailing lists (postings to the newsgroup are also sent to the mailing list subscribers and vice versa) which provides an alternative means of accessing the newsgroup postings. In these cases, I have provided a link to the mailing list description contained in the mailing list section of the file. Additional information on genealogy newsgroups can be found in Frequently Asked Questions (FAQ) files.

- alt.war.civil.usa
- alt.adoption (for adoptees, birthparents, adoptive parents)
- alt.genealogy (general genealogy topics). Gatewayed with the ALT-GENEALOGY mailing list.
- alt.scottish.clans
- dk.historie.genealogi (general genealogy topics, mostly in Danish)
- fido.eur.genealogy
- fido.ger.genealogy
- fr.comp.applications.genealogie (genealogy software used by French genealogists). Gatewayed with the GEN-FF-LOG mailing list.
- fr.rec.genealogie (French-speaking people, mostly in French). Gatewayed with the GEN-FF mailing list.
- news.groups (discussions on newsgroup "administration")
- no.fritid.slektsforsking.diverse (general genealogy topics, mostly in Norwegian)
- no.fritid.slektsforsking.etterlysing (searching relatives/ancestors, mostly in Norwegian)
- no.fritid.slektsforsking.it (computer programs, mostly in Norwegian)
- rec.heraldry
- sfnet.harrastus.sukututkimus (mostly in Finnish)
- soc.genealogy.african. Gatewayed with the GEN-AFRICAN mailing list.
- soc.genealogy.australia+nz. Gatewayed with the GENANZ mailing list.
- soc.genealogy.benelux. Gatewayed with the GEN-BENELUX and the GENBNL-L mailing lists.
- soc.genealogy.britain. Gatewayed with the GENBRIT mailing list.
- soc.genealogy.computing (genealogical computing and net resources). Gatewayed with the GENCMP mailing list.
- soc.genealogy.french. Gatewayed with the GEN-FR mailing list.
- soc.genealogy.german. Gatewayed with the GEN-DE mailing list.
- soc.genealogy.hispanic. Gatewayed with the GEN-HISPANIC mailing list.
- soc.genealogy.ireland. Gatewayed with the GENIRE mailing list.
- soc.genealogy.italian. Gatewayed with the GEN-ITALIAN mailing list.
- soc.genealogy.jewish. Gatewayed with the JEWISHGEN mailing list.
- soc.genealogy.marketplace. Gatewayed with the GEN-MARKET mailing list.
- soc.genealogy.medieval. Gatewayed with the GEN-MEDIEVAL mailing list.

John Fuller and Chris Gaunt offer an extensive list of Usenet genealogy discusssion lists on the web at **http://rootsweb.com/ ~jfuller/gen_use.html**.

News groups can be a bit intimidating at first for the novice user. Remember *flames* in our discussion of Usenet rules? Flames are nasty messages you get back should you overstep the bounds of net etiquette. There are very good and strong reasons for this sometimes rather instant irritability on the part of news group users. For a more detailed explanation of these reasons, we encourage you to subscribe to and read **news.newusers** and **news.newusers.questions**.

However, here's a summary of Usenet etiquette (*netiquette*) garnered from posted suggestions on the net itself. And these rules also apply to the, now, more popular web-based discussion boards like **genforum.genealogy.com**, which we'll look at later in this chapter. Here are the rules:

- Always remember that the people reading your posts are human (i.e. take into account their feelings).
- Don't blame system administrators for users' misbehavior.
- Take care in what you say about others.
- Be brief.
- Use descriptive titles (nothing more annoying than scrolling through 400 postings looking for what's of interest to you but the postings have no titles!).
- Think about your audience and keep to the topic of the news group.
- Use humor and sarcasm with care.
- Post a message only once. Remember, your message is going to propagate itself to thousands of computers. Let's not waste space with unneeded repetition.
- If you are posting an answer to another message, summarize what you are replying to, otherwise the reader might have to scroll back through hundreds of messages trying to find what the heck you are talking about.
- If your reply is only for the author of the post, send him or her e-mail, don't waste the net's bandwidth to reach just one person! (That really irritates flamers.)
- Read all the follow-ups that have been posted and don't repeat what other people have already said.
- Be careful about copyrighted material.
- Cite references, if they add to what you are saying.
- Don't flame about spelling or grammar errors. Just because someone else is not as educated as you, or simply was in a hurry

and got a bit sloppy, doesn't mean what they are posting is not significant.

- Keep signatures moderately short. (A *signature* is such things as your name and address, cute sayings, or anything else you want to add to the bottom of messages.)
- Limit the length of lines and don't use control or other special characters. Remember, messages are read on a wide variety of computers—keep things as generic as possible.

Now, all that said, don't be afraid of news groups. Dive in and *use* them. News groups are a highly helpful part of the entire internet arsenal of information gathering tools.

ELECTRONIC MAIL

Of course, the best and most intimate way to correspond with your friends and others on the net is electronic mail. We gave one method of finding e-mail addresses above. Another is from the web pages you visit. Most authors of web pages include an e-mail address for those who wish to contact them.

My own email address is **ralph@abooks.com**. Feel free to send me email on whether you liked or even did not like this book. After writing over 90 books, people who dislike a particular book no longer bother me—since most people seem to like my stuff yet I know that you can't please everyone. But thanks to all of you who do appreciate the blood I sweat in bringing information to you.

Anyway, keep lists of email addresses just like you would mail addresses. That way, when a question pops up, you most likely have the address of an expert on that subject to whom you can pose your question.

Email has replaced letters, faxes, and phone calls as the preferred method of contacting people.

ELECTRONIC MAIL LISTS

I belong to several electronic or email lists. An *email list* allows those interested in a particular topic an easy way of receiving and sending email messages about that topic. Several hundred people or more may belong to a list. All emails sent to the list automatically get forwarded to everyone belonging to the list. You read and reply to list messages at your convenience.

Mailing Lists | Usenet Newsgroups | Telnet Sites | Gopher Sites | Web and other sites | Email sites

Genealogy Resources
on the Internet

MAILING LISTS

URL: http://www.rootsweb.com/~jfuller/gen_mail.html

Last update: March 9, 2002 by John Fuller. johnfl4246@aol.com

Register Resource | Update Resource | Report a Broken Link

Welcome packages are generally provided when you subscribe. Please keep these on file since they contain important information about posting, unsubscribing, and other aspects of list membership. A number of lists are included for various countries and areas of the world where the list descriptions do not specifically address genealogy. While these lists are not devoted to genealogy, the list owners have indicated that genealogy is an acceptable, though in some cases unusual, topic for the list.

When subscribing, please make sure that the subscribe command is the only text in the body of the message unless the list description states otherwise. In general, you must be a subscriber to post to these mailing lists and posting instructions will be contained in the Welcome message you receive when you subscribe.

PLEASE NOTE: First, I do not own any of these lists so sending a subscribe message to me will not work. Please see the description of the mailing list you are interested for the applicable subscribe instructions. Second, I am probably not researching these surnames and geographic areas, so please do not write to me to see if I have information on your ancestors. Finally, all of these lists are free.

The mailing lists contained in this section are divided into the following categories ... just click on the one that interests you.

- COUNTRIES OTHER THAN USA
- USA
- SURNAMES
- Adoption
- African-Ancestored
- Cemeteries/Monuments/Obituaries
- Computing/Internet Resources
- Emigration/Migration Ships and Trails
- Family History, Folklore, and Artifacts
- Genealogical Material/Services
- General Information/Discussion
- Jewish
- LDS
- Native American
- Newspapers
- Nobility/Heads of State/Heraldry
- Occupations
- Religious/Churches (other than Jewish/LDS)
- Societies
- Software
- Translations and Word Origins
- Vital Records (census, BDM)
- Wars/Military
- Uncategorized (some great lists)

COUNTRIES OTHER THAN USA. Click on one of the following for geographic lists dealing with countries other than the USA.

| General | Afghanistan | Albania | Algeria | Angola | Antigua and Barbuda | Argentina | Armenia | Australia | Austria | Bahamas | Bangladesh | Belarus | Belgium | Belize | Benin | Bhutan | Bolivia | Botswana | Brazil | British Virgin Islands | Bulgaria | Burkina Faso | Burundi | Cameroon | Canada | Cape Verde | Cayman Islands | Central African Republic | Chad | Chile | China | Colombia | Comoros | Republic of the Congo | Costa Rica | Croatia | Cuba | Czech Republic | Denmark | Djibouti | Dominican Republic | Ecuador | Egypt | El Salvador | England | Equatorial Guinea | Eritrea | Estonia | Ethiopia | Finland | France | Gabon | Gambia | Germany/Prussia | Ghana | Greece | Guatemala | Guinea | Guinea-Bissau | Guyana | Haiti | Honduras | Hungary | Iceland | India | Indonesia | Iran | Ireland | Israel | Italy | Ivory Coast | Kenya | Korea | Kuwait | Latvia | Lebanon | Lesotho | Liberia | Libya | Liechtenstein | Lithuania | Luxembourg | Macedonian Republic | Madagascar | Malawi | Mali | Malta | Mauritania | Mauritius | Mexico | Micronesia | Moldova | Montenegro | Morocco | Mozambique | Namibia | Nepal | Netherlands | New Zealand | Nicaragua | Niger | Nigeria | Norway | Panama | Papua NewGuinea | Paraguay | Peru | Philippines | Poland | Portugal | Reunion | Romania | Russia | Rwanda | Samoa | Sao Tome and Principe | Saudi Arabia | Scotland | Senegal | Serbia | Seychelles | Sierra Leone | Slovak Republic | Slovenia | Somalia | South Africa | Spain | Sri Lanka | Sudan | Suriname | Swaziland | Sweden | Switzerland | Syria | Tanzania | Togo | Tunisia | Turkey | Uganda | Ukraine | United Kingdom and Ireland | Vatican City | Wales | West Indies | Western Sahara | Yemen | Yugoslavia | Zaire | Zambia | Zimbabwe |

USA. Click on one of the following for USA geographic lists for your State/territory of interest.

| General | AK | AL | AR | AZ | CA | CO | CT | DC | DE | FL | GA | HI | IA | ID | IL | IN | KS | KY | LA | MA | MD | ME | MI | MN | MO | MS | MT | NC | ND | NE | NH | NJ | NM | NV | NY | OH | OK | OR | PA | RI | SC | SD | TN | TX | UT | VA | WA | WI | WV | WY | American Samoa | Puerto Rico | Virgin Islands |

SURNAMES. Click on one of the following for alphabetized surname lists. If you can not find a list specifically for your surname, it may be addressed as a variant for another list (e.g., the Abshire mailing list includes Ipsher, Habisch, Upsher and other variants). Chris has created a script that gathers the surnames and variants included in the mailing list entries and creates links to each applicable list. Just go to the Surnames Found in Mailing Lists Entries web page.

Also from John Fuller and Chris Gaunt (thanks again, guys!), an equally extensive and useful group of links to genealogy mail lists (see **http://www.rootsweb.com/~jfuller/gen_mail.html**).

The illustration on page 268 (opposite) shows John Fuller and Chris Gaunt's list of genealogy related mail lists. Thousands exist! You can find lists specializing in geographical area (such as counties, states, or countries), family surnames (I belong to the Roberts mailing list, for example), and many other topics of interest to us family researchers.

Email lists give you the advantage of concentrated information about very narrow topics and it's all interactive—you can ask questions! You'll find email lists an invaluable adjunct to your research and I encourage you to seek them out and use them.

CHAT GROUPS

A even more interactive mode of communication on the internet are *chat groups*. Chat groups allow you instant communication (i.e. two-way conversations) with others having similar interests to your own. You engage in conversation by typing instant messages to each other. Anywhere from two to scads of people can participate and chats are great fun.

Again using genealogy as an example, go to a search engine and do a search for "genealogy chat" and you'll find

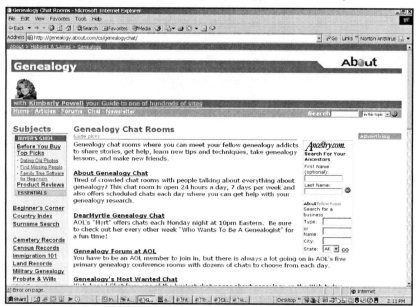

Kimberly Powell lists several genealogy chat rooms at **http:// genealogy.about.com/cs/genealogychat/**.

bunches of them. We recommend Digital's Alta Vista (**http://altavista.com**) for this because it handles search terms in quotes better than most. HOTBOT (**http://hotbot.com**) also works well for this exercise if you click on the complete phrase option.

There are many,other ways of *conferencing* (talking in real time) on the internet. Microsoft's NetMeeting program, for example, is free. You can find out how to get it and other Microsoft products at **http://microsoft.com**.

But whatever method of making and chatting with friends you choose, doing so online widens your scope of acquaintances. It also adds greatly to your ability to find out more about the topics you research on the net. Plus, it's downright fun!

FORUMS

Think of genealogy *forums* as virtual (existing on computers instead of physically) bulletin boards. The old fashioned bulletin board was made of cork and one pinned messages or notices to it with thumbtacks. Several drawbacks exist. First, you have to be in the building in which the board is to see it and, after awhile, there's more papers pinned to it than

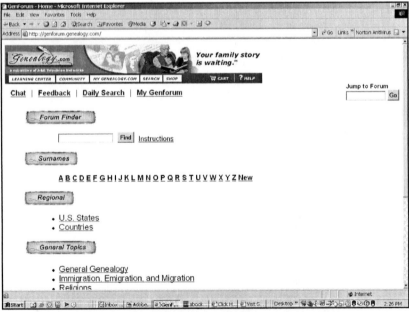

The entry page at **http://genforum.genealogy.com/**.

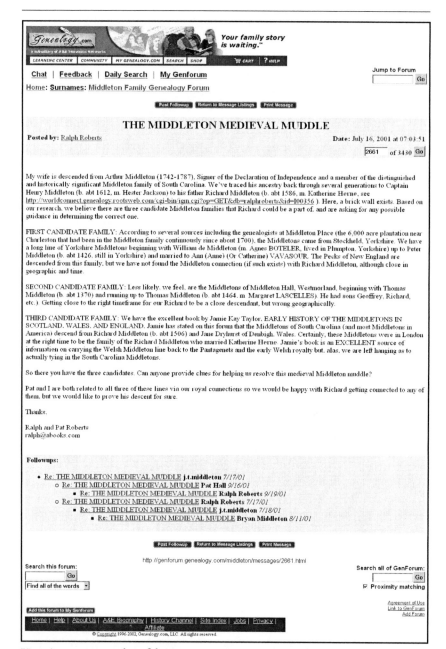

Here's an example of how you post a request for information. The above is an actual post of mine in the Middleton family forum on **http://genforum/genealogy.com**. We're looking (still) for the ancestral line of Arthur Middleton, especially who the parents of Richard Middleton were. A temporary impasse, by the way, we call a "brick wall" in genealogical research.

leaves on a tree—you can't *find* anything! But virtual bulletin boards—those on the world wide web—can be accessed from anywhere and you can have as many as you like to make organization and finding things a lot easier.

For example, one of the largest genealogy-oriented forums is at **http://genforum.genealogy.com** (a free service from the people who publish Family Tree Maker and Family Origins software). There are separate boards for hundreds (probably thousands) of surnames, thousands of U.S. counties, all 50 states, and much more.

Moving to a specific forum—let's say the Middleton family since my wife descends directly from Arthur Middleton, Signer of the Declaration of Independence—is as simple as typing the name of the forum you wish.

However, before you post a query, good etiquette requires you to do a search to see if the question has already been answered. Also, it's an excellent idea to read over all the previous postings. Something might just jump out at you, answering questions about your family's history you did not even realize you had! Forums are marvelous resources, indeed. Spend the time learning their usage, you'll be glad!

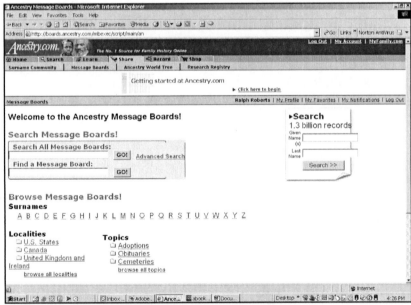

Another collection of genealogy forums worth your attention is at **http://boards.ancestry.com** (over 100,000 boards!).

ROOTSWEB,
A GOOD STARTING POINT!

RootsWeb (**rootsweb.com**) is the largest and oldest free genealogy site on the world wide web. As already mentioned in this book, it's my favorite genealogy site. While thousands upon thousands of other great sites now exist, RootsWeb remains the starting point I highly recommend as you begin your family history research or turbo charge an already ongoing project.

In a mission statement at **http://searches. rootsweb.com/share.html** you'll read: "The primary purpose and function of RootsWeb, is to connect people so that they can help each other and share genealogical research. Most resources on RootsWeb are designed to facilitate such connections."

RootsWeb recently gained the sponsorship of **ancestry.com**, the largest commercial genealogy site. While I suggest you start with a free site, hence this chapter, there is nothing wrong with occasionally paying for research data when you can't find it on your own. The Ancestry service offers access to billions of records—I use it some myself—and some of the profits go to keeping RootsWeb online.

SHARING RESEACH

The operative concept (not just of RootsWeb but family history in general) is *sharing*. The underlying strong foundation enabling online genealogy rests on the fact that everyone

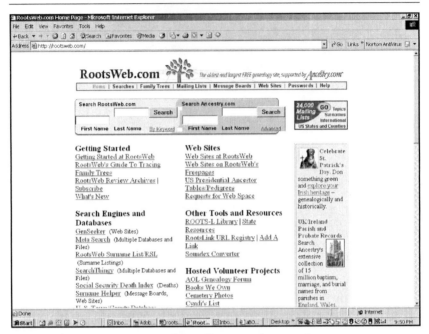

RootsWeb's main page at **http://rootsweb.com** is your gateway to loads of free family research resources.

shares a common pool of ancestors. The topic of full genealogy introduced in Chapter 1 of this book and emphasized throughout bases its power on this very fact—our *commonality*, cousin, our commonality (white, red, pink, black, brown, yellow, polka-dotted, we all share the same ancestors). In practical terms, this means your family research—as you move it back through the generations—ties into that of many, many other people.

RootsWeb provides easy-to-use, wide ranging methods of accessing a vast amount of already completed research that you can just drop in place (add hundreds of relatives a night, see the next chapter). Of course one should not just take advantage of all the many thousands of hours contributed by those who did the original research you pull into your own family history, so RootsWeb also supplies ways for you to give back to the huge community of genealogy researchers—remember, they are all you cousins anyway, be nice to the kinfolk.

One more mention here of the clash of cultures between 'serious' genealogists and the majority of us, who love computers, the internet, and like pushing the envelope to the max. Many thousands of people contribute to RootsWeb and the other online genealogy repositories, both free and commercial. Not all facts—births, marriages, deaths, burials, the basic building blocks of family data—are correct. In fact, a good percentage of it *is not*. People being people, we make mistakes or we sometimes don't properly verify data before entering it. Computerized genealogy runs at a much faster pace than old-fashioned "serious" genealogy, but this means mistakes also proliferate faster.

Don't let the above slow down your research, but do remember to continually check facts. This is yet another advantage of sharing. If you publish your GEDCOMs on a service like RootsWeb's WorldConnect project (like I do, database *ralphroberts*), then lots of people email you pointing out mistakes. A great way to find and fix errors in a huge database of relatives, as you will soon be accumulating. Plus, by this sharing of your own work, you help others who share common lines with your family.

ROOTSWEB'S METHODS OF SHARING

It's awesome when you understand all RootsWeb offers free! The *hundreds of gigabytes* of data on RootsWeb are a byproduct from the generosity of millions of online genealogists sharing their hard-wrought research.

Here are some ways RootsWeb suggests you share your own research:

- Submit records you have transcribed for inclusion in our user-contributed databases. Only a small fraction of genealogy-related information is on the Web. Most is in the form of books, documents (many handwritten), photographs, microfilm, and microfiche held by tens of thousands of libraries, genealogy societies, churches, local, state and national government archives, and other organizations. Much of the best information is located in the attics, file cabinets, bookshelves, and computers of millions of individual genealogists.

- Upload your family tree to the RootsWeb WorldConnect Project, a database of family trees submitted by thousands of RootsWeb researchers. There are currently more than 196,120,634 ancestor names. With your family tree posted here, other researchers with common ancestors can find you.

- Post your family surnames on the RootsWeb Surname List (RSL). The RSL is a registry of more than 1,001,380 surname entries that have been submitted by more than 231,685 online genealogists. Associated with each surname are dates, locations, and information about how to contact the person who submitted the surname. The RSL is one of the primary tools on RootsWeb that online genealogists use to contact each other and share information.

COMMUNICATION

The quickest way to make progress in genealogical re-search—both advocated by RootsWeb and myself—is to connect with someone who is further along or is more experienced than you are in family history research.

Keep in mind, RootsWeb stresses and I heartily endorse, that a large part of the fun of genealogy is the relationships you develop with people along the way. Be kind, courteous, helpful, slow to take offense, and quick to forgive, and you will be rewarded. Here are some of the ways they suggest (and which emphasize what I've been showing you all along in this book):

- Join a mailing list. A mailing list is simply an e-mail party line: every message that a list subscriber sends to the list is distributed to all other list subscribers. There are more than 24,432 genealogy-related mailing lists on RootsWeb covering surnames, U.S. counties and states, other countries and regions, ethnic groups, and other topics. Subscribing to a mailing list is one of the best ways of connecting to people who share your interests. If you do not find a mailing list covering your topic of interest, start one.

- Post a message to a message board. A message board is a computerized version of the old-fashioned bulletin board. There are more than 177,390 message boards on RootsWeb related to surnames, localities, and other topics. By posting a message to the appropriate message board, you create a record through which other researchers can find you. If you do not find a message board covering your topic of interest, start one.

- Add Post-em Notes to the Social Security Death Index (SSDI), the WorldConnect Project, or to other databases at RootsWeb. A Post-em is the electronic equivalent of a yellow sticky note. It allows you to attach your e-mail address, a link to another Web address, or other information to the record of any individual. Search for your ancestors and leave your calling card attached to their names.

- Build your own genealogy Web site on RootsWeb. Request free unlimited Web space. Building a basic Web site is not as difficult as you might imagine; millions of people have done it, and RootsWeb offers an online editor for those who wish to use one.

- Add a link to your Web site using RootsLink. RootsLink is RootsWeb's Web address registry, where users can add and categorize a genealogy link from anywhere on the Web.

- Link your Web site to the relevant surname, county, state, and/or country resource cluster. Thereafter, a link to your Web site will appear at the top of whatever surname, county, and/or state resource cluster(s) you have chosen. Users specifically interested in the information on your Web site will see this link whenever they use the RootsWeb surname resources, U.S. county and state resources, or world resources. This feature is ONLY available for Web sites located at RootsWeb.

VOLUNTEER

RootsWeb hosts many of the largest volunteer genealogy projects on the Internet. Volunteers locate, transcribe, and publish genealogical data and help new users. Through this work they meet other genealogists with similar interests. You will find a listing of some volunteer efforts on RootsWeb's main page (**http://rootsweb.com**). Your own interests may lead you to others.

ROOTSWEB IS HUGE

It would take a book the size of an encyclopedia (yep, much larger than this one in its entirety) to do justice to all the marvelous features offered at **http://rootsweb.com**. Thankfully, such a weighty tome is not required, simply go there and explore. You'll be glad you did.

RootsWeb provides guides to getting started in online genealogy, databases of all sorts, search engines to help you find more, tens of thousands of mailing lists, celebrity genealogy, message boards, research templates, and much, much more.

Part of that "much, much more" is the WorldConnect project (**http://worldconnect.rootsweb.com/**) with (as of this writing) over 196 million names on file (earlier in this book, I said 192 million, that's how fast it's growing—an additional 4 million names added in just a few weeks). I use WorldConnect a lot in my own family research, implementing the techniques of FULL genealogy. So, as promised, I show you how in the next chapter.

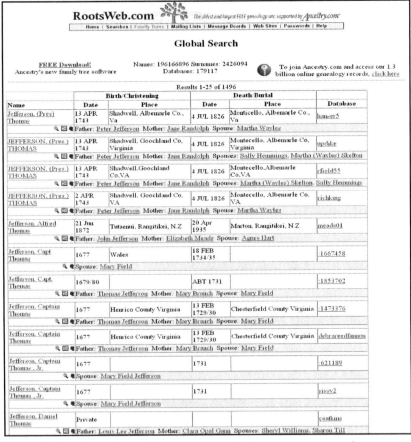

One of the first things I'll show you is how to narrow down your searches on WorldConnect. Above is a search for Thomas Jefferson. I got over 1400 Thomas Jeffersons (and imagine how many John Smiths you'll get). We can use dates of birth or death, spouses, and several other factors to hone search results down to a reasonable number. All that coming up. Stay tuned to the pages of this book.

18

WHOLESALE GENEALOGY

O n looking into any technical endeavor—including your family history research—you'll usually find two ways of doing it, *fast* and *slow*. Not right and wrong, mind you; a person has the potential of making just as many mistakes doing things slowly, the errors simply take longer to accomplish. What I'm talking about here really is *efficiently* and *non-efficiently*.

Let me use an analogy to **ahem** drive the point home. The way some genealogists use computers and the internet is like owning a fast sports car but *pushing it* everywhere—after all, it is a convenient container, keeps the groceries dry, doncha know, eh? In other words, they still do family research the same way they always have, one *sloooow* entry at a time.

Should you get nothing else from this book (albeit I trust *that's* not true), it would please me greatly and benefit you immensely if your mindset changes to accommodate the power and speed of computerized genealogy combined with the almost infinite resources of the internet. Don't put your milk and bread in that sports car and *push it*, hop in and peel rubber!

How? Instead of taking months to get your family reseach moving by finding, verifying, and painfully entering one person at a time, roam **http://worldconnect.com** (and all the other great sources on the internet) and download hundreds of relatives a night!

Yes, you will have errors and you need to find and fix those, but make it a continuing process rather than letting it hold up progress. You'll find this method much faster and results in a markedly larger database far faster than the old traditional methods. You'll also find full genealogy works great with this larger base of kinfolk (instead of that narrow old ancestor genealogy, as we discussed in Chapter 1).

So, let's get to doing wholesale genealogy. The process of importing large groups of relatives and exporting them back out (sharing your work) lends itself nicely to the speed of today's personal computers and fast internet connections.

So, turn the ignition key on your new mindset and let's roar!

The first thing you must learn about is the format in which family data must be for transfer to and from your system.

GEDCOMS, THE MEDIUM OF EXCHANGE

GEDCOM is an acronym for **GE**nealogical **D**ata **COM**munications and is a file format developed by the Family History Department of The Church of Jesus Christ of Latter-day Saints (LDS, the "Mormons"). GEDCOMs give you a standardized format for sending and receiving family research data, allowing you to share files with other researchers no

A GEDCOM file—the standard format for exhange of genealogy data—is a plain text file but with tons of specialized tags. Good genealogy software reads in these files (imports) and exports them for you in the right format.

matter what genealogy software they might use. GEDCOMs may be thought of as a universal language, or at least as close as we can get to that concept today.

At first, you'll *download* (copy from the internet) GEDCOMs containing family history data that ties into what you already have entered. For example—after consulting other family members—you may have your father's line (or at least one of them) back to your 2nd great grandfather. After searching WorldConnect (and I'll show you how to search later in this chapter) you find someone who has published a GEDCOM that has you 2nd great grandfather in it.

You look at this file and it looks pretty accurate with good sources. So you download as much of it as the person who published allows (usually on WorldConnect, this is 6 or 10 generations). Once the file is on your computer (takes a few seconds), you use the facilities in your genealogy program to *import* the file and *merge* it with your current data, thus adding several more generations and 30, 40, or more relatives almost instantaneously.

Each software package varies in how importing is accomplished, so consult your manual or online help. In Family Tree Maker, for example, just click on *File, Append/Merge Family File...*, choose *GEDCOM* in the *Files of type* box, then click on the title of the GEDCOM file you just downloaded.

FTM guides you through the importing and merging steps. *Merging* means joining together individuals that might already be in your file to those in imported GEDCOM, otherwise you'll have duplicates. Additional data (like a birthdate you did not have) will then appear. Of course, occasionally you'll need to do additional research to resolve conflicts like a wrong spouse or incorrect dates, and so forth. Merging is critical because it ties together your existing data with all the new people you are importing, giving your software the ability to add them to relationship reports, pedigrees, descent charts, and all the other neat stuff computerized genealogy does for you.

To create a GEDCOM for *uploading* (copying) to WorldConnect or to share with a fellow family researcher, you *export* from your genealogy software.

In FTM, choose *File, Copy Export Family File...*, choose *GEDCOM* in the *Save as type* box, and decide on the name to save it under (like *roberts.ged* or *taylor.ged*—it must have a .ged extension).

FINDING AND DOWNLOADING GEDCOMS

Now, let's find a GEDCOM to download. Go to **http:// worldconnect.rootsweb.com/cgi-bin/igm.cgi** and you will see a search form. As an example, we'll look for the ancestors of President George "yes, I chopped down the durn cherry tree" Washington. Enter 'Washington' in the last name and 'George' in the first name boxes. Now, to narrow the search (there's been lots of guys named George Washington) type Martha Dandridge in the spouse box (so we'll be sure to get President George Washington). Click on the *Search* button.

Boom, we get over 600 results but they are all President George Washington. I click on the top name. Hmmm. Lots of good info, but there's no *Download GEDCOM* button—this person has opted not to share his data, unless you type it in the old fashioned way. Please folks, *share* your data.

So we look at the next. Ah! A Download GEDCOM button is there. We click on it. A nice person indeed, he or she allows us to download ten generations of ancestor or ten generations of descendants! Choose which you want, then click on the *Download* button. Your computer will guide you though where to put the GEDCOM (usually in the same directory as your genealogy software). It takes just seconds and, in a 10-generation GEDCOM, there can be hundreds of people.

Once the file is on your computer, import and merge it as we discussed previously.

It's that simple.

Now, you can go down through all the new generations you have and pick new people to search for and, thus, add new generations.

See! Hundreds of people a night! Wholesale genealogy.

But... yes, remember verification of facts remains an ongoing process. Never accept anyone's data as 100% correct—chances are, it's not, just don't let that slow you down. Think of it like building a house. Get the roof on and the sheetrock nailed up. You can come back and paint it later.

Downloading the ancestors of George Washington from Pat's and my database at **http://worldconnect.rootsweb.com**.

SHARING GEDCOMS

A lot of people have been kind enough to share their family research on WorldConnect, that's where those 196 millions names (and more added every day) came from. In all fairness, you should return the favor, as I do (using the built in privacy safeguards to avoid publishing birthdates of living people).

To protect the databases of WorldConnect submitters, as is pointed out in the online help for this wonderful free service, researchers are not permitted to download a GEDCOM in its entirety. If you would like to have a copy of an entire GEDCOM, you should contact the submitter privately. Many GEDCOM owners are willing to share their information on a personal basis.

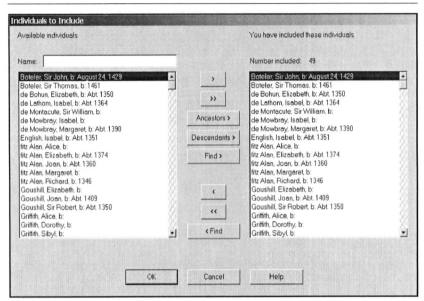

Using Family Tree Maker to import a GEDCOM. This file contains 49 people but GEDCOMS can have anywhere from one person to literally hundreds of thousands.

GEDCOM submitters may allow a portion of their file to be downloaded, but not everyone chooses this option. On the standard set-up page, if the submitter has selected "yes," six generations of the GEDCOM may be downloaded. The advanced set-up page allows the submitter to specify the number of generations to be downloaded ranging from two to 10, and also allows for the inclusion of a message in the notes for each individual in the GEDCOM to be downloaded. You'll be able to do this as well when you submit your own GEDCOMs.

GO FORTH AND MULTIPLY YOUR DATABASE RAPIDLY

And that is essentially it as far as getting started in wholesale genealogy goes. Read the helpful FAQs (frequently asked questions) and other informative pages at **http:// worldconnect.rootsweb.com**. Then practice finding and downloading GEDCOMs appropriate to your family history database (i.e. ones that tie in).

Thanks for reading my book and I hope you got a lot out of it—after all, you and I, we're definitely cousins and I always try to do right by mah kinfolk!

INDEX

Genealogy via the Internet—cousins finding cousins by the dozens.